UNQUIET DREAMS

THE BESTIARY OF WALERIAN BOROWCZYK

BY SIMON STRONG

WHAT IS MADNESS? To have erroneous perceptions, and to reason correctly from them? Let the wisest man, if he would understand madness, attend to the succession of his ideas while he dreams. If he be troubled with indigestion during the night, a thousand incoherent ideas torment him; it seems as if nature punished him for having taken too much food, or for having injudiciously selected it, by supplying involuntary conceptions; for we think but little during sleep, except when annoyed by a bad digestion. Unquiet dreams are in reality a transient madness.

Madness is a malady which necessarily hinders a man from thinking and acting like other men. Not being able to manage property, the madman is withheld from it; incapable of ideas suitable to society, he is shut out from it; if he be dangerous, he is confined altogether; and if he be furious, they bind him. Sometimes he is cured by baths, by bleeding, and by regimen.

This man is not, however, deprived of ideas; he frequently possesses them like other men, and often when he sleeps. We might inquire how the spiritual and immortal soul, lodged in his brain, receives all its ideas correctly and distinctly, without the capacity of judgment. It perceives objects, as the souls of Aristotle, of Plato, of Locke, and of Newton, perceived them. It hears the same sounds, and possesses the same sense of feeling—how therefore, receiving impressions like the wisest, does the soul of the madman connect them extravagantly, and prove unable to disperse them?

If this simple and eternal substance enjoys the same properties as the souls which are lodged in the sagest brains, it ought to reason like them. Why does it not? If my madman sees a thing red, while the wise men see it blue; if when my sages hear music, my madman hears the braying of an ass; if when they attend a sermon, he imagines himself to be listening to a comedy; if when they understand yes, he understands no; then I conceive clearly that his soul ought to think contrary to theirs. But my madman having the same perceptions as they have, there is no apparent reason why his soul, having received all the necessary materials, cannot make a proper use of them. It is pure, they say, and subject to no infirmity; behold it provided with all the necessary assistance; nothing which passes in the body can change its essence; yet it is shut up in a close carriage, and conveyed to Charenton.

This reflection may lead us to suspect that the faculty of thought, bestowed by God upon man, is subject to derangement like the other senses. A madman is an invalid whose brain is diseased, while the gouty man is one who suffers in his feet and hands. People think by means of the brain, and walk on their feet, without knowing anything of the source of either this incomprehensible power of walking, or the equally incomprehensible power of thinking; besides, the gout may be in the head, instead of the feet. In short, after a thousand arguments, faith alone can convince us of the possibility of a simple and immaterial substance liable to disease.

The learned may say to the madman: "My friend, although deprived of common sense, thy soul is as pure, as spiritual, and as immortal, as our own; but our souls are happily lodged, and thine not so. The windows of its dwelling are closed; it wants air, and is stifled."

The madman, in a lucid interval, will reply to them: "My friends, you beg the question, as usual. My windows are as wide open as your own, since I can perceive the same objects and listen to the same sounds. It necessarily follows that my soul makes a bad use of my senses; or that my soul is a vitiated sense, a depraved faculty. In a word, either my soul is itself diseased, or I have no soul."

One of the doctors may reply: "My brother, God has possibly created foolish souls, as well as wise ones."

The madman will answer: "If I believed what you say, I should be a still greater madman than I am. Have the kindness, you who know so much, to tell me why I am mad?"

Supposing the doctors to retain a little sense, they would say: "We know nothing about the matter."

Neither are they more able to comprehend how a brain possesses regular ideas, and makes a due use of them. They call themselves sages, and are as weak as their patient.

If the interval of reason of the madman lasts long enough, he will say to them: "Miserable mortals, who neither know the cause of my malady, nor how to cure it! Tremble, lest ye become altogether like me, or even still worse than I am! You are not of the highest rank, like Charles VI. of France, Henry VI. of England, and the German emperor Wincenslaus, who all lost their reason in the same century. You have not nearly so much wit as Blaise Pascal, James Abadie, or Jonathan Swift, who all became insane. The last of them founded a hospital for us; shall I go there and retain places for you?"

N.B. I regret that Hippocrates should have prescribed the blood of an ass's colt for madness; and I am still more sorry that the "*Manuel des Dames*" asserts that it may be cured by catching the itch. Pleasant prescriptions these, and apparently invented by those who were to take them!

— Voltaire

This book has been produced by The LedaTape Organisation on behalf of the author, who retains all rights in their material.

All copyrights in screen grabs, promotional material and other images remain the property of their respective owners.

© Simon Strong, 2015.

Acknowledgements

I started this book back in pre-Internet days but it's ended up being mostly cobbled together from shit on wikipedia and imdb.com, beefed up with the results of a good few googles. These sites in particular kept coming up:

- betedugevaudan.com
- chantrellposter.com
- filmpolski.pl
- mondo-digital.com
- mondo-erotico.com
- sheffieldhistory.co.uk

Actually, that's kinda bullshit because I wouldn't have even bothered revisiting the project if it hadn't been for the awesome staff and resources at the AFI Research Collection, and, of course, the generosity and inspiration of Mr Michael Helms.

Conventions

Foreign films are usually listed under their original title followed by a translation [in square brackets]. The translation is capitalised if this is the English title, otherwise the English title is given afterwards. Non-roman scripts are transliterated.

Exceptions to these conventions include Borowczyk's own films, which are often referred to by their English titles, and filmographies and captions which provide only English titles to conserve space, although the supplementary data is given in the index.

Most films are dated by their year of domestic release.

Book Production
War Economy standard

This book has been prepared in complete conformity with the authorised economy standards.

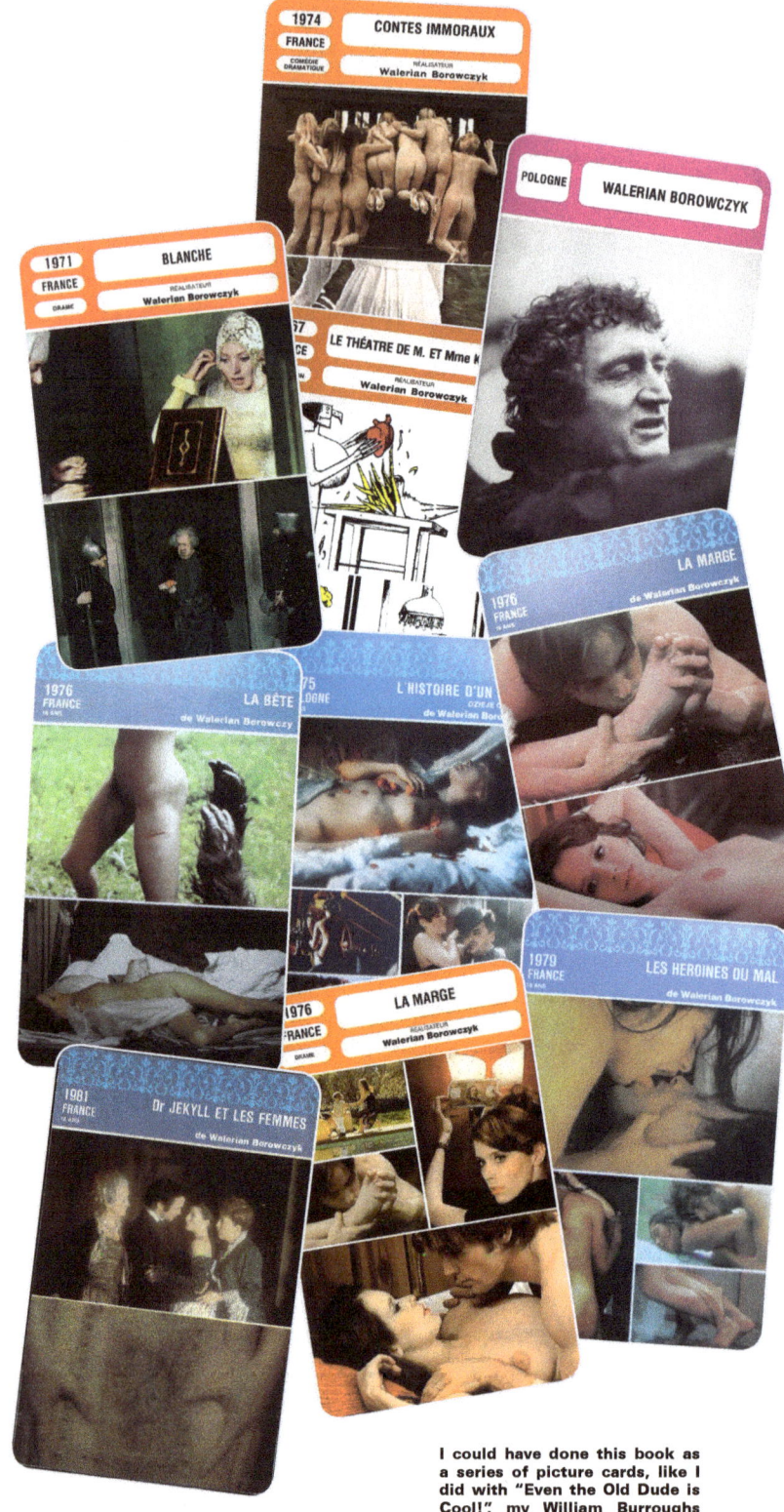

◀ **Page 2**
Szał Uniesien [Frenzy of Exultations], a famous Polish symbolist painting by Władysław Podkowinski features prominently in Borowczyk's film. The original measures 310 cm × 270 cm.

I could have done this book as a series of picture cards, like I did with "Even the Old Dude is Cool!", my William Burroughs book, but the dudes at Fiches Mr Cinema beat me to it... GAH!

CONTENTS

— INTRODUCTION The Studio 5-6-7 6
  Borowczyk's Posters 10
— BOROGRAPHY 12
— THEATRE OF MR AND MRS KABAL . . . 18
— GOTO, ISLAND OF LOVE 20
  Ligia Branice 22
— BLANCHE 24
  Anatole Dauman 26
— IMMORAL TALES 30
  Erzébet Báthory / Lucrezia Borgia /
  Thérèse Philosophe 32
  Les Rendez-vous en Forêt 34
— THE BEAST 38
  Assailed by a Snail 45
  Sirpa Lane 46
— STORY OF A SIN 50
— LA MARGE 52
— BEHIND CONVENT WALLS 54
  Nunsploitation 56
— THREE IMMORAL WOMEN 58
  Marina Pierro 60
  L'Armoire / Collections Privées 62
— LULU 64
  Wedekin's Lulu / Jack the Ripper . . . 66
— DR JEKYLL AND THE WOMEN 68
  Jeksploitation 70
— THE ART OF LOVE 72
— EMMANUELLE 5 74
  The Emmanuelle Series 77
— LOVE RITES 78
  André Pieyre de Mandiargues 80
— ZOOPHILMOGRAPHY
  Simulations of bestiality in
  (not very) mainstream cinema 82
  THE BIGGEST SCREEN 89
  Further Reading 92
— ADDENDA
  The Actual Facts about
  the Beast of Gevaudan 96
  Beauty and the Beast
  by Marie Leprince de Beaumont . . . 100
  Lokis
  by Prosper Mérimée 106
  Studio 5-6-7 (Pink Stainless Tail) 119
  Index 120

As is customary, I shall commence this belated volume berating my better qualified peers for not beating me to the punch. Obviously, it would have been much easier for me to pick up a book by someone like Daniel Bird or Marc Morris or Scott Murray than to spend nigh on twenty years cobbling together this, my own poor excuse. I'm confident that any of their works would have turned out more conventionally useful than this did. To their credit, these (and other) Boro fans have been busy, slogging away for years in print, online, and on and behind the camera, working hard to get Borowczyk into the pantheon. And what with the recent (2014) spate of retrospectives and reissues it appears that they have succeeded definitively. Surely the "definitive" volume on Borowczyk is not far off now?

But, in the meantime, here is this: my own account of The Oeuvre, focussed — or, more accurately, blurred — on his most notorious work.

It has not been necessary to devote any special effort to avoid pissing on any respective bonfires. My primary agenda is at significant odds with my colleagues. As a militant enthusiast I utterly repudiate all the empty fetishes and affectations of the academy, that abattoir of dreams where our cherished films are mere carcass to be butchered and sold. There's just no excuse. You could work in a zoo or a circus at least. So I will not be providing anything so crass as capsule reviews of the films, let alone critical readings, formal analyses or other such wankery. In any case, I am not so much concerned here with Borowczyk's work as with the milieu in which it occurred. By way of compensation, there will be jokes (some even funny) and pictures of topless women.

It's entirely possible that the reader may find all this talk of taboo genres (nazisploitation, nunsploitation, zoosploitation etc.) confronting in the extreme, but consider for a moment the wealth of material excluded: women in prison films, rape revenge films, unsimulated death films, extreme gore, and the fringes of Japanese pinku. This material is relatively benign. If you don't believe me, on no account read Robin Bougie's *Cinema Sewer* books to get some perspective. At best you'll get a nosebleed.

And finally, you shouldn't need me to tell you that sexual abuse of animals is Wrong on every conceivable level. Not only is it illegal and commonly physically dangerous to all parties involved, but there is no meaningful moral defence for the practice as there are no recorded fatalities due to sexual frustration. It's tautological to state that simulations of any proscribed act can be distinguished from their actualised counterparts by virtue of the very fact that they are simulated. As a vegetarian of many years I have no aversion to faux-meat whether derived from soy or mycoprotein, and this remains my position.

Introduction

I BELONG TO THE BEAST GENERATION

Just in case you don't know, Sheffield is the capital city of South Yorkshire in the north of England. And it's fucking massive. There's like half a million people live there, making it the third biggest city in the UK. It used to be famous for its steel industry (we were especially good with knives) but we got fucked by Thatcher in the eighties and there's nothing much left of that now. Since its foundation, built on seven hills like Rome, the city has had a reputation for militancy. George III called it a "damned bad place" and it was. The toffs down south had always done mostly all of their northern business through Manchester, which is in neighbouring Lancashire, and they studiously ignored us in the Steel City, and that was fine with us. In those days, our major cultural exports were Tony Christie and Joe Cocker, whilst Lancashire had The Beatles, Cilla Black and Jimmy Tarbuck. The emblem of Yorkshire is the white rose, whilst the Lancashire sports the more obvious and ostentatious red one. In the fifteenth century the two counties had a war on the topic of their respective flora, the relevance of which may become apparent later. But don't hold your breath.

As an early teen in the mid-seventies I used to go and hang out at the amusement arcade just up from the big Pond Street bus station. For hours I'd play video games like *Asteroids*, *Galaxians* and a strange one called *Tail Gunner* that never really caught on. When my supply of 5p pieces was exhausted I'd head home – briskly – past the gang of skinhead girls outside the chip-shop and they'd usually call out some incoherent abuse. I'd have to get away by vaulting down four flights of escalators, always jammed, with my spare bag of pickled onion Monster Munch bulging dangerously out of my snorkel parka pocket.

Waiting for a 265 back to S5, I'd sometimes wonder about the strange films that were playing at the CineCenta Twin there. It had opened in 1969 and was a members only club till 1981. That meant they could play spicier fayre than the High Street cinemas where I watched sf and spy films like a posh little twat who couldn't hack the kung fu and horror slop that my classmates were digging. Mind you, I was curious about the films at the CineCenta simply because they never got reviewed by Barry Norman or written up in *The Star*.

At that age, my interest in curves didn't extend to girls, but I was certainly interested in typography! These distinctive film posters intrigued me with their fonts that reminded me of my weekly comics. Not the classics like *Dandy* and *Beano* but the more modern prolecentric titles like *Whizzer and Chips* and *Whoopee!* To my naive eyes, the posters appeared gaudy and sophisticated at the same time. If I'd known what sleaze and glamour were back then, I would have described them as a hybrid.

◀ **Studio 5-6-7 at night. c.1979 as films include "Seven Women for Satan" (France, 1970, d. Michel Lemoine) and "Savage Weekend" (USA, 1979, d. David Paulsen) ▲ CineCenta, Flat St. ◢ The Wicker, with 5-6-7 at right, bus stops and newsagents on left of picture. Both early 1980s, photographers unknown.**

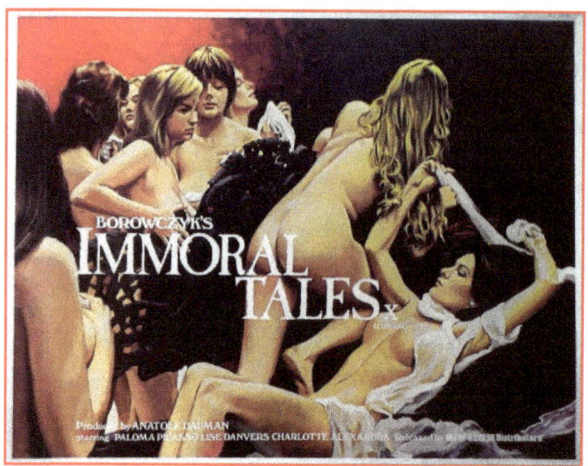

Borowczyk on the UK High Street: "Immoral Tales" was only permitted to be projected publicly in London. The painting was done by Tom Chantrell, the most recognisable of all British poster artists, who did over 7,000 posters starting in 1938. By the end of the 1970s hand-painted posters were being replaced illustrations based on photographs.

There was one other cinema where these kind of films played too and that was the Studio 5-6-7 on The Wicker. Sometimes I'd head down Waingate and over Lady's Bridge to check out the paper shop (i.e. newsagent) opposite it. the paper shop was stacked to rafters with back issues of old sf mags and they used to get in new ones from the states, *Starlog* and others. Tatty old copies of *Continental Film Review* lined the front window. I think they had a darkened back room, which must have been full of porno rags, so it could be that the other mags were used for some kinda importation cover racket, or maybe I'm addled and remembering the whole thing wrong.

Like the CineCenta, the 5-6-7 went through phases of screening what passed for filth back before switching to more uh general interest films and then back again. Representative films that played the 5-6-7 were: *What The Swedish Butler Saw* (Sweden/USA, 1975, d. Vernon P. Becker), *Emmanuelle* (France, 1974, d. Just Jaeckin), *Playgirls and the Vampire* (Italy, 1960, d. Piero Regnoli), *Supervixens* (USA, 1975, d. Russ Meyer).

Sometimes as I waited for a bus I'd try to freak out the furtive clientele by staring at them as they went in and out. They also showed *The Beast*, but I'm inclined to think that it more likely the 1974 Sergio Corbucci film than Borowczyk's epic. The 5-6-7 closed in 1989 and was demolished to make way for a ring road.

As far as I know, all that's left of it is a recurring dream that comes back to me every three months or so. I find myself back in a replica of the 5-6-7 faithfully recreated down to the last detail. This is weird because I'm pretty sure I never set foot in the place, and I'm not sure why it's a replica as dreaming about the actual cinema would make more sense. Just as I'm hitting up the snack bar for some Spangles I realise I'm asleep and I better get into the auditorium to check out the big show sharpish but as I shove through the curtains to the auditorium I always wake up.

So I quit Sheffield in 1983 and moved to Brighton (Hove actually) on the south coast where employment prospects were better and getting-the-shit-kicked-out-of-you-on-a-regular-basis prospects were worse. By this time I was, of course, interested in kung fu and horror films, and girls. I decided it would be a good idea to familiarise myself with arty shit so I could chat up the sophisticated south coast women. Not just films you dig, but books and paintings too. I bought the whole fucking shithouse and started hanging out at the Duke of Yorks on Preston Circus. They showed selections from the art-house canon but when the pubs turned out on Friday and Saturday they'd have cool double-bills where you could sit and piss on with your take-out or even spark up if you was holding.

Back in those days before the internet, the first "cult classics" were just coming on stream and exploitation films were just starting to be rescued from oblivion but there weren't screens or prints enough to make much of a canon yet. There was the VHS underground, of course, but I didn't have a tv set let alone a VCR so I wasn't connected and I had a better chance of seeing a Jack Smith than a Lucio Fulci.

Borowczyk was lucky that Anatole Dauman's Argos Films were widely distributed in the UK and this allowed *Immoral Tales* and *The Beast* to become popular late-night selections for art-house cinemas, although the latter was still uncertified and could only be played at cinema clubs, like the Duke of Yorks was.

So one Friday I rolled out of the Stanford Arms and instead of *Easy Rider* (USA, 1969, d. Dennis Hopper) or *Up in Smoke* (USA, 1978, d. Lou Adler) or *The Blues Brothers* (USA, 1980, d. John Landis) I got to see *Immoral Tales*, which struck me as a sexed-up French Hammer film. I hoped that the second feature was just as hot. Well, next was *The Beast*, so the rest is history. I became Borowczyk's leading evangelist on the south coast, even though it took me five years to find someone who could tell me how to pronounce his name (roughly boroff-chick). I went back to the Duke's every time they showed one of his films, whether I'd seen it before or not, dragging along enthusiastic mates or less enthusiastic girlfriends.

One time they double-billed *The Beast* with Pasolini's *Salo* (Italy, 1975). Not in the mood for the cruelty and coprophagy, I decided to skip *Salo* and waited outside for the second film. I could hear screams and gunshots from the auditorium as I snarfed my filter coffee and carrot cake in the foyer. Suddenly the moth-eaten red curtains parted and shabby old bastard in a macintosh stumbled out looking dazed.

"That's really not my kind of thing at all..." he went.

"I'm only here for *The Beast*." I replied waggishly, spitting a few orange crumbs.

The disappointed and traumatised old pervert lurched out into the past midnight and never knew what he missed.

★

It turned out later that I'm not the only Sheffielder disproportionately enamoured of Borowczyk's film. Pulp front-man and "lovable" pundit Jarvis Cocker appeared on *Red Light Zone*, a 1994 Channel 4 tv season of banned films, raving about *The Beast* and his personal reflections on it. The cunt. Jarvis is always jumping my bandwagons. It gives me the shits but he's a funty dude so I guess that's okay. More impressively, Adi Newton, of industrial-electro pioneers Clock DVA, used some Borowczyk references on the sleeve notes to his disc *The Act*. Sadly, when I checked, the girls out of the Human League were unavailable for comment.

★

In 1995 I started up my CodeX publishing outfit and wanted to commission the great English pulp hack Guy N. Smith to write to write a novelisation of *The Beast*. Unfortunately I had to leave the UK suddenly and the idea was shelved. I had met the great author the year before at the London Paperback Fair, where I had co-incidentally picked up a flyer blurbing the forthcoming publication of Cathal Tohill and Pete Tombs' book *Immoral Tales*, which featured long articles on Borowczyk alongside Jesús Franco, Jean Rollin, Alain Robbe-Grillet, and other names that will likely crop up in the following pages. The films therein had just started trickling out via Redemption Video, and soon other vendors were getting in on the action too. In 2001 Nouveaux Pictures put out the first uncut English subbed version of the film on VHS. I had a VHS (and a TV) by then, and it became the first purchase I made online.

Upon viewing I realised that, given the film is 94 minutes long, if I wrote 400 words for each minute of video I would have 37,600 words, enough for a novel. With hindsight, this turned out to be a stupid idea, the scant fruits of which you may find later in this book.

Over the next decade or so, still convinced that the world needed a full-length book on Borowczyk, I revisited the project several times, always abandoning it as something more pressing cropped up or if it took a nasty turn in the subject matter department.

Eventually, it was the twenty-first century and I was using the AFI Research Collection to help research Adrien Clerc's book on William Burroughs' pal Antony Balch. The AFIRC held an incredible array of film journals from the 20th century, including many copies of *Continental Film Review*. Scouring the archive for Balch-related goodies I blundered into a number of interesting articles on Borowczyk. By this stage I wanted to do a tribute to CFR and, given the massive hoard of research, I thought it would be funty to start the Borowczyk project again. So I did. As the book progressed I heard of Arrow Films plan to reissue all Boro's early films in remastered versions with a comprehensive book. I was skint as all fuck and by the time I'd saved up for the ten-disc set it had sold out on pre-orders. Which is a bastard as it would probably have been helpful. What ya gonna do? Like I said, this book has been almost twenty years coming. I'll be fucked if I'm going to wait any longer. Sorry.

★

Coverage of Borowczyk in Continental Film Review. ▶ "Immoral Tales" from September 1974. ◀ "Story of a Sin" from April 1976.

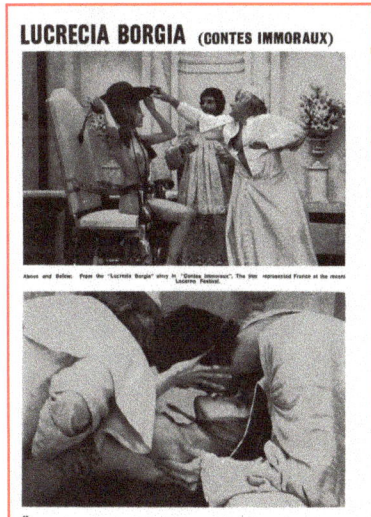  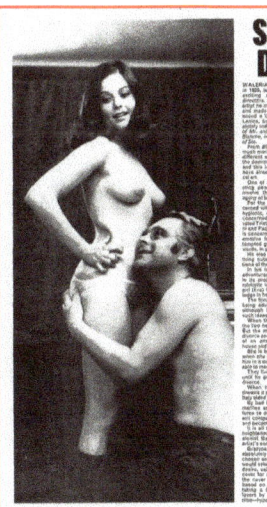

SZTUKA ULICY

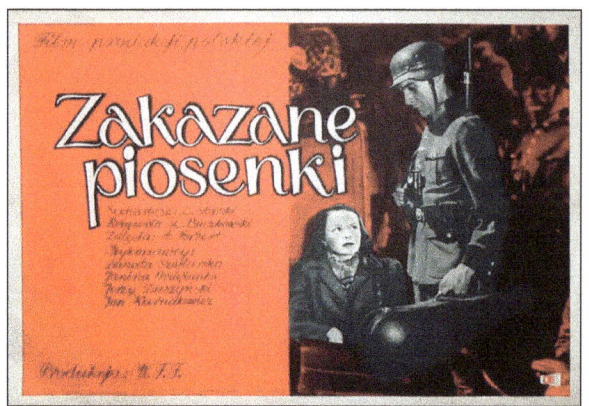

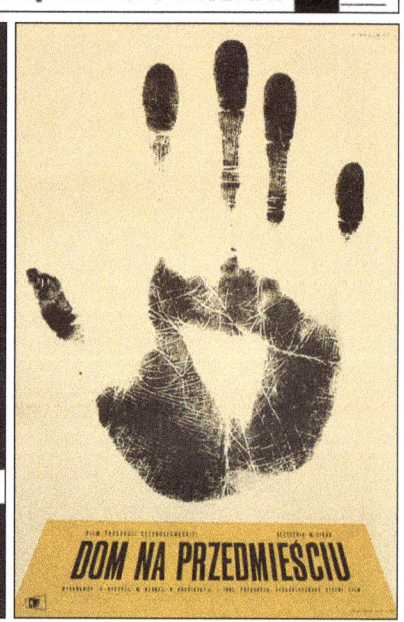

BOROWCZYK
4 1 3 1 4 3 10 4 5

These are just a few of the many posters that Borowczyk designed between graduating from the Cracow Academy of Art in 1951 and moving to Paris in 1958.

◀▼ *Zakazane Piosenki* [forbidden songs] Poland, 1946, d. Leonard Buczkowski. This farcical musical dealing with life under the nazi occupation was the first post-war Polish feature film. It remains well-known and is still often shown on Polish TV.

▼ *Korzenie* [roots] (Mexico, 1954, d. Benito Alazraki) A portmanteau film about the plight of indigenous Mexicans based on stories by Francisco Rojas Gonzáles.

◀◀ *Wieczor Trzech Kroli* [*Twelth Night*] (USSR, 1956, d. Jakow Fried). An adaptation of the Shakespeare play.

◀ *Do Ostatniej Kropli Krwi* [to the last drop of blood] (USSR, 1956, d. Borys Buniejew) Polish release of За власть Советов [for the power of the soviets].

◀◀▲ *Prawdziwy Koniec Wielkiej Wojny* [the real end of the great war] (Poland, 1956, d. Jerzy Kawalerowicz). The director would follow this with *Matka Joanna od Aniołów* [*Mother Joan of the Angels*] (Poland, 1961) and become one of the most celebrated of Polish directors.

◀▲ *Siodma Pieczec* [*The Seventh Seal*] (Sweden, 1957, d. Ingmar Bergman).

▲ *Dom na Przedmiesciu* [house in the suburbs] (Czech, 1955, d. Miroslav Cikan). Polish release of *Na Konci Mesta* [at the end of the city].

The word **borowczyk** is a verb meaning "to utterly destroy an opponent in a game of Scrabble" and it will get you 35 points just by itself without any bonus squares, and the chances are that you'll get the seven letter bonus. Or perhaps it's an esoteric chemical formula, half gas, half metal.

For many years fans were hampered in their research for ignorance of a definitive pronunciation. I asked a Polish Battle of Britain veteran but I couldn't understand what he said. In those days we didn't even have a reliable birthdate. There were conflicting reports. It could have been 12 September or 21 October. Turns out it was 2 September. Probably. We used to be told that he was born in 1923, but 1932 is currently more favoured. Borowczyk was a very private man and I have found no biographical details of his youth, and nothing in his films appears autobiographical.

In 1949, following the nazi defeat and the establishment of communism in Poland, Borowczyk commenced studies in painting and printmaking at the Cracow Academy of Art. It was there that he started making amateur documentary shorts. After graduating in 1951 he worked as a litho artist and designer of posters (often for films) and in 1953 was awarded a national prize for his work.

In 1954 Boro (as he was forgivably abbreviated) visited Paris and made two short films before returning to Poland to work with fellow lithographer Jan Lenica on more short films and newsreel segments before leaving again, settling permanently in Paris in 1958.

Some time prior to that he had married Ligia Branice, from Krasnystaw in the east of Poland. She would go on to appear in several of his shorts and features, and they would remain together until his death.

In 1960 Boro wrote a script for *Le Dernier Voyage de Gulliver* [the last voyage of Gulliver] but the film was unproduced. and the early sixties saw him making adverts, sometimes for Italian TV, and this was the provenance of *Holy Smoke*, *Gancia*, *Le Petit Poucet*. In the middle of the decade he provided animated title sequences for René Clément's *Les Félines* and Jean-Paul Rappenau's *Le Vie de Château*. Boro's star was rising, and his shorts began to collect festival prizes.

Throughout the early sixties Boro worked on his animated feature, *Le Theatre de M. et Mme Kabal*, which debuted in 1967. He also provided animations for a surreal historical drama, *20.000 Ans à la Française* (known in English as *The French Way of Looking at It*), which was directed by the producer of *Kabal*, Jacques Forgeot and filmed by Boro's cameraman Guy Durban.

By 1968 Boro was ready to produce his first live action feature...

BOROGRAPHY

Byl Sobie Raz

Strip-Tease

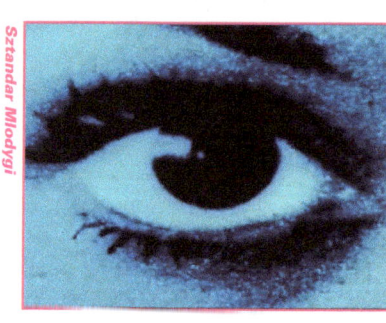

Sztandar Mlodygi

Nagrodzone Uczucie

Sierpien [August]
Poland | 1946 | 1 min

Glowa [the head]
Poland | 1949 | 1 min

Boro's rarely-seen first (live action) films were made principally for his own education and very little data about them has come to light yet.

Zywe Fotografie [living pictures]
Poland | 1954

A short documentary filmed in Paris.

Atelier de Fernand Léger [Fernand Léger's studio]
Poland | 1954

Boro's first of several shorts about his favourite artists. This is a short documentary made in Gif-sur-Yvette, France, at the studio of Fernand Léger, whose remarkable surrealist film *Ballet Mecanique* (France, 1924) seems to have exerted a profound influence of Boro's work.

Jesien [Autumn]
Poland | 1955 | 7 min

A short live-action film of a stroll in a deserted park in the autumn, where the colours of summer suddenly return for a moment.

Byl Sobie Raz [once upon a time]
Poland | 1957 | 9 min   with Jan Lenica

⚜ Silver Lion, Venice
⚜ Third Prize, Warsaw / Warsaw Mermaid
⚜ Gold Ducat, Mannheim

Influenced this time by Joan Miró, Boro and Lenica used paper cut-outs and magazine clippings to show an abstract avian love story that may or may not have metaphorical implications.

Strip-Tease
Poland | 1957 | 1 min   with Jan Lenica

Dni Oswiaty [school days]
Poland | 1957 | 1 min   with Jan Lenica

Short segments made for the Polish newsreel service.

Sztandar Mlodygi [banner of youth]
Poland | 1957 | 2 min   with Jan Lenica

A trippy cut-up style promotional film made at the Documentary Film Studios to promote a newspaper for young people, originally the journal of ZMP (Polish Youth Union), published in the years 1950-1997.

Nagrodzone Uczucie [love requited]
Poland | 1957 | 9 min   with Jan Lenica

One of the most spectacular instances of the Repollero method of animation, using a rostrum camera on still images, that was popular for children's cartoons especially in Eastern Europe.

This short film uses the beautiful folk art of Jana Plaskocinskiego set to music by the Orkiestra Deta Gazowni Miejskiej to relate a simple love story, presumably that of the artist and his wife.

Sztuka Ulicy [art of the streets]
Poland | 1958 | 12 min   d. Konstanty Gordon

Boro provided the commentary (co-written with art historian Szymon Bojko) for this short documentary on poster art.

Boro's involvement seems likely to have been attributable to his own award-winning poster designs.

Dom [House]

Poland | 1958 | 12 min   with Jan Lenica

🏆 BAFTA nomination
🏆 Grand Prix, Brussels.

With an unsettling score by Włodzimierz Kotoński and featuring Ligia Branice in her first role for her husband, this creepy masterpiece was Boro and Lenica's stab at synthesising their diverse animation techniques into a coherent whole.

Amos Vogel pointed out that this film "brought to the West the first intimation of a Polish avant-garde film movement opposed to prevailing sterilities of Polish social realism."

Stadion [stadium]

Poland | 1958 | 20 min   d. Stanislaw Jedryka

Boro was a consultant on this short film that starred his wife Ligia.

Szkola [School]

Poland | 1958 | 9 min

🏆 Special mention, Oberhausen.

A display of military drill is told in animated stills. A humble private is frustrated first by a fly then by a faulty rifle. Exhausted he retires to dream of promotion and disembodied legs. Ardent fans of this uncommon animation technique may want to seek out the universally derided *An Eye for the Girls* (USA, 1966, d. Harold Klein).

Terra Incognita

France | 1959 | 3 min | b/w

An animated film in which Borowczyk utilized Alexandre Alexeieff's pin screen technique to achieve a shadow and movement effect. The most celebrated example of this rare technique is Alexieff's prologue to *The Trial* (France/W. Germany/Italy, 1962, d. Orson Welles).

French TV spots

France | 1961 | 4 × 1 min   📺

After arriving in France, in 1961 Boro made several one minute spots for ORTF, the French TV network: *Le Magicienne* [the magician], *La Foule* [the crowd], *La Tete* [the head] and *La Boite a Musique* [the music box]. We have been unable to trace any further details of these.

Les Astronautes [The Astronauts]

France | 1959 | 14 min   with Chris Marker

🏆 FIPRESCI Prize, Oberhausen
🏆 Prix du film de recherche, Venice
🏆 Special Prize & Gold Medal, Bergamo

Boro's first outing for Argos Films is the story of an amateur astronaut and his owl travelling in a cardboard spaceship. Features cameos by Argos Films founders Anatole Dauman and Philippe Lifchitz, as well as Ligia Branice, whom Marker would cast in his 1962 masterpiece *La Jetée*.

Marker reportedly did not contribute to the film, but lent his name for bureaucratic reasons as a favour. Marker didn't work in the field of animation, but his short masterpiece *La Jetée* is composed (almost) entirely of still images in a manner that seems to owe much to both this film and Borowczyk's earlier *Szkola*. Viewers may also notice similarities between *Les Astronautes* and *Yellow Submarine* (UK, 1968, d. George Dunning).

Le Concert de M. et Mme Kabal [the concert of Mr. and Mrs. Kabal]

France | 1962 | 6 min

A precursor to Borowczyk's *Kabal* feature. Mme. Kabal's piano recital (with music actually by Avenir de Monfred) begins unpromisingly but turns out quite nicely, though not for M. Kabal, whose grisly demise propels their piano into a strange hyperspatial dimension.

L'Encyclopedie de Grand'maman en 13 Volumes [Grandmama's encyclopedia in 13 volumes]

France | 1963 | 7 min | b/w

Reminiscent of Max Ernst's collage novels such as *Une Semaine de Bonté* but funnier, Boro's animations of 18th century etchings are his most Gilliamesque creations. It's a shame he only made the entries for the first three letters of the alphabet.

Renaissance

France | 1963 | 10 min | b/w

🏆 Jury's Special Prize, Tours.

A homage to the neglected experimental film-maker Hy Hirsh. Destroyed objects

Dom

Szkola

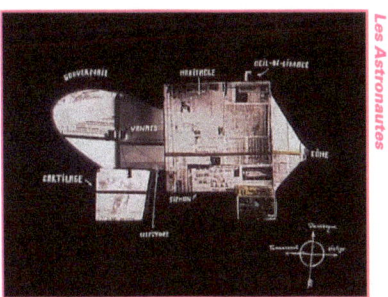

Les Astronautes

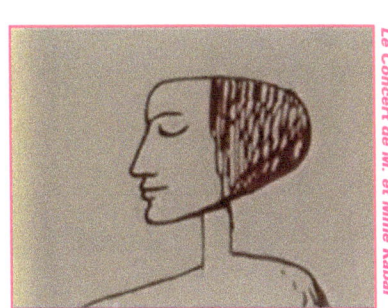

Le Concert de M. et Mme Kabal

L'Encyclopedie de Grand'maman

Renaissance

Les Félins

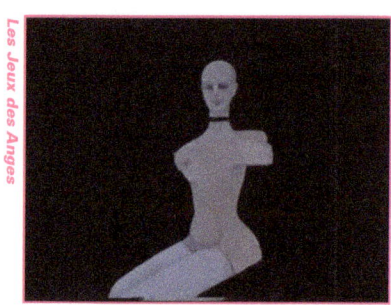
Les Jeux des Anges

Le Petit Poucet

Le Dictionnaire De Joachim

are restored to existence thanks to the miracle of reverse-motion. "Useless leftovers of different kinds attract and find one another and unite to give birth to a new world of commonplace, magical things. A haunting, disturbing work." (Amos Vogel)

Holy Smoke

France | 1963 | 10 min

A promotional film for Wills tobacco.

TV ads

Italy | 1963-64 | 7 × 2 min   **TV**

From 1963-64 Boro made several approx. two minute TV spots for the Italian market. These could have been ads or informational films. The titles were: *Les Bibliotheques* [libraries], *Les Écoles* [schools], *Le Musée* [the museum], *La Fille Sage* [the wise girl], *L'Écriture* [handwriting], *Les Stroboscopes: Les Magasins du XIXe Siecle* [stroboscopes: shops of the nineteenth century] and *Gancia*. No further details are currently available.

Les Félins [felines]

France | 1964 | 2 min | b/w   d. René Clément

Boro provided the animated title sequence for Réne Clément's thriller starring Alain Delon and Jane Fonda, known in England as *The Love Cage* and the USA as *Joy House*.

Les Jeux des Anges
[The Games of Angels]

France | 1964 | 12 min

♛ Special Jury Prize & Int'l Critics Prize, Tours

This profoundly unsettling abstract piece bears the unmistakable influence of Léger and De Chirico. Amos Vogel described Borowczyk's allegory of the Polish concentration camps as "a masterpiece of modern art" and Terry Gilliam remarked "*Jeux des Anges* was just extraordinary: the sense that you're on a train with the walls of the city going past, and then the sound of angels' wings – incredible."

La Prima Donna

France | 1964 | 10 min   d. Philippe Lifchitz

Boro provided artistic advice for this short film shot at the Palace of Versailles by the co-founder of Argos Films.

Le Petit Poucet
[Tom Thumb]

France | 1965? | 2 min | b/w   **TV**

A short TV ad for pasta that starts as an woodcut-style animation of the fairy tale that suddenly takes a more culinary twist.

Un Été Torride
[a torrid summer]

France | 1965 | 2 min

An episode from the full-length film *Le Théâtre de M. et Mme. Kabal*, which had been originally intended as a series of episodes for TV.

Le Dictionnaire de Joachim
[Joachim's dictionary]

France | 1965 | 9 min

Having attempted an encyclopedia, Boro now provides a tour of the alphabet based on drawings by Ligia Branice. The jury of Tours Film Festival were less impressed than they had been with *Renaissance* and deemed this one "detrimental to the prestige of art".

Camera Obscura

France | 1965

Made as a trailer for programmes of Boro's shorts, also used as an introduction to the programmes.

Rosalie

France | 1966 | 15 min

♛ Special Mention, Locarno
♛ Silver Bear, Berlin
♛ Golden Dragon, Krakow

Boro's first significant live-action short was a rendition of Guy de Maupassant's story *Rosalie Prudent* with Ligia in the title role, confessing the murder of an infant, punctuated with stills showing evidence of the crime.

La Vie de Château
[life in a castle]

AKA *A Matter of Resistance*

France | 1966 | 2 min | b/w
     d. Jean-Paul Rappeneau

Given Boro's later penchant for making films about life in castles, it's no surprise he provided the animated titles for Jean-Paul Rappeneau's film with Catherine Deneuve.

Vingt Mille Ans a la Française
[20,000 years of the French]

AKA *The French Way of Looking at it*

1967 | France | 80 min   d. Jacques Forgeot

Boro animated engravings for this comic documentary, directed by the producer of *Goto* and photographed by Guy Durban.

Gavotte
France | 1967 | 10 min

🏆 Gold Ducat, Mannheim.

The travails of a 17th century dwarf in his battle for somewhere to sit, set to the sounds of a peaceful gavotte.

One of the diminutive stars, Roberto, went on to play in Boro's *Blanche* (1972) and many works for other directors including a role in Jerry Lewis's legendary *The Day the Clown Cried* (1972). The other, Ludo, fared less well but did land some TV roles. The director of photography is Guy Durban who went on to photograph all of Boro's features up till *Immoral Tales*.

Diptyque [diptych]
France | 1967 | 8 min

🏆 Interfilm Award, Mannheim.

A film of two halves. A silent monochrome clip of an agricultural worker, followed by sentimental images set to Georges Bizet's "The Pearl Fishers". This one was also photographed by Guy Durban.

Le Théâtre de M. et Mme Kabal
[*The Theatre of Mr. and Mrs. Kabal*]

France | 1967 | 80 min   **F**

Goto, L'Ile d'Amour
[*Goto, Island of Love*]

France | 1967 | 93 min   **F**

Feature films. See following pages for more information.

Le Phonographe
[the phonograph]

France | 1969 | 6 min

Another Durban-lensed riff on *Renaissance*, this time featuring an exploding gramophone.

Blanche
France | 1972 | 92 min   **F**

Live action feature. See following pages for more information.

La Véritable Histoire de la Bête du Gévaudan
[the true story of the Beast of Gévaudan]

France | 1973 | 18 min

In 1972 Boro was commissioned by Dauman to shoot an ending for Alain Fleischer's film *Les Rendez-Vous en Forêt.* [meetings in the forest].

Boro's work was vehemently rejected by Fleischer and the film suppressed by court order. Boro went on to screen his footage as a segment of his then forthcoming *Immoral Tales* the at the 17th Regus London Film Festival (24 & 25 Nov. 1973) and won the London Festival Choice award. However, the footage was dropped from that project and resurfaced as the climax to his subsequent feature, *The Beast*.

Une Collection Particulière
[*A Private Collection*]

France | 1973 | 14 min

In this fascinating and educational short film, Boro's friend and frequent collaborator Mandiargues gives us a conducted tour of highlights of Boro's collection of erotic artefacts. Or maybe they're really clever fakes constructed by Borowczyk himself? Either way, etchings, optical toys and mechanical devices are all featured. This was originally intended as a prelude to *Immoral Tales* and it's a shame it wasn't included as it would provide a nice framework to hang the episodes on.

The film premiered at the Oberhausen Film Festival in 1973 and its salacious content provoked something of a scandal. The film was subsequently re-issued in a version with fingers obscuring the most offending details and shorn of a short vintage clip of a woman with a dog that poses censorship challenges to this day.

Rosalie

La Vie de Chateau

Gavotte

Diptyque

Une Collection Particulière

Escargot de Venus

Brief von Paris

L'Amour Monstre de Tous les Temps

Collections Privée / L'Armoire

Scherzo Infernal

Contes Immoraux
[*Immoral Tales*]

France | 1974 | 103 min 🅵

La Bête [*The Beast*]

France | 1975 | 102 min 🅵

Dzieje Grzechu [*Story of a Sin*]

Poland | 1975 | 128 min 🅵

Live action features. See following pages for more information.

Escargot de Venus
[*Venus on the Half-Shell*]

France | 1975 | 5 min

Produced by Argos Films as a supporting feature for *The Beast*, this is a miniature portrait of Bona Tibertelli De Pisis (1926-2000) whose erotic pencil drawings of hermaphrodite couplings were inspired symbolist poet Remy de Gourmont's *Physique de l'Amour* (1903). Here she reads from the work in her atelier while Borowczyk tracks over some of her paintings whilst a record of Rumanian folk music play. Bona was the niece of renowned Italian painter Filippo de Pisis and, not coincidentally, wife of André Pieyre de Mandiargues.

Brief von Paris [letter from Paris]

France/W. Germany | 1975 | 37 min 📺

Originally made for German tv, and little-seen since, Boro's montage-style documentary on the inhuman face of the Eternal City has no narration or spoken dialogue, relying instead on a musique concrète soundtrack by Tom Schmitt and Borowczyk himself.

La Marge [the margin]

AKA *The Streetwalker*

France | 1976 | 91 min 🅵

Live action feature. See following pages for more information.

L'Amour Monstre de Tous les Temps
[the greatest love of all time]

France | 1977 | 10 min

🏆 Grand Prix, IIIeme
🏆 Best Direction, Montreal.

Produced by Argus films, this is a portrait of Serbian erotic surrealist Ljubomir Popović, known as Ljuba, shot mostly in his atelier and devoid of dialogue. We see him at work on one of his elaborate canvasses from the first brush-strokes to the finished work. Again, there is a Mandiargues connection, as the author had produced a monograph on Ljuba in 1972.

Interno di un Convento
[inside a convent]

AKA *Behind Convent Walls*

Italy | 1978 | 95 min 🅵

Les Heroines du Mal
[heroines of evil]

AKA *Three Immoral Women*

France | 1979 | 111 min 🅵

Live action features. See following pages for more information.

Jouet Joyeux [happy toys]

France | 1979 | 3 min

A short on the topic of praxinoscopes produced to tie in *Les Heroines Du Mal*.

Collections Privées
[*Private Collections*]

France/Japan | 1979 | 103 min

Borowczyk contributed *L'Armoire* [the wardrobe] to this portmanteau film. See following pages for more information.

Hyper Auto Erotic Art — Hayashi

France (?) | 1980 | 75 min 🅵

A hard-to-find feature length documentary about Yoshifumi Hayashi who was born in Fukuoka, Japan, in 1948 and moved to Paris in 1974 where he began making highly detailed erotic pencil drawings, influenced by Hans Bellmer. A couple of years earlier Borowczyk had provided the introduction to a monograph by Hayashi.

Lulu

W.Germany/Italy/France | 1980 | 86 min 🅵

Docteur Jekyll et les Femmes [*Dr Jekyll and the Women*]

France | 1981 | 92 min 🅵

L'Art d'Aimer [*The Art of Love*]

France/Italy | 1983 | 100 min 🅵

Live action features. See following pages for more information.

Scherzo Infernal
[infernal symphony]

France | 1984 | 6 min

Boro's final assignment for Anatole Dauman was also his final short. This beautiful short composed of his own drawings, telling the story of a love affair between an errant angel and devil. It's narrated by Yves Robert (director of *Le Château de ma Mère* and *La Gloire de mon Père*) and has a score by electronic musical genius Bernard Parmegiani.

Emmanuelle 5

France | 1987 | 85 min (versions) [F]

Cérémonie d'Amour
[*Love Rites*]

France | 1988 | 98 min [F]

Live action features. See following pages for more information.

---

further reading

Cahiers du Cinéma, vol.16 no.96, June 1959, p.28, (in French.)

Chaplin, no.63, April 1966, p.151, (in Swedish.)

Coniam, Matthew. "Angel Games: The Early Films of Walerian Borowczyk" in Andy Black (ed), *Necronomicon: Book Two*, (London: Creation Books, 1998), p. 79–87.

Durgnat, Raymond, "Borowczyk and the Cartoon Renaissance." *Film Comment*, Jan/Feb 1976. p.37-47.

Film Dope, no.4, March 1974 p.25-26.

Film Dope, no.8, October 1975, p.24b.

Film Quarterly, vol.19 no.2, December 1965, p.52.

Films and Filming, vol.11 no.7, April 1965, p.54.

Image et Son, no.136/137, December 1960, p.22, (in French.)

Image et Son, no.207, July 1967, p.25-30, (in French.)

Pierre, Sylvie. "The Theatre of Monsieur Borowczyk." *Afterimage* no.13, October 1987, p.79-83.

Polish Film Polonaise, no.5/6, September 1976, p.17. (in English, French and Polish.)

Série Rose [pink series]

In the early 1990s, Borowczyk directed four episodes of this popular French tv series that ran for 26 episodes from November 1986. It featured the historical international classics of literary erotica adapted by directors including Harry Kümel and Michel Boisrond. Most writers only got one story featured, but Boro's fave Guy de Maupassant had no less than four featured, none by Boro, who had visited the author for his episode of *Private Collections*. In addition to predictable authors such as de Sade, Restif de La Bretonne, Comte de Mirabeau, the series featured the work of many names unfamiliar in the anglosphere. An English-dubbed version was aired in the US under the title *Softly from Paris*.

Almanach des Adresses des Demoiselles de Paris
[almanac of addresses of ladies of Paris]

France | 1991 | 30 min [TV]

Episode 13 was based on the anonymous 1791 annotated directory of Parisian brothels. For dramatic purposes Boro added a framing story concerning a young aristocrat discovering a copy of the almanac in a bookshop.

Un Traitement Justifié
[a justified treatment]

France | 1992 | 30 min [TV]

Episode 14 was based on Giovanni Boccaccio's short story "La Précaution Inutile" [the useless precaution] which is probably drawn from the Decameron. This version starred Marina Pierro in her last role for Borowczyk.

Le Lotus d'Or
[the golden lotus]

France | 1992 | 30 min [TV]

Episode 18, Borowczyk's personal favourite of the four, is based on the 16th century Chinese classic by Jin Ping Mei, which is regarded as one of the earliest and most sophisticated sustained narratives.

L'Expert Halima
[Halima the expert]

France | 1992 | 30 min [TV]

Episode 19 is based on a tale from the *Thousand and One Nights* of Scheherazade.

Théâtre de M. et Mme Kabal
THEATRE OF MR. AND MRS. KABAL

France | 1967 | 77 min

🏆 Interfilm Award, Mannheim

Directed by	Walerian Borowczyk
Screenplay and original story by	Walerian Borowczyk

•••••••••••••••••••• **CAST** ••••••••••••••••••••

Louisette Rousseau	Voice of Mme Kabal
Pierre Collet	Voice of M. Kabal
Louis Jojot	
Renata Astruc	
Jacqueline Boivin	
Edith Catry	
Yvonne Landry	
Kathy Luc	
Maïté Mansoura	
Mei-Chen	

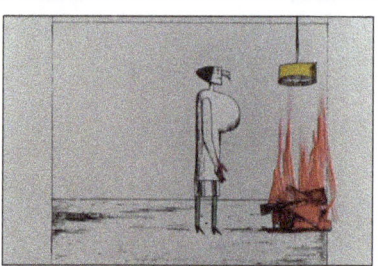

•••••••••••••••••••• **CREW** ••••••••••••••••••••

André G. Brunelin	executive producer
Jacques Forgeot	producer
Music by	Avenir de Monfred
Cinematography by	Guy Durban
	Francis Pronier
Film Editing by	Claude Blondel
Production Design by	Walerian Borowczyk
Claudette Coulant	makeup artist
Serge Groffe	
Jean Guerbette	unit manager
Daniel Pauquet	production manager
Madeleine Quiquandon	unit production manager
Claude Copin	assistant director
Brigitte Duvorgé	
Claude Blondel	foley artist
Louis Perrin	sound
Gérard Cox	stop-motion photographer
Philippe Malémont	
Francis Pronier	
Marcellin Lerouge	key grip
Daniel Mamet	electrician
Umbert Pieri	assistant camera

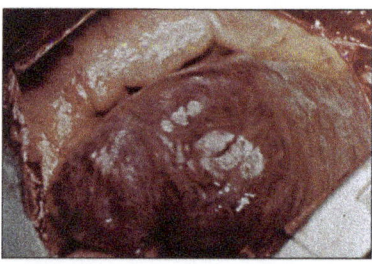

• • • • • • • • • • • • • • • • SYNOPSIS • • • • • • • • • • • • • • • •

Borowczyk's first full-length feature was an animated film drawn (or designed, the sub-title is ambiguous in French) for adults. The spare line-drawings are rendered mostly in washed-out monochrome with soberly coloured highlights, and occasionally interspersed with live-action sequences such as the introduction by Borowczyk himself or mutoscope-style footage of girls undressing.

The film was conceived as a series for television and this is betrayed in its episodic structure. Raymond Durgnat's remarkable essay on Borowczyk refers only briefly to this film but usefully designates the episodes: The Creation of Mr and Mrs Kabal, Mr and Mrs Kabal at the Seaside, Mr and Mrs Kabal at Home, Mr Kabal's Fantastic Voyage into Mrs Kabal, Mrs Kabal's Atom Bomb, Mr Kabal Goes Big Game Hunting, Mr Kabal Photographer, Mrs Kabal Sings a Lullaby, Mr and Mrs Kabal Throw a Party. Boro's 1962 short **The Concert of M. & Mme Kabal** is not included in the feature.

Mme. Kabal herself is a monstrous machine-like creature given over to all manner of destructive impulses whilst M. Kabal, her doting, if lecherous, spouse is no less sinister in his docility and attentiveness. They seem well-adapted to their mechanical home and the weird landscape that they inhabit, and their marriage is realistic perhaps in its mixture of affection and violence. The couple remind one of Ma and Pa Ubu from Alfred Jarry's Ubu Plays. The most touching moment occurs when Mme. Kabal is poisoned by a butterfly and M. Kabal, having briefed himself by viewing **Corps Profond** [deep body] (France,1960, d. Igor Barrère & Etienne Lalou), miniaturises himself to embark on a Fantastic Voyage to save her.

• • • • **FURTHER READING** • • • •

Allombert, Guy. **Image et Son**, no.222, December 1968, p.76, in French.

Cervoni, Albert. **Cinéma 68**, no.124 p.110, March 1968, in French.

Durgnat, Raymond, "Borowczyk and the Cartoon Renaissance." **Film Comment**, Jan/Feb 1976. p.37-47.

Johnston, Claire. **Monthly Film Bulletin**, vol.36 no.427, August 1969, p.166.

Marcorelles, Louis. **Living Cinema: New Directions in Contemporary Film-making.** London: George Allen & Unwin Ltd, 1973.

Thirard, Paul-Louis. **Positif**, April 1968, no.94 p.70, in French.

French poster

Goto, l'Île d'Amour

GOTO, ISLAND OF LOVE

France | 1968 | 93 min | b/w with colour sequences

🏆 Grand Prix du Challenge Intl des Cinemas d'art et d'essai
🏆 Georges Sadoul Prize, France

Directed by	Walerian Borowczyk
Original scenario	Walerian Borowczyk
Dialogue	Walerian Borowczyk
	Dominique Duvergé

············· CAST ·············

Pierre Brasseur	Goto III
Ligia Branice	Glossia, his wife
Guy Saint-Jean	Grozo
Jean-Pierre Andréani	Lt Gono
Ginette Leclerc	Gonasta, Glossia's mother
René Dary	Gomor, Glossia's father
Fernand Bercher	Tutor
Michel Charrel	Grymp
Pierre Collet	
Raoul Darblay	General Gwino
Rudy Lenoir	Magistrate
Maritin	
Colette Régis	Head of brothel
Michel Thomass	Gra
Ari Arcadi	Dog executioner
Guy Bonnafoux	Gurto
Canari	
Robert Capia	
André Cassan	Doctor
Hubert Lassiat	General with glasses
Allain Marco	
Noël Mickely	Man with musical saw
Paul Pallardi	
Percival Russel	Gotudo
Pascale Brouillard	Gauda
Alain Noël	
Steve Kalfa	Gilo

············· CREW ·············

René Thévenet	executive producer
Louis Duchesne	producer
Cinematography by	Guy Durban
Film Editing by	Charles Bretoneiche
Serge Groffe	makeup artist
Renée Coulant	assistant makeup artist

Louis Duchesne	production manager
Claude Cheutin	assistant production manager
Théo Michel	unit production manager
Georges Combes	assistant unit manager
Alain Pottiez	assistant unit manager
Patrick Saglio	first assistant director
Gérard de Lagarde	sound
Norbert Gernolle	
Jacques-Clément Duval	sound mixer
Alain Dagbert	still photographer
Jean-Pierre Platel	first assistant camera
Noël Véry	assistant camera
Colette Cueille	assistant editor
Victor Kerdoncuff	press attaché
Anne Mirmant	assistant to director
Suzanne Ohanessian	script supervisor
Alain Poirier	administrator
Gisèle Thénaisie	production assistant
Jacques Tréfouel	assistant to director

Polish poster

French poster

SYNOPSIS

Borowczyk's first live action feature is set on the (fictional) island of Goto, isolated from contact with the rest of humanity since a catastrophic earthquake in 1887. It is a bleak world of stone and iron, ruled over by the tyrannical Goto III. The small population (whom, for undisclosed reasons, all have names starting with the letter 'G') are put to work in quarries and transgressors are forced to fight in gladiatorial contests to provide meagre diversion. It is through a victory at one such contest that the victorious Grozo is pardoned and set to work as apprentice fly-catcher, dog-keeper and boot-polisher. Tragically, Grozo falls in love with Goto's beautiful wife Glossia, who is herself in love with Gono, the captain of the stables. The web of various deceptions unravels with tragic results. The final scene, of Glossia opening her eyes, cannot help but recall her moment of motion in Chris Marker's **La Jetée** [the jetty] (France, 1962).

Borowczyk took great pleasure in the fact that his film was banned in his native "communist" Poland and in Franco's fascist Spain.

FURTHER READING

Armes, Roy. **The Ambiguous Image**. London: Secker & Warburg, 1976, p.165-175.

L'Avant-Scène du Cinéma, no.93, June 1969, p.52-54, in French.

Benayoun, Robert. **Positif**, no.105, May 1969. p.61, in French.

Cornand, André. **Image et Son**, no.226, March 1969, p.112, in French.

Johnston, Claire. **Monthly Film Bulletin**, vol.36 no.431, December 1969. p.257.

Spanish press ad

Ligia Branice on the cover of *Positif* (April 1967) from *Rosalie* at the Tours Film Festival.

Born Ligia Branice on 7 December 1932 in Krasnystaw, in eastern Poland. Before working with Boro she made two features, the drama *Zimowy Zmierzch* [winter twilight] and a comedy *Spotkania* [meetings], both in 1957 for Stanislaw Lenartowicz. The following year she made a 20 minute short, called *Stadion* [stadium], for Stanislaw Jedryka on which her husband acted as a consultant.

She appeared in several Boro shorts and his features *Goto* (1968), *Blanche* (1971) and *Behind Convent Walls* (1978). Other than her work with Boro, she only appeared in Chris Marker's influential sf short *La Jetée* (1962) and a 45 minute Polish TV movie, *Kamizelka*, in 1971, again directed by Stanislaw Jedryka.

Ligia Branice

FILMOGRAPHY

1932   Born 7 December 1932 in Krasnystaw, Poland.
1957 — Spotkania [meetings] (Stanislaw Lenartowicz)
     — Zimowy Zmierzch [winter twilight] (Stanislaw Lenartowicz)
1958 — Krzyż Walecznych [cross of valour] (Kazimierz Kutz)
     — **Stadion [stadium] (Short by Stanislaw Jedryka)**
1959 — Dom [home] (Short by Walerian Borowczyk)
     — Les Astronautes [the astronauts] (Short by Walerian Borowczyk)
1962 — La Jetée [the pier] (Short by Chris Marker)
1966 — Rosalie (Short by Walerian Borowczyk)
1969 — Goto, Island of Love (Walerian Borowczyk)
1971 — Kamizelka (TV movie by Stanislaw Jedryka)
1972 — **Blanche (Walerian Borowczyk)**
1976 — Złote Ekrany [golden screen] (Documentary)
1978 — **Behind Convent Walls (Walerian Borowczyk)**

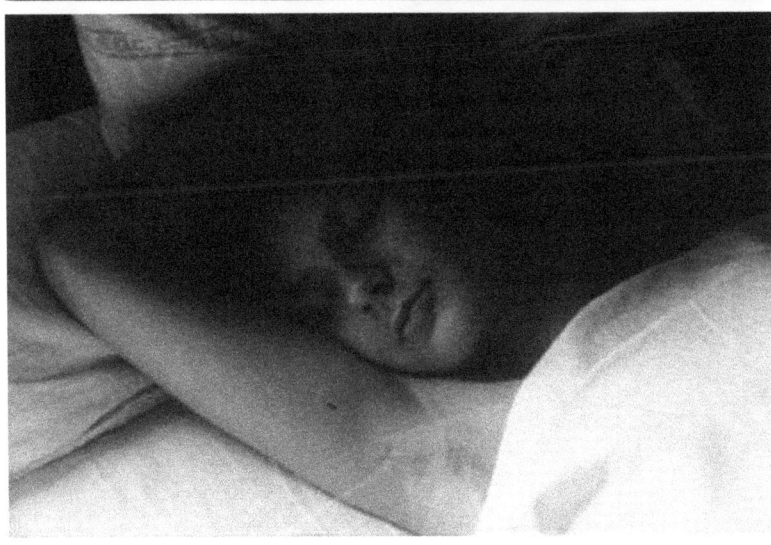

▲ Krzyz Walecznych
▼ Zimowy zmierzch
◀ La Jetée

BLANCHE

France | 1971 | 92 min

🏆 Grand Prix, International Film Festival, Berlin, 1972

Directed by — Walerian Borowczyk
Script by — Walerian Borowczyk
Based on the play **Mazepa** by — Juliusz Slowacki

•••••••••••••••••• CAST ••••••••••••••••••

Ligia Branice — Blanche
Michel Simon — Baron
Georges Wilson — King
Jacques Perrin — Bartolomeo
Denise Péronne — Madame d'Harcourt
Jean Gras — Captain of the guard
Lawrence Trimble — Nicolas
Michel Delahaye — Monk
Roberto — Dwarf
Genevieve Graves
Stanley Barry
Guy Bonnafoux
Christian Boissonnade
Annie Challan
Roger Cotte
Agnès Faucheux
Maurice-Pierre Gourrier
Florence Lassailly
Michel Maurice
Micheline Rolla

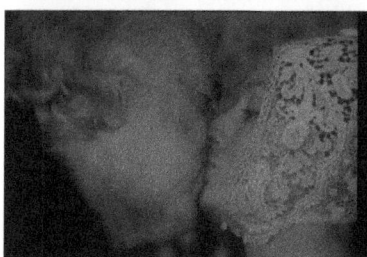

•••••••••••••••••• CREW ••••••••••••••••••

Philippe d'Argila — producer
Dominique Duvergé — producer
Music by — Christian Boissonnade
Annie Challan
Agnès Faucheux
Maurice-Pierre Gourrier
Florence Lassailly

Cinematography by — André Dubreuil
Guy Durban
Film Editing by — Walerian Borowczyk
Charles Bretoneiche

Production Design by — Walerian Borowczyk
Jacques D'Ovidio
Art Direction by — Jacques D'Ovidio
Costume Design by — Piet Bolscher
Christine Fornelli — makeup artist
Trieste Sarnelli — hair stylist
Madeleine Quiquandon — unit production manager
Daniel Riché — production manager

Bernard Cohn	second assistant director
Patrice Leconte	
Christiane Regnault	
Robert Dauphy	construction coordinator
Roger Mocati	head painter
Roger Parreton	head carpenter
Daniel Brisseau	boom operator
Jean-Clément Duval	sound mixer
Robert Pouret	foley artist
Jean-Pierre Ruh	sound
Georges Beaumont	key grip
Robert Cesar	still photographer
Robert Danglade	electrician
Jérome Gesbert	key grip
Noël Véry	first assistant camera
Jean-Pierre Platel	second assistant camera
Joëlle Loucif	costumer
Françoise Thévenot	assistant editor
Suzanne Ohanessian	script supervisor

French poster

SYNOPSIS

Borowczyk's first colour feature was an adaptation of Juliusz Słowacki's play **Mazepa**, written in 1839 and considered a classic of modern Polish literature. Borowczyk moved the action to 13th century France and, as with **Goto**, the narrative concerns the intrigues and duplicities of castle life. Here Ligia plays the young wife of an ageing baron. She is lusted after by all the men who see her, and a visit from the king starts a chain of events that inevitably leads to tragedy.

I AIN'T NO HOLOUBEK GIRL

Although he has nothing to do with Borowczyk's version, we will here celebrate the Polish actor Gutaw Holoubek (1923-2008) who appeared in such classics as Wojciech Has's **Rekopis znaleziony w Saragossie** [**The Saragossa Manuscript**] (Poland, 1965) and **Sanatorium pod klepsydra** [**The Hourglass Sanatorium**] (Poland, 1973). He had been performing a version of **Mazepa** on stage since 1953 and directed tv versions in 1965 and 1969 before making a faithful cinematic version in 1975, and another tv version in 1992.

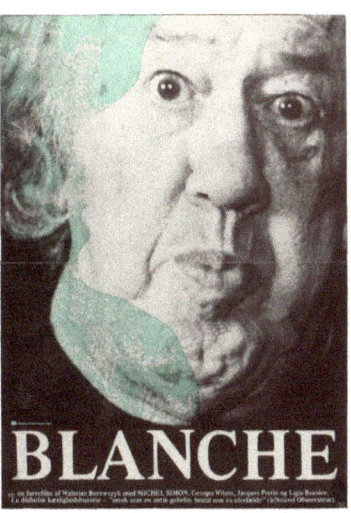

Danish poster

FURTHER READING

Armes, Roy. **The Ambiguous Image**. London: Secker & Warbutg, 1976.
Cervoni, Albert. **Cinéma 72**, no.164, March 1972, p.116-119, in French.
Cornand, André. **Image et Son**, no.258, March 1972, p.91-97, in French.
Trémège, Bernard. **Jeune Cinéma**, no.61, February 1972, p.11-12, in French.
L'Avant-Scène Cinéma, no.125, May 1972, p.50-51, in French.
Philip Strick. **Monthly Film Bulletin**, vol.40 no.473, June 1973, p.120.
Kempna-Pieniazek, Magdalena. **On two adaptations of "Mazepa" by Juliusz Słowacki.** Silesian Journal of Polish Studies 2 2/2012 p.105-116 in Polish.

Spanish poster

  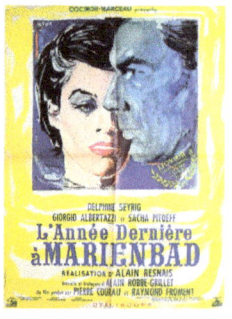  
 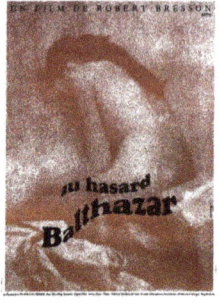 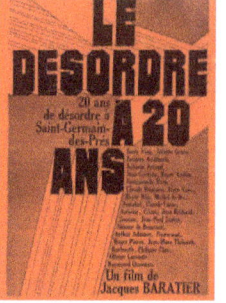  
 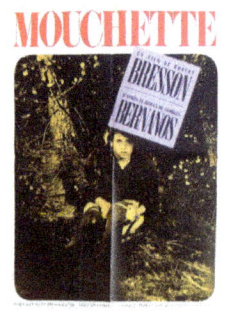  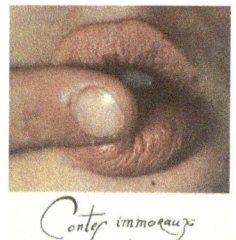  
  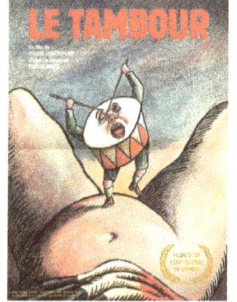  

ANATOLE DAUMAN

A name that towers over half a century of French cinema, Anatole Dauman was born into a Russian Jewish family in Warsaw, Poland on 7 February 1925. During the later years of the second world war he was active in the resistance and afterwards helped investigate nazi war crimes.

Following the war, most of his family's businesses were nationalised by the communist government and his family moved to France where they held some property. It was there that he, along with Philippe Lifchitz, founded Argos Films in 1949. Despite its relatively humble origins, it would go on to become one of the most influential production companies in the history of cinema.

By the time Borowczyk moved to Paris in the late fifties Dauman had made his name with a number of acclaimed short films including Alain Resnais' definitive short documentary about the nazi death camps *Nuit et Brouillard* [*Night and Fog*], and Chris Marker's second feature *Lettre de Siberie* [*Letter from Siberia*].

Dauman took Boro under his wing and introduced him to friends and colleagues such as filmmakers Chris Marker and Mario Ruspoli, and painters including the Serbian surrealist Ljuba Popović who would become the subject of a short film in 1977. Dauman also introduced Borowczyk to the writer André Pieyre de Mandiargues, who would become a frequent collaborator, and to Mandiargues' artist wife Bona, who would become the subject of a 1975 short.

Borowczyk's first commission for Dauman was his 1959 short *Les Astronautes*, which was co-signed by Dauman's friend Chris Marker for bureaucratic reasons. In 1962 Marker cast Boro's wife Ligia in his classic *La Jetée*, which used the same technique of animated photos that Borowczyk had used in his 1958 short *School*.

Meanwhile Dauman had produced more films for Resnais from out of the nouveau roman literary movement, with adaptations from Marguerite Duras and Alain Robbe-Grillet. Throughout the sixties Dauman continued to produce fiction, documentary and experimental films, particularly on overtly political subjects that reflected popular disillusionment with the Vietnam war that the US had entered after the French departed their former colony. Although not produced by Dauman, *Loin du Vietnam* [*Far from Vietnam*] (France, 1967, d. various), a portmanteau film supervised by Marker, was put together by many of the Argos milieu. Then, in 1967 Argos co-funded two Jean-Luc Godard features that marked the start of Godard's transition to political commitment.

Dauman also distributed films. His catalogue included several shorts by Jan Lenica and René Laloux's *Les Escargots* [*The Snails*] and features including *Goto* alongside Andy Warhol and Paul Morrissey's *Flesh* (USA, 1968) and Sergio Leone's *Il Était Une Fois la Révolution* [once upon a time the revolution] (AKA *Duck You Sucker!*, Italy/Spain, 1971).

◀ Posters from just a few of Argos Films productions. ▼ New Realm picked up many Argos Films productions for distribution in the UK. ◢ If this is the first thing you see when the film starts, prepare to have your head fucked.

By the start of the seventies Argos's projects were becoming less politically committed and were more concerned with the fantastic and erotic, such as Alain Fleischer's *Les Rendez-Vous en Forêt* (see following article) and René Laloux's mind-blowing feature-length sf animation *La Planète Sauvage* [wild planet] (AKA *Fantastic Planet*).

In the intervening years Borowczyk had made his first three features for diverse producers before Dauman financed *Immoral Tales* which marked a more graphically erotic direction for Argos, leading to Oshima's *Empire of the Senses* and *Empire of Passion*, as well as Schlöndorff's *The Tin Drum*, which became an arthouse smash hit after winning the Palme d'Or at Cannes in 1979.

During the 1980s Argos's output slowed but still brought us Terayama's *Fruits of Passion* (based on the sequel to *The Story of O* and starring Klaus Kinski) and Robbe-Grillet's *La Belle Captive*, which includes several nods to Jack Cardiff's *The Girl on The Motorcycle* (UK/France, 1968), adapted from Mandiargues' novel. Dauman bowed out with three of the most lauded films of the decade: Wim Wenders' *Paris, Texas* and *Wings of Desire*, and Andrei Tarkovsky's last film *The Sacrifice*. Dauman's last short commission was Borowczyk's also final animation, *Scherzo Infernal*, which finally fused his twin interests in animation and the erotic.

In 1989 Dauman was honoured with a four-month retrospective at the Centre Georges Pompidou, the catalogue of which became Jacques Gerber's book, cited below.

A cinephile to the end, in 1995 Dauman helped save the Accattone cinema (a historic venue in the 5th arrondissement that had been managed Guy Debord's murdered producer Gerard Lebovici amongst other luminaries) by allowing them to project the Argos catalogue free of charge. Then, in 1997, Dauman brought his production credits full circle with Marker's *Level Five* marking forty years since *Lettre de Siberie*.

Dauman's relationship with the French establishment was ambivalent at best and he lamented the direction that the cinema chains were leading the industry. In the years of his death he was ignored by the Cannes festival's tribute to producers.

Dauman died 8 April 1998 in Paris, but Argos Films is still operated by his daughter Florence who, incidentally, had served as a young woman as assistant editor on... *The Beast*.

further reading

Gerber, Jacques. *Anatole Dauman: Pictures of a Producer*. London: BFI, 1992.

Brunette, Peter. "The Producer and the Script Girl". *Sight and Sound*, vol.58 no.1, December. 1988.

Reader, Keith. "Obituary". *Sight and Sound*, vol.9 no.3, March 1999. p.30.

▼ Cameo by Anatole Dauman (L) and Philippe Lifchitz (R) in Borowczyk's *Les Astronautes*.

ARGOS FILMS – Features and Selected Shorts

1951 — L'Affaire Manet (Short by Jean Aurel)
1953 — Les Crimes de l'Amour (Alexandre Astruc, Maurice Barry, Maurice Clavel)
1955 — Night and Fog (Documentary short by Alain Resnais)
1957 — Letter from Siberia (Documentary by Chris Marker)
1958 — Broadway by Light (Short by William Klein)
— Du Côté de la Côte (Documentary short by Agnès Varda)
— La Joconde: Histoire d'une obsession (Short by Henri Gruel)
1959 — Les Astronautes (Short by Walerian Borowczyk, Chris Marker)
— Monsieur Tête (Short by Henri Gruel, Jan Lenica)
— Hiroshima Mon Amour (Alain Resnais)
1961 — Le Rendez-vous de Minuit (Roger Leenhardt)
— Strangers of the Earth (Short documentary by Mario Ruspoli)
— Chronicle of a Summer (Documentary by Edgar Morin, Jean Rouch)
— Madame se Meurt (Short by Jean Cayrol, Claude Durand)
— Last Year in Marienbad (Alain Resnais)
1962 — La Fête Prisonnière (Documentary short by Mario Ruspoli)
— **La Jetée (Short by Chris Marker)**
1963 — Muriel, or The Time of Return (Alain Resnais)
1964 — La Femme Fleur (Animated short by Jan Lenica)
— "A" (Animated short by Jan Lenica)
1965 — Mona, l'Étoile sans Nom (Henri Colpi)
— Valparaiso (Documentary short by Joris Ivens)
— Les Oiseaux sont des Cons (Short by Chaval)
— The Heat of a Thousand Suns (Short by Pierre Kast)
1966 — Demain la Chine (Documentary by Claude Otzenberger)
— The War is Over (Alain Resnais)
— Masculin Féminin (Jean-Luc Godard)
— Au Hasard Balthazar (Robert Bresson)
1967 — Mouchette (Robert Bresson)
— Two or Three Things I Know About Her... (Jean-Luc Godard)
— Eden Miseria (Documentary short by Jacques Baratier)
— Tu Imagines Robinson (Jean-Daniel Pollet)
— A Question of Rape (Jacques Doniol-Valcroze)
1968 — 17e Parallèle (Documentary by Joris Ivens)
— Les Deux Marseillaises (Jean-Louis Comolli, André S. Labarthe)
— La Femme-Bourreau (Jean-Denis Bonan)
1970 — À Nous Deux France (Désiré Ecaré)
1971 — Love Is Gay, Love Is Sad (Jean-Daniel Pollet)
— La Chavalanthrope (Short by Mario Ruspoli)
1972 — Meetings in the Forest (Alain Fleischer)
1973 — Une Collection Particulière (Short by Walerian Borowczyk)
— **La Vèritable Histoire de la Bête du Gévaudan (Short by Walerian Borowczyk)**
— Fantastic Planet (René Laloux)
1974 — Immoral Tales (Walerian Borowczyk)
— Le Beau Samedi (Short by Renaud Walter)
— Ô Gaule (Documentary short by Pierre-Marie Goulet)
1975 — The Beast (Walerian Borowczyk)
1975 — Venus on the Half-Shell (Short by Walerian Borowczyk)
1976 — Coup de Grâce (Volker Schlöndorff)
— In the Realm of the Senses (Nagisa Ôshima)
— Singing During the Occupation (Documentary by André Halimi)
1977 — The Greatest Love of All Times (Short by Walerian Borowczyk)
1978 — Empire of Passion (Nagisa Ôshima)
1979 — The Tin Drum (Volker Schlöndorff)
1981 — Circle of Deceit (Volker Schlöndorff)
— Fruits of Passion (Shûji Terayama)
1982 — La Belle Captive (Alain Robbe-Grillet)
1983 — Sans Soleil (Documentary by Chris Marker)
1984 — Scherzo Infernal (Short by Walerian Borowczyk)
— Paris, Texas (Wim Wenders)
1986 — The Sacrifice (Andrei Tarkovsky)
1987 — Wings of Desire (Wim Wenders)
1997 — Level Five (Chris Marker)

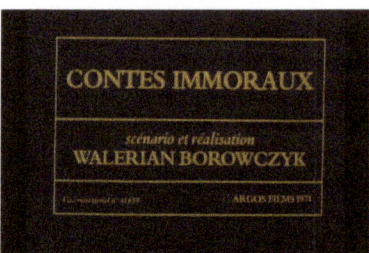

Contes Immoraux
IMMORAL TALES

France | 1974 | 103 min

🏆 Le Prix de l'Age d'Or from the Royal Film Archive, Brussels, 1974

Directed by	Walerian Borowczyk
Screenplay and dialogue by	Walerian Borowczyk
First episode based on "La Marée" by	André Pieyre de Mandiargues

•••••••••••••••••••••CAST•••••••••••••••••••

Lise Danvers	Julie
Fabrice Luchini	André
Charlotte Alexandra	Thérèse
Paloma Picasso	Erzébet Bathory
Pascale Christophe	Istvan
Florence Bellamy	Lucrezia Borgia
Jacopo Berinizi	Pope Alexander VI
Lorenzo Berinizi	Cesare Borgia
Philippe Desboeuf	Friar Hyeronimus Savonarola
Nicole Karen	
Thomas Hnevsa	
Mathieu Rivollier	
Robert Capia	
Gerard Tcherka	
Kjell Gustavsson	

•••••••••••••••••••••CREW•••••••••••••••••••

Anatole Dauman	producer
Music by	Maurice Leroux
Cinematography by	Bernard Daillencourt
	Guy Durban
	Noël Véry
	Michel Zolat
Film Editing by	Walerian Borowczyk
Production Design by	Walerian Borowczyk
Costume Design by	Piet Bolscher
Dominique Duvergé	assistant director
Alain Cayrade	production assistant
Bernard Grignon	
Maxine Groffsky	
Alain Herpe	
Jean-Pierre Platel	

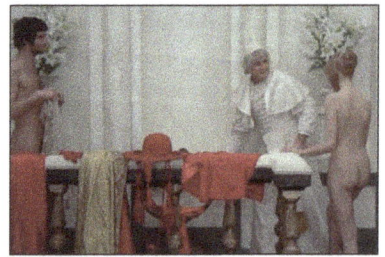

NOTES

Borowczyk's fourth feature film was his first in the portmanteau format, exploiting his mastery of the short film. It was originally intended to comprise of prelude **Une Collection Particulère**, followed by **La Véritable Histoire de la Bête du Gévaudan**, **La Marée**, **Thérèse Philosophe** and **Erzébet Bathory**. The first three segments were premiered at the 17th Regus London Film Festival on Saturday 24th and Sunday 25th November 1973, coincidentally (?) the tenth anniversary of the assassination of JFK, at 8:45pm and 1:30pm respectively. These extracts screened with Carmelo Bene's **Un Amleto di Meno** [one Hamlet less] (Italy, 1973) and the programme warned the "easily offendable" of the "explicit treatment of the subjects". Borowczyk won the Festival Choice Award.

Immoral Tales marked Borowczyk's first commercial success, not hindered by Argos Films' expert marketing and distribution, and a directive that he make the film more accessible with extra sex and violence. Unfortunately, it was received with critical ambivalence which is usually attributed to disapproval of Borowczyk's willing embrace of salacious and violent themes that were regarded as better suited to exploitation fayre. Whilst this cultural myopia was prevalent at this time, I would postulate that the true motivation of the critics was more likely their reactionary disapproval of Borowczyk's contempt for the criminal excesses of the aristocracy and the hypocrisy that eventuates thereby.

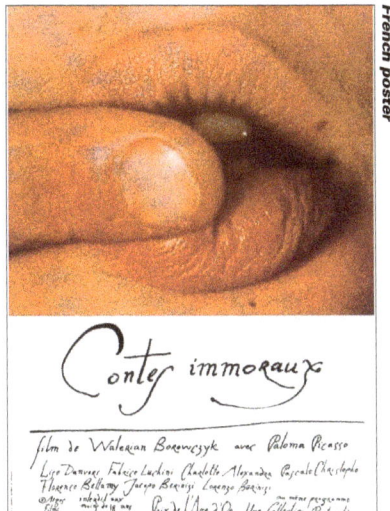

French poster

SYNOPSIS

The first episode of the film (as it was released) was "La Marée", based on a story by Borowczyk's pal André Pieyre de Mandiargues from his collection **Mascarets** [tidal bores] (1971). Set in the (then) present day, it's a straightforward though effective story of Julie's sexual initiation by her cousin André on a desolate beach.

The second episode, "Thérèse Philosophe", is set in 1890 and inspired by the 1748 politico-erotic tract of that name. Here a young girl, locked alone in a room, discovers the joys of masturbation courtesy of some courgettes and assorted religious paraphernalia. This is the first overt manifestation of Borowczyk's Voltairian strand of anti-clericism.

The third episode "Erzsebet Bathory" is set in 1610 and inspired by the story of the Bloody Countess but it grafts on some narrative twists harking back to the palace intrigues of **Blanche**, albeit in a bloodier and sexier style.

The final episode, not intended in the original sequence, and often regarded as lackluster, is "Lucrezia Borgia", set in 1498 as based on the incestuous appetites of the daughter of Pope Alexander VI.

US poster (hand censored to obscure arses)

FURTHER READING

Darnton, Robert. **The Corpus of Clandestine Literature in France, 1769-1789.** New York: W. W. Norton & Company, 1995.

Darnton, Robert. **The Forbidden Best-Sellers of Pre-revolutionary France.** New York: W. W. Norton & Company, 1996.

Milne, Tom. **Monthly Film Bulletin** vol.44 no.521, June 1977, p.120-121.

Penrose, Valentine trans. Alexander Trocchi. **The Bloody Countess: Atrocities of Erzsébet Báthory.** London: New English Library, 1972.

Reid, Gordon ?. **Continental Film Review**, vol.21 no.11, September 1974, p.14-17.

Variety, 21 August 1974, p.22.

Yugoslavian poster

 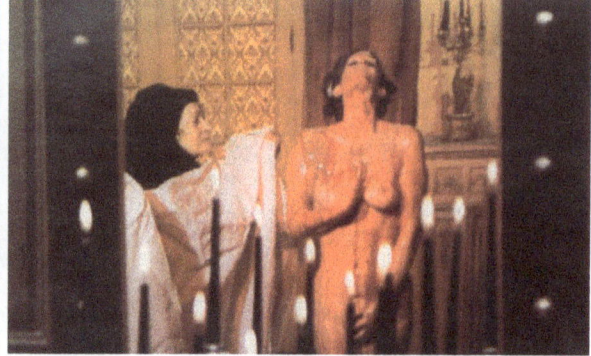

▲ Ingrid Pitt in Hammer's *Countess Dracula* (UK. 1970, d. Peter Sasdy). ◣ Lucia Bosé (and friend) in *Ceremonia Sangrienta* [blood ceremony] (Spain/Italy, 1973, d. Jorge Grau) ▲ Lina Romay in *The Female Vampire* (France/Belgium, 1973, d. Jesus Franco). ▼ *Krvavá Pani* [the bloody lady] (Czechoslovakia, 1980, d. Viktor Kubal), an animated feature.

Erzébet Báthory la Comtesse Sanglante

Countess Elizabeth Báthory de Ecsed (8 August 1560 – 21 August 1614) was a countess from the renowned Báthory family in Hungary. She is widely considered the most prolific female serial killer in history and the number of her victims runs into the hundreds. Despite the testimony of more than 300 witnesses and survivors, plus physical evidence and the presence of mutilated corpses and dying imprisoned girls in her chateau, her family's wealth and influence kept her from facing trial. She was imprisoned in a suite of rooms in 1610 and died four years later.

After her death stories started to circulate ascribing vampiric tendencies to her, most notably the story that she bathed in the blood of virgins to maintain her youth. Historians generally consider these stories unreliable, and there even exist revisionists who claim that she was the innocent victim of a political conspiracy. She is often compared to Vlad the Impaler or Gilles de Rais in the field of homicidal sadistic aristocrats who were held accountable, albeit belatedly.

There have been a number of books about Báthory, by far the most interesting being the one by surrealist poet Valentine Penrose, translated into English by Alexander Trocchi, whose name seems to crop up at the juncture of most interesting twentieth century tropes.

Characters based on her appear in many films, most famously Hammer's 1970 *Countess Dracula*. Sometimes the Báthory character adopts a different name, as in Jess Franco's *The Female Vampire* (1973) where Lina Romay plays Countess Irina Karlstein who, like Romilda in *The Beast*, kills her victims through sexual rapacity, and like Báthory bathes in blood although we do not see any sequences of blood-letting and her bloodbath seems heavily diluted. In Harry Kümel's critically acclaimed *Daughters of Darkness* (Belgium/France/W.Germany, 1971) she dispenses entirely with her customary bloodbath. The trope is easily conflated with Le Fanu's *Carmilla*, and by the 21st century she had become just another vapid icon of the goth/burlesque crossover industry.

Lucretia de borgia

Second only to the Bloody Countess in the Goth Girl's iconography, Lucrezia Borgia was born 18 April 1480 to Spanish cardinal Rodrigo Borgia (later Pope Alexander VI) and his mistress.

The exploits of the Borgia family came to be synonymous with the Machiavellian political and sexual corruption of Renaissance Italy, but little is known about Lucrezia herself, and the degree her complicity in the excesses of her father and brothers is still hotly debated, with Lucrezia's image being constantly revised to suit the prevailing political climate of the times. Although hard evidence is scant, she is accused of adultery, plotting, poisoning, participating in orgies, and assisting her father and brother's (better proven) crimes as well as freely indulging in incest with them. It goes without saying that Borowczyk focuses his attention on the last of these. Given the coincidence of initials, one may have expected Ligia Borowczyk (née Branice) to play Lucrezia, but the role in *Immoral Tales* was taken by Florence Bellamy.

The first film adaptations of Lucrezia's story were *Lucrèce Borgia*, a French production by Albert Capellani in 1909, and a Brazilian version by Antônio Serra in the same year, followed the next year by an Italian version by Mario Caserini. Abel Gance's more elaborate feature (France, 1935) created a scandal due to its raunchy "banquet of chestnuts" orgy scenes and a brief shot showing star Edwige Feuillère naked. There was a chaster French version, directed by Christian-Jaque, in 1953 with Martine Carol in the title role. The 1980s saw another spike in borgiasploitaion with the classic BBC tv series of 1981, starring Anne-Louise Lambert, and the not-so-classic *The Secret Nights of Lucrezia Borgia* (Italy, 1982, d. Roberto Montero) with Lucrezia played by none other than... Sirpa Lane.

THÉRÈSE PHILOSOPHE

The celebrity of the Marquis de Sade gives the impression that he was somewhat of a renegade anomaly of his time, whereas his work is representative of a much wider field. Robert Darnton's exemplary book (and its companion bibliography) masterfully outlines the underground publishing milieu of prerevolutionary France and the canon of *philosophes*: salacious, blasphemous and illegal bestsellers of their time, mixing sexual and political subversion with explosive results! It includes an English translation the full text of *Thérèse Philosophe*, a 1748 French erotic novel usually ascribed to Jean-Baptiste de Boyer, Marquis d'Argens. The narrative describes the stages of education of naive Thérèse as she is schooled first by a secretly materialist Jesuit, in a convent, by an experienced prostitute and finally by a libertine nobleman who wagers that she cannot last a fortnight in a library of erotic books and paintings without succumbing to the temptations of onan. This episode provides the inspiration for Boro's zucchini interlude.

There are many contested portraits of Lucrezia Borgia, all subject to varying degrees of disputation. Bartolomeo Veneto's "fanciful" portrait (left) is included here since it is the most immodest.

LES RENDEZ-VOUS EN FORÊT

AKA Meetings in the Forest

France, 1971 | 80 min / 88 min

d/wr: Alain Fleischer. *p:* Anatole Dauman, Peter Schamoni. *ph:* Marcel Grignon. *ed:* Eric Pluet. *m:* Michel Fano. *w:* Heinz Bennent, Renée Gardès, Catherine Jourdan, Maria Meriko, Lawrence Trimble.

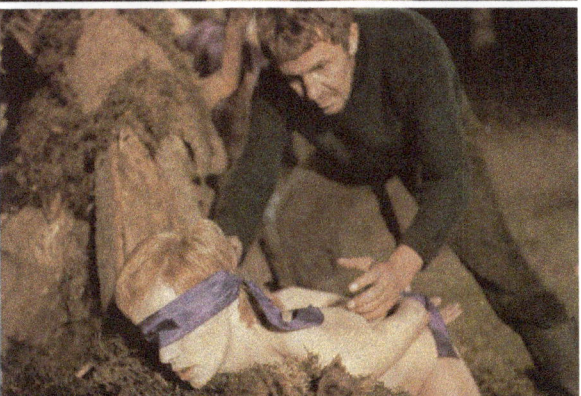

Alain Fleischer was born on 10 January 1944 in Paris and studied modern letters, linguistics, anthropology and semiology at the Sorbonne. A true renaissance man, he practised painting, photography, sculpture and cinema, whilst also teaching in universities and schools. His early shorts and features were heavily experimental, and he usually wrote, shot and edited his films himself.

In the summer of 1971 Argus Films produced Fleischer's first commercial feature, *Les Rendex-Vous en Foret* [meetings in the forest], a self-consciously literary conflation of *Alice in Wonderland* and *Beauty and the Beast*. The lead role was taken by Catherine Jourdan, who had recently starred in Alain Robbe-Grillet's *Eden et Apres* (France, 1970) and, prior to that, appeared in the Mandiargues adaptation *The Girl on a Motorcycle* (UK/France, 1968, d. Jack Cardiff).

The story goes that Svea (Jourdan) dismounts from a car and places her foot in a recent print that fits hers exactly. She is in a river valley with a castle on one bank and a forest on the other. She undresses and puts on a dress she has found in a package under a nearby bush. The castle is inhabited by her cousin Adrien and his governess Maria and they spend their time playing the piano. On the other side of the valley, in the forest, is a cabin which is home to Akos, the chief woodcutter. He photographs Svea, whilst Adrien has recorded her actions in his journal, which serves as a screenplay for the film. As Svea's amorous advances are thwarted it becomes clear that a special ceremonial role awaits her...

Dauman wasn't satisfied by Fleischer's ending for the film and commissioned Borowczyk to supply a climax with more oomph. To this effect, Boro constructed his own beast and had Fleischer's cinematographer Marcel Grignon shoot a new sequence, featuring Sirpa Lane.

Fleischer did not approve of these developments and went to court to prevent the new ending being used. The film was screened for the press at Club 13 on Avenue Hoche, 8eme, Paris on 13 January 1972 and is reported as having a brief provincial release before being suppressed. It is often listed as unreleased.

◀ Alain Fleischer c. 1971
Catherine as The Queen in "The Four Charlots Musketeers" ▶
Catherine and Marianne Faithfull in "The Girl on a Motorcycle" ▼
Catherine on the poster for Robbe-Grillet's "Eden and After" ▼▼
Catherine on the cover of Vogue (US) February 1971 ▼▼▼

ALAIN FLEISCHER

SELECT FILMOGRAPHY

1968 — Montage IV
1969 — Le Règlement
1972 — Meetings in the Forest
1975 — Dehors-dedans
1979 — Zoo Zéro (shot 1977)
1982 — Règles, Rites (shot 1969)
1982 — Histoire, Geographie (Documentary)
1984 — Photographie et Cinema (Documentary)
1989 — Contacts (TV documentary)
1989 — La Nuit des Toiles (Short)
1992 — Rome Roméo
2000 — Un Monde Agité (Documentary)
2001 — Cités de la Plaine (producer, d. Robert Kramer)
2007 — Fragments of Conversations with Jean-Luc Godard (Documentary)

Borowczyk showed his footage, retitled *La Véritable Histoire de la Bête du Gévaudan* [*The True Story of the Beast of Gévaudan*] at the 1973 London Film Festival, along with *Une Collection Particulière* and *La Marée*, as a preview of his forthcoming *Immoral Tales* portmanteau film but, as we all know, Boro instead chose to use the footage instead as the climax to an original feature inspired by Prosper Mérimée's *Lokis*.

Meanwhile, Fleischer followed up with the uncompromisingly experimental *Dehors-dedans* and then with *Zoo Zéro*, both featuring Catherine Jourdan. In the latter she plays opposite Klaus Kinski as a chanteuse in Robbe-Grillet-esque hybrid zoo/night-club with the expectable bestiality undertones. After that, as the eighties dawned, Fleischer switched his emphasis to teaching and photography, occasionally returning to cinema to make documentaries, usually on the topic of contemporary art.

further reading

L'Avant-Scène Cinéma. no.126 (June 1972) p.50-54.
Continental Film Review. July 1972 p.3/35.
Variety. 26 January 1972. p.24.

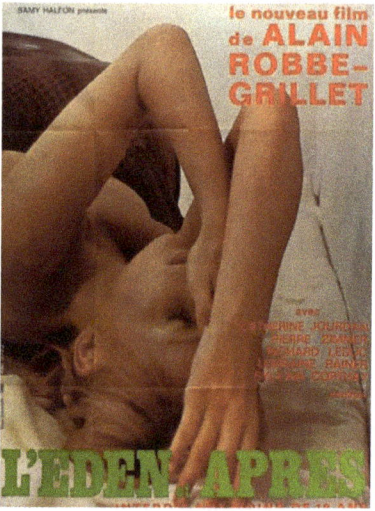

CATHERINE JOURDAN

FILMOGRAPHY

1948 Born 12 October at Azay le Rideau, France.
1967 — Le Samouraï (Jean-Pierre Melville)
1968 — Love in the Night (Marcel Camus)
— The Girl on a Motorcycle (Jack Cardiff)
1969 — L'Amore (Jean-Luc Godard segment in "Love and Anger")
— Un Merveilleux Parfum d'Oseille [a sweet smell of cash] (Rinaldo Bassi)
1970 — Eden and After (Alain Robbe-Grillet)
1971 — Early Morning (Jean-Gabriel Albicocco)
— N. a Pris les Dés... (Alain Robbe-Grillet)
1972 — Meetings in the Forest (Alain Fleischer)
1973 — Marriage a la Mode (Michel Mardore)
1974 — The Four Charlots Musketeers / The Four Charlots Musketeers 2 (André Hunebelle)
1975 — Dehors-dedans (Alain Fleischer)
1976 — Vortex (AKA Blondy) (Sergio Gobbi)
1979 — Zoo Zéro (Alain Fleischer)
1982 — Aphrodite (Robert Fuest)
— Pourvoir (Patrice Enard)
1984 — The Devil and the Lady (Ariel Zúñiga)
1986 — L'Araignée de Satin [The Satin Spider] (Jacques Baratier)
1989 — La Nuit des Toiles [night of the canvasses] (Short by Alain Fleischer)
2011 Died 18 February in Paris.

VHS and DVD art from around the world

La Bête

THE BEAST

AKA Death's Ecstasy

France | 1975 | 93 min

Written and directed by — Walerian Borowczyk

•••••••••••••••••••••••• **CAST** ••••••••••••••••••••••••

Sirpa Lane	Romilda de l'Esperance
Lisbeth Hummel	Lucy Broadhurst
Elisabeth Kaza	Virginia Broadhurst
Pierre Benedetti	Mathurin de l'Esperance
Guy Tréjan	Pierre de l'Esperance
Roland Armontel	Priest
Marcel Dalio	Duc Rammendelo De Balo
Robert Capia	
Pascale Rivault	Clarisse De l'Esperance
Hassane Fall	Ifany
Anna Baldaccini	Théodore
Thierry Bourdon	Modeste
Mathieu Rivollier	
Julien Hanany	
Marie Testanière	Marie
Stéphane Testanière	Stéphane
Jean Martinelli	Cardinal Joseph de Balo

•••••••••••••••••••••• **CREW** ••••••••••••••••••••••

Anatole Dauman	Producer
Cinematography by	Bernard Daillencourt
	Marcel Grignon
Film Editing by	Walerian Borowczyk
Production Design by	Jacques D'Ovidio
Set Decoration by	Alain Guillé
Costume Design by	Piet Bolscher
Odette Berroyer	makeup artist
Dominique Duvergé	production manager
Michel Laurent	sound
Jean-Pierre Ruh	
Alex Pront	sound mixer
Serge Boiron	chief electrician
Noël Véry	camera operator
Gérard Wurtz	photographer
Florence Bory	assistant editors
Alain Cayrade	
Florence Dauman	
Claude Delon	
Jean-Pierre Platel	
Monique Prim	
Michel Valio	
Robert Atellian	chief machinist
Jean Duguet	auditorium sound recording

• • • • • • • • • • • • • • • FURTHER READING • • • • • • • • • • • • • • •

Continental Film Review, vol.22 no.12, October 1975, p.8
Monthly Film Bulletin, vol.45 no.537 October 1978.
Positif, no.174, October 1975, p.72 in French.
Screen International, 26 August 1978, p.1.
Screen International, 23 September 1978, p.17.
Sharp, Kerri. "Hairy Hands Make Light Work". ***Headpress***, no.19, 1999, p. 37-40.
Thompson, David. "Forbidden cinema: that hairy monster." ***Sight and Sound,*** vol.11 no.6, June 2001, p.12-13.
Variety, 27 August 1975, p.16.

French poster

• • • • • • • • • • • • INTRODUCTION TO THE SUMMARY • • • • • • • • • • • •

Borowczyk's masterwork functions on at least three levels.

1. A conventional Gothic melodrama, albeit one that degenerates into an uncharacteristic level of sexual detail.
2. A pastiche or homage to the imagery and folklore (i.e. the vocabulary) of human/animal relations. The three most prominent influences are Prosper Mérimée's story "Lokis", the tale of "Beauty and the Beast" most famously rendered by Jeanne-Marie Leprince de Beaumont, and the legend of the Beast of Gévaudan. Transcriptions or descriptions of each of these may be found in the addenda of this book.
3. A narrative of the recurrence of several objects and motifs recurring in a (potentially) significant sequence. This technique is most famously evoked in literature in Georges Bataille's ***The Story of the Eye***.

These three readings, and potentially others, coexist and complement each other. They correspond to three views on dream analysis.

1. Dreams as reconciliation and organisation of elements of waking life, as characterised by the dismissive and reductionist "garbage collection" hypothesis favoured by cognitive scientists.
2. Dreams as synthesis of conscious and unconscious memories. The Freudian reading favoured by out-of-fashion psycho-analysts.
3. Dreams as distorted recollections of past events and precognitions of events to come. The Serialist reading favoured by experimental novelists and few others.

The recurrence of certain symbols through the films in the course of Borowczyk's oeuvre is itself analogous to the recurrence of certain symbols through different dreams in the course of any individual's life.

In order to isolate these components, it was necessary to analyse the film scene-by-scene. I put the bootleg of Disc Three of the Deluxe boxed set into my $90 region-free player. I used the Dutch version as it subtitled both the English and the French dialogue, easing transcription, plus it included scenes deemed superfluous in other versions.

Italian poster

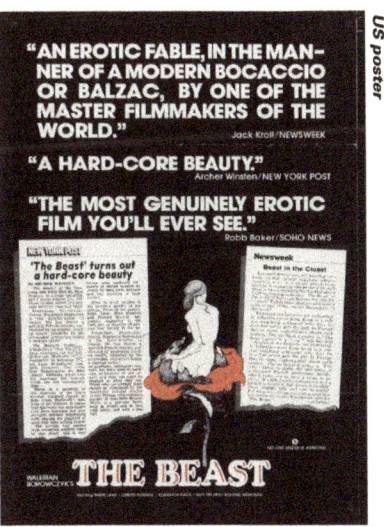

US poster

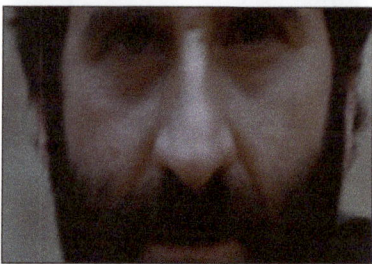

• • • • • • • • • • • • • SUMMARY & OBSERVATIONS • • • • • • • • • • • • •

Sound of horse hooves and neighing. Credits in a bold sans serif face[1], names in capitals. A Voltaire quote: "Les rêves inquiets sont réellement une folie passagère[2]."

Cut. A bearded man with his hand in a cast leads a horse out a stable into a courtyard. A big horse penis. A horse galloping round. It's cold out today. A big horse vagina[3]. Generously leaking juice and steam[4]. Literally. Breath from horsey nostrils. Maybe the first equine cream pie[5] shot in cinema history. Mathurin[6] gazes on transfixed.

In the château[7] Pierre de l'Esperance wields a feather duster at an elaborate clock while his wheelchair-bound uncle, Raymonde, Duc de Balo, presses leaves in an album. He moves on to dust a portrait of his ancestor Romilda de l'Esperance and the two men argue about Mathurin's imminent wedding to Lucy Broadhurst, an American heiress who will rescue their estate from insolvency. The Duke is convinced that the marriage licence will be Mathurin's death warrant. A painting of nude on a horse[8] – Pierre blackmails Raymonde with a vial of poison that the Duke had used to murder his wife years before, to help him obtain the blessing of Raymonde's brother, the Cardinal de Balo.

The horses continue their copulation as the men continue their argument, summoning Mathurin by telephone as the priest and two altar boys arrive for his baptism. Pierre and the priest briefly discuss carnal desires and their suppression by intellect. The Duke is assailed by a snail[9], and summons their black servant, Ifany, to dispose of it. Pierre shaves Mathurin's copious beard. A bucket of snails. Lucy and her aunt Virginia arrive by Roll Royce. "Beautiful France has always lived in lust" remarks Virginia. Pierre baptises Mathurin as the priest waits outside the bathroom. Lucy and Virginia stop at the run-down gatehouse, close to what Mathurin calls his "desert romantique" and Lucy takes a Polaroid[10]. She dons a leopard skin coat. "It's a jungle." Virginia chases Lucy as she runs off exploring, discovering a displaced truncated column and a strange underwater spring, all the time snapping Polaroids. "Nature is serious but never sad. I'll have that column restored and painted white" she declares. They arrive at the château and encounter the still-copulating horses. Lucy photographs to the admonishments of her aunt. The duke greets them and they enter past a tapestry depicting a unicorn hunt.

A fat cat sits atop a glass case containing an antique corset. Lucy asks the Duke about ghosts mentioned in a book by Romilda, two centuries previously. The Duke denies the existence of the book but produces her

1 Univers. Coincidentally this font..
2 Translating as "Troubled dreams are in fact a passing moment of madness". The quote is from **Dictionnaire Philosophique** [*Philosophical Dictionary*] (1764).
3 We can postulate that the hardcore inter-animal sex here stands in for human hardcore in the same way that photographs of topless "savages" were used in silent newsreels and soiled copies of **National Geographic**. In those instances the effect was bidirectional as the "savages" were dehumanised at the same time. Here, it is characteristically unclear whether Borowczyk is exploiting or parodying the technique of explicitness by proxy. An analogous "snuff" technique, especially popular in mid-seventies Italian cannibal films, sees animals being killed on-camera in the absence of legislation permitting homicide.
4 Insert pun/joke about "opening segment" here?
5 Porno jargon for a frontal shot of vagina (or anus) immediately post-ejaculation.
6 Mathurin's name may be intended to recall Charles Maturin, the Irish author of **Melmoth the Wanderer**, an exemplary Gothic novel.
7 Le Maison de André Ciganer was also used as the setting for Jean Rollin's **Fascination** (France, 1979).
8 "Frenzy of Exultations", an 1893 painting by Polish artist, Władysław Podkowinski,
9 The first of many references to snails in the film. Borowczyk professes that he is predominantly interested in their spiral shape.
10 Lucy's Polaroid camera is anomalous in Borowczyk's films. Even in his stories with entirely contemporary settings, he assiduously avoids the inclusion of any artefacts postdating the invention of cinema.

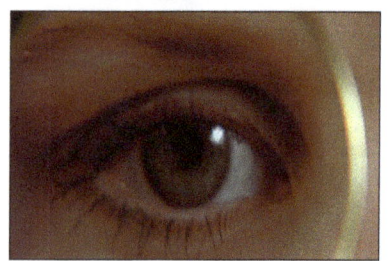

"herbal" from beneath his covers "Voila le fameux album". An album of pressed leaves she had collected. He directs her to page 115B., a map of the woods, annotated with a figure of a tree, and a beast, "I met him and overcame him..." The Duke tells them her corset was found at the bottom of a pond and still bears the claw-marks. He hears Pierre coming and departs in haste, scattering the herbal. On the reverse of a picture Lucy finds a drawing[11] of a dog and a woman in congress. Pierre derides the legend but succeeds only in compounding it: "since time immemorial, every 200 years, the same day, same time, when mercury moves away from the sun, a beast arrives at our house blah blah blah." The introductions are made again. Lucy: "I like forests and animals." Ifany is summoned to help the ladies to their rooms. He is busy with Pierre's dreadlocked foxy daughter and his premature departure is to the benefit of the bedhead with which she consoles herself. Alone, Aunt Virginia reviews a copy of Lucy's father's will she has concealed in her garter. Lucy examines the paintings and books in her room[12], one has an engraving of a winged ass buggering a woman. It is **La Pucelle d'Orléans** [the maid of Orleans] by Voltaire. One of the altar boys plays the harpsichord[13] downstairs. The priest seems overly affectionate. Still in the bathroom, Mathurin tells his father of his fears. They meet with the priest, whom Pierre bribes with the promise of a bell for the church tower if he testifies that Mathurin's baptism followed church rules.

Ifany and Clarisse are at it again. Once more they are interrupted and Ifany has trouble fitting his erection into his uniform. Once again the bedhead is the beneficiary. The children she is minding have been hidden in the wardrobe,[14] playing hide-and-seek. Pierre finishes a note for Lucy, ostensibly by Mathurin, and Ifany takes it to Lucy in the grey room[15] with a single rose. In an often excised scene, the cook lays the table, forgetting the sixth seat, for the cardinal? The prominence of the snail-tongs is noted. In the grey room, Lucy arranges her Polaroids, including the horse copulations, and starts to masturbate. She is interrupted by Ifany. It seems that daytime sex is doomed to frustration in the château. The cook is at work, a basket of snails on the bench. Another excised scene as the Duke examines Mathurin's hair collected from the bathroom. A plate of snails. Dinner. A discussion of the reasons for the cardinal's ongoing absence. Virginia is not pleased to hear of the promised bell. The wedding must take place within 48 hours or the will is null and void. Mathurin, who lacks social graces, explains how the vet to his horses cured him of smoking. He embarrasses himself and has to be restrained as the party breaks up. The priest composes himself and Clarisse and the children come in. The children are dressed for the wedding, a little girl (Marie) with the cat, and the boy (Stéphane) with a huge bouquet. They are dismissed and Pierre and the priest await the cardinal.

11 The drawing is probably by Borowczyk himself, but bears a striking resemblance to the work of Hans Bellmer (1902-1975). Bellmer had illustrated Bataille's **Story of the Eye**, and an important 1969 monograph on Bellmer was annotated by Mandiargues.
12 In a scene reminiscent of one from **Thérèse Philosophe** from **Immoral Tales**.
13 The piece is "Sonata in D Major (K.119)" by Domenico Scarlatti (1685–1757).
14 Borowczyk referred to wardrobes more directly in his segment for **Private Collections** (see elsewhere). In 1992 British pop-group Pulp released their single **Babies**, a celebration of wardrobe-bound voyeurism. This becomes significant when we note that their front-man, Jarvis Cocker, had contemporaneously presented a short TV segment (for Channel 4 Red Light Zone) discussing **The Beast**. A wardrobe also features prominently in Georges Bataille's novel **Story of the Eye**.
15 Although it seems unlikely that Borowczyk would consciously invoke a modernist writer, the "grey room" is an image derived from the work of William Burroughs, referring to the human brain, hence "breakthrough in grey room".

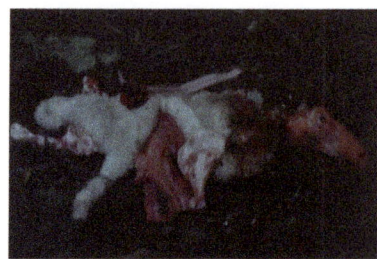

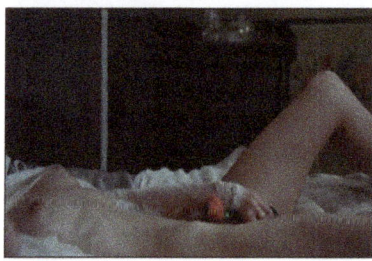
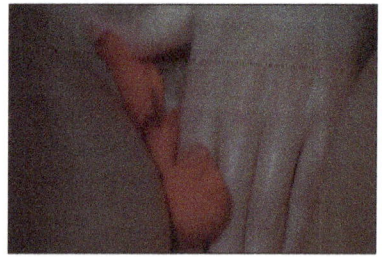

Cut to a diaphanous gauze. Buttocks. Mons Venus. Lucy admiring herself in a three-panelled mirror. Beneath the veil, she is naked but for her pearls. She takes up the rose and rubs it briefly on her face and between her breasts. She is almost asleep. She dreams of the gatehouse. Beneath the gaze of a stone goat-god gargoyle, the countess Romilda de l'Esperance is playing on a harpsichord[16]. She watches over a sheep and lamb as she plays. The cry of the Beast rings out. The lamb breaks its tether and escapes. Romilda, clad in a blue shepherdess[17] gown grabs her little shawl and dashes out after it, holding up her flowing blue skirts. Behind the lone column two huge black claws are glimpsed. Bleating, the lamb follows the path of Lucy earlier in the film, though the events are taking place two centuries before. The harpsichord music really kicks in now. Romilda finds the disembowelled lamb. Her hands fly to her face in horror. The Beast is still dissecting its prey.

Back in the château, Virginia, the children, the altar boys and the priest, and Pierre are all asleep when the phone rings. The Duke pleads with the cardinal to stay in Rome and not consecrate the wedding. He is convinced that Mathurin will die and is about to reveal the truth about the baptism when Pierre breaks in and cuts him off. Pierre takes the razor[18] out of his pocket. The Duke's cry wakes the priest and the altar boys. "It was an illusion" says Pierre. "But you are also awake." says the priest. "The noisy spring in your chair must have woken me" he lies unconvincingly.

The Beast has been aroused by its kill, or by Romilda, as she cowers from its terrible erect phallus. She skips over the remains of the lamb and flees, her dress coming apart in her haste. The Beast pursues but is frustrated in catching her by the layers of skirts and petticoats. These are one-by-one discarded or stripped away in the chase through the forest. The Beast foaming at the mouth, and elsewhere, as she is reduced to her stockings, corset, and wig.

Flashes of sunlight between the leaves illuminate the fleeing buttocks, the cords of the corset dangling between the cheeks. As she runs, her breasts come free of their restraint. She throws a shoe at the Beast and takes refuge behind an ancient tree, trying to climb it. There is a wound on her left leg. The Beast observes and sates his erection on a tree trunk, ejaculating copiously[19]. Romilda is dangling from a branch, terrified. The Beast approaches and licks at her sex. She screams in terror and disgust. Unable to get a purchase on the tree, her feet flail at the penis of the Beast, inflaming his desire anew as he continues his cuntish ministrations. Her remaining shoe drops off and the Beast spurts on her stockings, but she is able to drop from the tree, landing in a shamefully exposed posture. The Beast advances, and she pulls off her wig and presses it to her cunt to afford some meagre defence. The Beast seizes the wig and wanks with it, giving Romilda time to escape. His semen[20] drips from the powdered hair[21] and there is a cross-dissolve to Lucy's sleeping face. A brief shot of her thighs parting before her eyes open to the rose beside her on the pillow. She sneaks out to visit Mathurin but he passed out fast asleep. She removes his shoes and returns to her room. She takes a drink from the tap and wets her translucent veil. She lies on the bed, caressing her breasts and rubs the

16 The piece is again by Scarlatti's, this time the "Sonata in A Major, K. 209 (Allegro)".
17 Until the 19th century the church often encouraged the employment of women to tend animals as the practice of bestiality was thought so prevalent amongst herdsmen.
18 Recalling perhaps Luis Buñuel's ***L'Age D'Or*** [the golden age] (France, 1930).
19 The sequence of bestial ejaculation shots runs the gamut of pornographic convention and beyond: (1) tree (2) feet (3) wig (4) buttocks (5) breasts (6) feet (7) face.
20 Should this be "sebeasts"?
21 Despite extensive research, I have not been able to find any other instances of wig-sex in the pornographic canon. Ejaculation into hair itself is relatively infrequent, and generally unintentional when it occurs.

rose down her belly, drawing up her veil and spreading her legs. As she masturbates with the flower, the petals fall away. She forces it into her vagina, her face masked with perspiration, transfixed. Her fingers and pubic hair are dewy with the evidence of her arousal as the rose vanishes inside her. Fix on her vagina.[22] Six eggs in a nest. The Beast has caught Romilda from behind, she screams and struggles to free herself from the embrace, but it throws her face-down onto her cast-off petticoat. The monstrous penis plays between her thighs as she clutches the fabric and a snail climbs a discarded shoe. Her expression becomes resigned as the Beast enters her from behind, her tongue running round her teeth. Eyes half-closed as the terror transforms itself to ecstasy. The ground rises to meet her. Lens flare. Snail. Shoe. And the Beast's penis thrusting between the globes of her buttocks. She gasps as it withdraws and spills its Beastly seed[23] between them before re-entering until the two of them tumble over and the Beast withdraws. The petticoats are pooled with the blood of hymen. Lucy is thrashing on the bed. In a somnivalent[24] state she saws the veil between her legs and some stray rose petals are scattered till she rips it off and gives herself entirely to her desire. But as she does so, she awakens and is startled by her state. She throws the leopard-skin coat over her nakedness and again visits Mathurin. He turns in his disturbed sleep and pulls her coat from her. She flees, and back in her room she considers and caresses the bedknob. The bloody sheet is withdrawn and the corset discarded to the water of the lake where the spring will mark its position. Romilda now fondles her breasts, as if to re-excite the Beast. As the corset sinks, torrents of semen[25] erupt between her cleavage[26] and run down her belly to drip from her crotch. She uses her other hand to masturbate herself from behind. Gentle now, the Beast caresses her foot, and still the snail climbs the shoe. Now she uses her feet willingly on the Beast and he discharges yet again. A strange breeze blows through the foliage as she uses her mouth, the endless flow of semen smears her lips and chin and still the Beast comes[27]. The snail has ascended the slipper, it overtips and falls from its place. The Beast gives a final blow and its eyes glaze as it dies of ecstasy.

Lucy awakens still naked, but now concerned, in his room she finds Mathurin on the floor, as dead as a sex-crazed Beast. She screams and runs through the corridors. The household is awakened as she goes in grief and horror and searches for her aunt. Joined by Pierre, the priest and the altar boys they bring Mathurin's body out and say the last rites. Lucy puts on her coat. The cat runs down the hall. Ifany is summoned. He and Camille sneak out of the wardrobe past the sleeping children. Mathurin is carried to the drawing room and laid on the desk. Lucy is

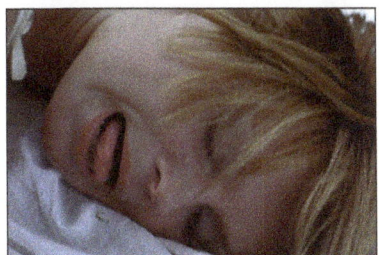

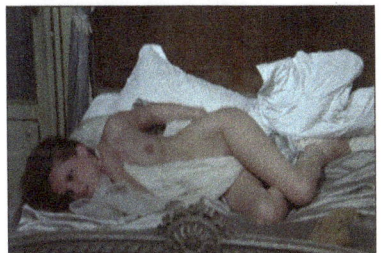

22 Reminds us of Gustave Courbet's "The Origin of the World" (1866), the Gioconda of split beavers.

23 At no stage does the Beast appear to ejaculate inside Romilda. So how was Mathurin fathered? Parthenogenesis? Immaculate Conception?

24 Sexually aroused during sleep, i.e. sleepwanking.

25 Unlike the real thing, the prop semen registers well on film and the illusion is quite convincing, which was not even the case with most gore effects at the time. A cinematic urban legend has it that Borowczyk used potato soup for this purpose but, despite arduous research, I have found no recipe that is visually analogous. In Poland, potato soup is known as Zupa Ziemniaczana (zoo-pah zhem-nyah-chan-ah) and is apparently served by loading it into a giant phallus and squirting it over the diners.

26 Pornotypically, a (heterosexual) sex scene ends with a male masturbating to ejaculation onto the buttocks, back, stomach or breasts of a woman. This renders the female skin a tabula rasa and the penis a rudimentary writing instrument. Does this conjunction represent the origin of written communication? Is the penis mightier than the pen is? Whilst it is certainly possible to ascertain glyphs in the patterns of semen traced on bodies in many pornographic films, examples of legible words have proved elusive. This exercise could be viewed as a sexy visual analogue of Raudive/EVP phenomena.

27 In cases where the male ejaculates between the female's lips, the DNA component of the semen literally puts his (genetic) words into her mouth.

hysterical "I didn't do anything" but Virginia is suspicious she strips off Mathurin's shirt and smashes the cast on his arm. Hirsute Mathurin has the tail and paw of the Beast.. the Beast.. the Beast![28] The priest sprinkles holy water on the body and the tail twitches in a death spasm. Lucy and Viriginia try to leave but their way is blocked by Pierre. Escaping up a spiral staircase in the library Lucy overturns a stack a books and discovers the body of the Duke. Their chauffeur is sleeping in the car. The cardinal and his assistant arrive at the château in the dawn, just as Virginia and Lucy, naked beneath her flapping coat, find the door. A sudden gust blows up a storm of leaves as they get into the car. Ifany and Camille observe from a balcony. The cardinal finds Lucy's Polaroid of the mating horses and pockets them. Pierre pleads with Virginia and Lucy uselessly as they depart. He takes the razor again from his jacket. The cardinal steps over the shattered remains of Mathurin's cast and the fallen portrait of Romilda to get to the corpse. He makes his pronouncement[29]:

> Bestiality, that is to say, copulating with an animal, is the most odious crime because it debases man, made in the image of God. It is most contrary to the laws of nature. That is why Leviticus... punished by death not only the guilty man or woman but also the beast itself.
>
> ...Unchaste caressing of a beast should not be forgotten at confession. For example, as if to defile herself, a woman has a dog or cat that lick her vulva, or if she touches the sex of the animal until it ejaculates... That's why Vernier advises confessors to ask women, particularly those of a lustful nature, if they have acted shamefully with an animal. Often in this way, shameful secrets are revealed.

On the back seat of the Rolls, Lucy is overcome, as Virginia embraces her and closes her coat over her breasts. Continuity error as it is dark now, the better to show the headlights of the cars behind like the yellow eyes of a following beast, and the sound of the engine and passing cars like its muted final cries.

Romilda awakens over the Beast to the harpsichord, she gathers armfuls of leaves[30] and buries the Beast beneath them by the column. She assumes the posture of Venus and finds a discarded transparent cloth to barely cover herself, reborn in shame, she skips down the path, looking back at first, but then hurrying down the path through the forest to the bright light of vanishing point. Running, the cords of her corset dangle between her buttocks, like the tail of a beast. Still running as the end credits scroll over her. Avec l'aimable concours de la Maison ANDRÉ CIGANER.

Fin.

---

28 The denouement of the film thus reveals that Lucy's dream is of Mathurin's great (great?) grandmother i.e. her maternal ancestor-in-law elect. She was turned on by her grandmother-in-law... What a pervert!

29 The most iconic example of this kind of "expert opinion" as denouement is found in **Psycho** (USA, 1960, d. Alfred Hitchcock), although it is more typical of fifties sf movies, particularly of the red-scare variety, such as **The Thing from Another World** (USA, 1954, d. Christian Nyby). Generally the message is "there are some things man was not meant to know" or "history shows again and again how nature points out the folly of men."

30 Leaves, symbol of shame in Genesis.

In Borowczyk's 1959 short *Les Astronautes* a snail is used to symbolise time accelerated due to relativity, and the periscopes of the ship resemble a snail's upper tentacles where its eye-spots are located. Perhaps this is some arcane word-play on gastropod vs astronaut?

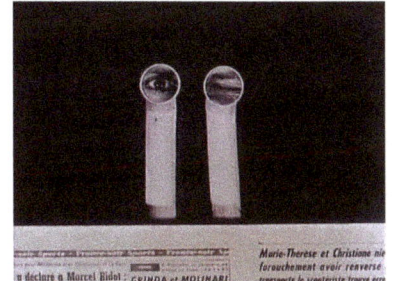 

ASSAILED BY A SNAIL

I saw in a basket thousands of live snails. Some, diverging from their number, crept along the edge. Terror staggered me: each was completely indistinguishable from another.

That epigraph, attributed to William Rowney (1223-1264), opened Borowczyk's 1965 interview in *Etudes Cinematographiques* (#41/42).

Despite their prominence in *The Beast* (and in *Escargot de Venus*, its supporting short) snails do not recur as frequently in Boro's oeuvre as some of his other fetishes.

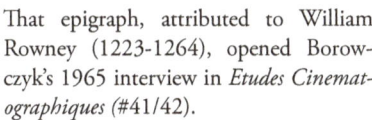

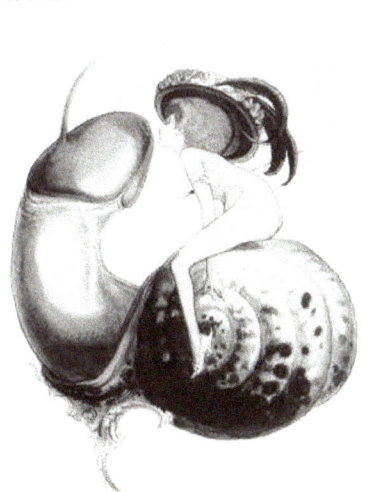

Precedents in film: *Les Escargots* (France, 1965, d. René Laloux), *Die Unendliche Geschichte* [The NeverEnding Story] (W.Germany/USA, 1984, d. Wolfgang Petersen), *Dr Dolittle* (USA, 1967, d. Richard Fleischer). *The Diary of a Chambermaid* (France/Italy, 1964, d. Luis Buñuel).

Precedents in art: A snail/penis hybrid by Franz von Bayros (1866-1924). Salvador Dali's *The Rainy Taxi*, detail of installation at the 1938 Exposition Internationale du Surréalisme in Paris. Giuseppe Arcimboldo (1527-93) *The Allegory of Earth* (detail).

Turku is a city on the southwest coast of Finland, the third largest after Helsinki and Tampere. It was where Lee Harvey Oswald said he intended to study so he could get a visa for the Soviet Union. After the collapse of the Soviet Union, the deputy mayor of Leningrad went there to study capitalist business practise. His name was Vladimir Putin. Fascinating as all of this may or may not be, much more relevant to matters in hand is the fact that the city was the first home of Sirpa Salo (no relation to the Pasolini film) who was born there on 30 November 1951.

Sirpa started out young as a fashion model and got some of her first assignments from English soft-focus expert David Hamilton before making her acting debut, aged 19, in a mysterious film called *Fluff*. This title is listed on IMDB as an Italian production, directed by Robert Paget, which was a pseudonym of Mario Gariazzo who is probably best known for his eurocrime *La Mano Spietata della Legge* [*The Bloody Hands of the Law*] (Italy, 1973). This info is squarely contradicted by the only other trace I've been able to find – a story in *Screen International* (27 September 1975, p.4,) that describes the film as an "X-rated *A Touch of Class*" produced and directed by the Notorious David Grant. (Convention dictates that we prefix Mr Grant's name with that title as a kind of inverted honorific.) Filming is listed due to start in October 1975 with Victor Spinetti and one of Grant's cars co-starring.

La Jeune Fille Assassinée
[a young girl murdered]

AKA *Charlotte: The Diary of a Nymphomaniac / Ein Wildes Leben* [a wild life]

France/Italy/West Germany | 1974 | 100 min

d/wr: Roger Vadim. p: Claude Capra. wr: Stash de Rola (Stash Klossowski). ph: Pierre-William Glenn. ed: Victoria Mercanton. mu: Mike Oldfield. w: Sirpa Lane, Michel Duchaussoy, Mathieu Carrière.

Sirpa's first real break came courtesy of none other than Roger Vadim, recently divorced from Jane Fonda he noticed her picture in a fashion magazine and made her his latest muse, touting her as "the next Brigitte Bardot." Here Vadim himself plays opposite Sirpa as the former lover of the murdered young girl. Already established as a maybe the classiest of the sleazier directors, Vadim had also acted in his own *Et Dieu... Créa la Femme* [*And God Ceated Woman*] (France/Italy, 1956), Cocteau's *Le Testament d'Orphée* [*Testament of Orpheus*] (France, 1960), and Warhol spin-off *Ciao Manhattan* (USA, 1972, d. John Palmer), and here he took the role a writer who tries to uncover the facts of the foxy corpse's last days which unfold, naturally enough, in flashback. The dialogue was co-written by the mysterious and ubiquitous Stash de Rola. It is reported that Sirpa's Finnish pronunciation required that her part be re-dubbed, and that this task fell to Brigitte Fossey, who was recommencing her film career after her retirement as the child star of *Jeux Interdits* [*Forbidden Games*] (France, 1952, d. René Clément).

The Beast

See previous chapter for technical data

Borowczyk's film remains the key film of Sirpa's career. It is the one for which she is best remembered and for many years was the only one in circulation in the anglosphere. Sirpa's unbridled performance made her the star of the film, even though she only appears an hour into it.

By this time Sirpa was regularly featuring in fashion magazines (Paris *Vogue* May and September 1975). Even Helmut Newton had a go at photographing her, but his snaps came out pretty lame.

The release of *The Beast* brought Sirpa instant fame, but it came at a cost. Like Sylvia Kristel, she was typecast into sex-charged films and with each role it became harder to break out and the films and roles became increasingly sordid.

SIRPA LANE

German lobby cards for Charlotte, known there as "Ein Wildes Leben" [a wild life].

 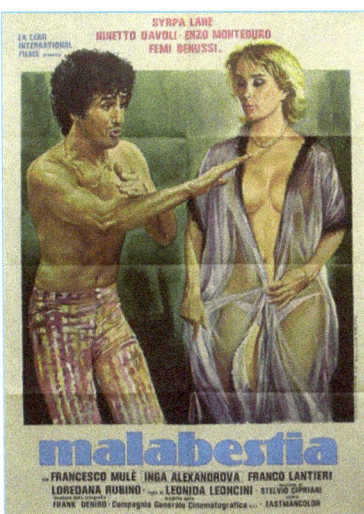 

La Svastica nel Ventre
[swastika on the belly]

AKA *Nazi Love Camp 27*

Italy | 1977 | 86 min

d/wr: Mario Caiano. *wr:* Gianfranco Clerici, Sandro Amati. *ph:* Sergio Martinelli. *ed:* Gianmaria Messeri. *mu:* Francesco De Masi. *w:* Sirpa Lane, Giancarlo Sisti, Roberto Posse.

Henceforth, Italian exploitation cinema would mostly be Sirpa's lot. In 1976, she was offered a starring role by Mario Caiano, a versatile and prolific director who had made peplums, spaghetti westerns, horror and violent crime films. Now he turned his hand to the new genre of nazisploitation. The (mostly) Italian nazisploitation cycle was inspired by the financial success of David Friedman's *Ilsa, She Wolf of the SS* (USA, 1975), which itself exploited art-house hits like *Salò* (Italy, 1975, d. Pier Paolo Pasolini) and *Salon Kitty* (Italy/W.Germany/France, 1976, d. Tinto Brass). These films had been prefigured, perhaps surprisingly, by a wave of porno novels in Israel during the 1950s that dealt with sexual exploitation in concentration camps. These in turn had been inspired by Ka-tzetnik 135633's fauxtobiography *The House of Dolls*.

The Italians produced less than a dozen nazisploitaters, including *La Bestia in Calore* [*The Beast in Heat*] (Italy, 1977, d. Luigi Batzella) which used to be often confused with Borowczyk's *The Beast* on wants lists.

In *La Svastica nel Ventre* [swastika on the belly] Sirpa Lane plays the role of a Jewish girl pressed into service as an SS whore, whose defiance impresses a nazi general and leads to her appointment as madame in a lush brothel for nazis.

Such effectiveness as the film has, it derives principally from Sirpa's performance and the strong script by Gianfranco Clerici, who was also responsible for *Non si sevizia un paperino* [*Don't Torture a Duckling*] (Italy, 1972, d. Lucio Fulci), *Cannibal Holocaust* (Italy, 1980, d. Ruggero Deodato), *La Casa Sperduta nel Parco* [*The House on the Edge of the Park*] (Italy, 1980, d. Ruggero Deodato).

Sirpa Lane's performance is quite good and the film has some powerful moments, somewhat at odds with the sleazier aspects of the production: graphic rape and torture sequences abound, with occasional flashes of hardcore that appear to have no erotic intent but rather to underscore the sadism. These contrast with the dropped-in stock footage that provides the action sequences.

It's a testament to Sirpa's interesting filmography that, even with the wall-to-wall sleaze here, maybe the most notable aspect of the film is that this time Sirpa is menaced by an Alsatian dog rather than a mythical or imaginary creature.

Malabestia [evil beast]

Italy | 1978 | 99 min

d/wr/ed: Leonida Leoncini. *ph:* Pasquale Fanetti. *mu:* Stelvio Cipriani. *w:* Inga Alexandrova, Bruno Amatucci, Femi Benussi.

Now installed in Italy, Sirpa's pickings were getting slimmer and she took a supporting role in this Italian "sexy" "comedy", this director's only film. She was alongside Femi Benussi, now remembered for his role in *Nude per l'Assassino* [*Strip Nude for Your Killer*] (Italy, 1975), directed by Andrea Bianchi, of whom more later. The title here probably did no favours in helping her avoid typecasting as the go-to star for "animal movies".

Papaya dei Caraibi
[Caribbean Papaya]

Aka: *Love Goddess of the Cannibals*

Italy | 1978 | 86 min

d: Joe D'Amato. *p:* Carlo Maietto. *wr:* Roberto Gandus, Renzo Maietto. *ph:* Aristide Massaccesi (Joe D'Amato). *ed:* Vincenzo Tomassi. *mu:* Stelvio Cipriani. *w:* Melissa Chimenti, Sirpa Lane, Maurice Poli.

The first entry in D'Amato's Caribbean Trilogy has Sirpa as a journalist who meets up with a friend who is constructing a nuclear power station, and then with the enigmatic Papaya who draws them into a mysterious netherworld of proto-voodoo rituals plus some sexy antics too. In addition to the characteristic D'Amato goriness, including a voodoo ceremony that seems to have been inspired by Hermann Nitsch before descending into

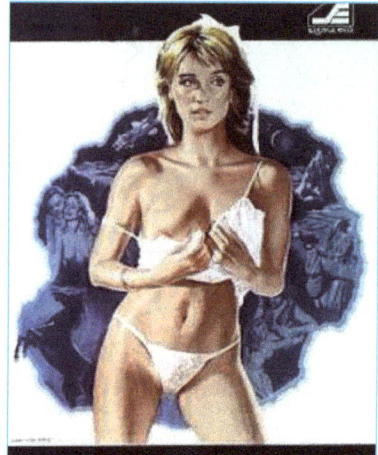
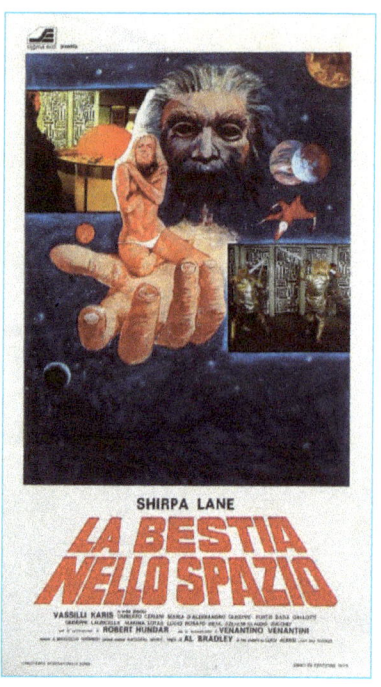

shit go-go dancing, there seem to be genuine attempts to elicit sympathy for the islanders and their struggle against the neocolonialists, in between all the writhing around in picturesque settings. Despite the alternative title, and a human sacrifice, there's no cannibalism in the film. Well, hardly any.

La Bestia nello Spazio
[the beast in space]

Italy | 1978 | 86 min

d/wr: Al Bradley (Alfonso Brescia). *wr:* Aldo Crudo. *ph:* Silvio Fraschetti. *ed:* Carlo Broglio. *mu:* Pluto Kennedy (Marcello Giombini). *w:* Sirpa Lane, Vassili Karisn (Vassili Karamesinis), Venantino Venantini, Umberto Ceriani, Robert Hundar (Claudio Undari), Dada Gallotti, Marina Lotar.

Alfonso Brescia (1930–2001) was an Italian low-budget director, now best remembered for his *Star Wars* inspired sci-fi films of the late seventies, of which this was the last instalment. In a quest for a new spin for the series, Brescia produced this unofficial sequel to *The Beast*, presumably influenced more by its profitability than its congruence with the tropes of the genre. Brescia's film centres around an overweight Han Solo character and a voyage to a strange planet populated by an omniscient computer, crap robots and gratuitous orgy action including a porn faun with the horn. Sirpa does a reasonable job of treating the whole thing seriously but the entire premise and delivery is so spectacularly bogus that there's no hope of salvaging anything approaching a "non-shit" movie. As if this wasn't seedy enough already, a hardcore version with xxx inserts (featuring other actors) was also produced. It must be grudgingly acknowledged that the film is so odd and misguided that it more than warrants the time wasted viewing it.

Le Notti Segrete di Lucrezia Borgia
[the secret nights of Lucrezia Borgia]

Italy/Spain | 1982 | 85 min

d: Roberto Bianchi Montero. *p:* Armando Novelli. *wr:* Ramón Llidó, Piero Regnoli. *ph:* Angelo Lannutti. *ed:* Cesare Bianchini. *mu:* Michael Serfran. *w:* Sirpa Lane, George Hilton, Willey Reynolds.

Depite making the front cover of French *Playboy* in August 1982, Sirpa's film roles didn't look up and she was cast next as Lucrezia Borgia in this tedious exercise that resembles nothing so much as a woefully unfunny Terence Hill/Bud Spencer movie with (slightly) more nudity and a soundtrack that is incongruous in a truly shit way.

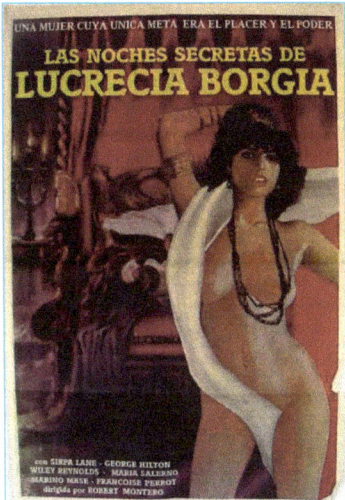

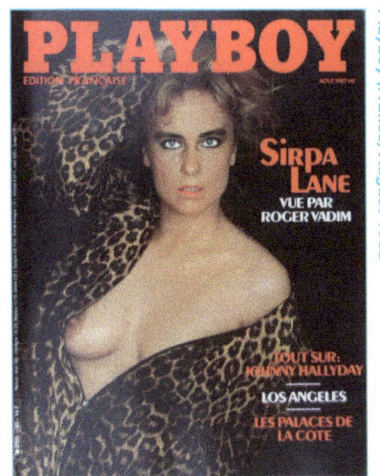

Playboy (France) August 1982

Apu (Finland) 1993? "Sirpa Salo-Lane to give AIDS a woman's face"

Giochi Carnali [carnal games]

AKA Exciting Love Girls

Italy | 1983 | 109 min

d: Andrea Bianchi. p: Oscar Santaniello. wr: Piero Regnoli. ph: Enrico Biribicchi. mu: Ennio Mancuso, Berto Pisano. w: Sirpa Lane, Franco Parisi, Domenico Anastasi.

Andrea Bianchi had made some very effective eurosleaze, notably *Nude per l'Assassino* [*Strip Nude for Your Killer*] (Italy, 1975) and *Malabimba* (Italy, 1979) but he completely lost the plot with this crime thriller about two rapists who drive around looking for victims, with one of the perps adopting a drag get-up for extra uh effectiveness. Sirpa plays a surgeon who gets kidnapped by the villains. Whatever its many other shortcomings, the film never gets boring. Its weird vibe is only enhanced by recurring woefully misplaced humorous episodes and obviously spurious hardcore inserts. The movie was actually shot in 1980 but had to wait three years till anyone was desperate enough to release it.

Trois Filles dans le Vent

[three girls on the wind]

Canada/France | 1982 | 108 min

d/p/wr/w: Jean-Marie Pallardy. wr: Jacques Wodkowski. ph: Max Monteillet. ed: Bruno Zincone. w: Sirpa Lane, Gordon Mitchell.

Jean-Marie Pallardy had started out as a male model but turned to directing softcore in the early seventies, soon switching to hardcore and directing Olinka, Brigitte Lahaie, Marilyn Jess and Alice Arno in such titles as *Le Journal érotique d'un Bûcheron* [*Erotic Diary of a Lumberjack*] (France, 1974), *L'Amour chez les Poids Lourds* [*Love in the Heavy Goods Vehicles*] (France, 1978), and *Emmanuelle à Cannes* [*Emmanuelle Goes to Cannes*] (France, 1978).

Here, two desperate actors kidnap Sirpa Lane and hide out on a small Mediterranean island but the crew from the film that Sirpa was working on track them down and the customary orgy eventuates. For bonus sleaze value, the film is stitched together from bits of other movies.

According to some internet sources, Sirpa turned to hardcore after this. Given her contacts and the milieu within which she worked, this does not seem unlikely, but no credible sightings have been reported yet. There are also rumours of appearances in unspecified films including the maybe apocryphal *Nympho-Teens of Roma Meet Son of the Wolfman* (Italy, 1979) which is sometimes credited to... Robert Paget. So did this just recycle the *Fluff* footage? I am barely satisfied that this film exists at all, and only then because the story provides a satisfying circularity to her career.

In the nineties, with her film career long-over, and forgotten by all but a few devout fans (such as myself) Sirpa tested positive for HIV and died from AIDS-related illness in 1999 in Formentera, Balearic Islands, Spain.

further reading

Fotogramas (Spain), 4 June 1976, vol. 31, no. 1442

Interview (USA), February 1978

Personas (Spain), 11 May 1975, no.70.

Playboy (France), August 1982, no.105

Playboy (Spain), May 1979, no. 7

Playboy (USA), June 1975, vol. 22, no. 6, p. 88

Playboy (USA), May 1979, vol. 26, Iss. 5, p. 167

Vogue, Nov 1974

Paris Vogue, May 1975

Paris Vogue, September 1975

49

Dzieje Grzechu

STORY OF A SIN

Poland | 1975 | 130 min

🏆 Golden Palm, Cannes.

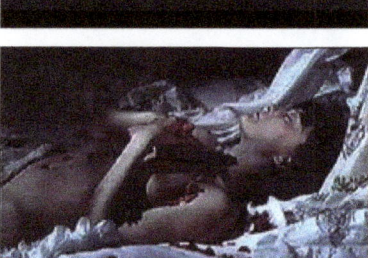

Directed by	Walerian Borowczyk
Scenario by	Walerian Borowczyk
from the novel by	Stefan Zeromski

• CAST •

Grazyna Dlugolecka	Ewa Pobratynska
Jerzy Zelnik	Lukasz Niepolomski
Olgierd Lukaszewicz	Count Zygmunt Szczerbic
Roman Wilhelmi	Antoni Pochron
Marek Walczewski	Plaza-Splawski
Karolina Lubienska	Mrs. Pobratynska, Ewa's mother
Zdzislaw Mrozewski	Mr. Pobratynski, Ewa's father
Mieczyslaw Voit	Count Cyprian Bodzanta
Marek Bargielowski	Adolf Horst
Jolanta Szemberg	Aniela
Zbigniew Zapasiewicz	Priest Jutkiewicz
Wladyslaw Hancza	Dr. Wielgosinski
Jadwiga Chojnacka	Leoska, servant
Boguslaw Sochnacki	

Janusz Zakrzenski	Editor of 'Tygodnik Naukowy'
Zbigniew Koczanowicz	Chief clerk
Jan Piechocinski	Stanislaw Liwicki, student
Henryk Hunko	Batasinski
Tomasz Lengren	Fajtas
Bogdan Wisniewski	

Paul Arenkens	Cabaret Singer
Thea Schmidt-Keune	
Jadwiga Siennicka	
Barbara Marszalek	
Maria Robaszkiewicz	
Barbara Dembinska	
Zofia Gienieczko	
Ewa Jez	

Maria Kowalik	Girl in the sewing room
Stanislaw Tylczynski	
Tadeusz Teodorczyk	Doctor in Cabaret
Irena Burawska	
Piotr Augustyniak	
Eugeniusz Korczarowski	
Józef Lodynski	
Zofia Wilczynska	
Czeslaw Piaskowski	
Dymitr Holówko	
Jan Pawel Kruk	Horst's friend

Mariusz Leszczynski	
Karol Obidniak	
Kazimierz Iwinski	
Walerian Borowczyk (uncredited)	Piotr Iwanycz, man in casino
Zygmunt Samosiuk (uncredited)	Piotr Iwanycz's wife

••••••••••••••••••••• **CREW** •••••••••••••••••••••

Cinematography by	Zygmunt Samosiuk
Film Editing by	Lidia Pacewicz
Art Direction by	Teresa Barska
Set Decoration by	Marek Iwaszkiewicz
Costume Design by	Jerzy Szeski
Zbigniew Dobracki	makeup artist
Zofia Macinska	
Jan Plazewski	
Helena Nowicka	production manager
Ewa Smal	assistant director
Felicja Blaszynska	assistant production designer
Boleslaw Pieczynski	
Andrzej Rafal Waltenberger	
Jan Czerwinski	sound
Andrzej Kubik	sound assistant
Zygmunt Nowak	
Marian Redlich	
Eugeniusz Gawrysiak	assistant camera
Kazimierz Pawlak	
Roswita Stern	costume assistant
Anna Izykowska	music consultant
Halina Gasior	filming manager
Stanislaw Moroszkiewicz	
Henryk Strzebiecki	
Lechoslaw Szuttenbach	

Polish poster by

••••••••••••••••••••• **NOTES** •••••••••••••••••••••

Stefan Zeromski (1864–1925) is one of Poland's most celebrated writers and was shortlisted for the Nobel Prize in literature in 1924. Many of his works had been adapted for the stage or screen, including his novel ***Popioły*** [the ashes] (Poland, 1965, d. Andrzej Wajda). ***Dzieje Grzechu*** had been filmed as early as 1911 by Antoni Bednarczyk, and then in 1933 by Henryk Szaro, but Boro's film is regarded as the most faithful and meticulously detailed adaptation of the novel. Produced during a period of liberalisation, it was the most explicit film to be released in Poland at the time.

French poster

••••••••••••••••••• **FURTHER READING** •••••••••••••••••••

Bouyxou, Jean-Pierre. ***Sex Stars System***, no. 12, April 1976, p.46.
Kino, vol.10 no.4, April 1975, p.12-19, in Polish.
Monthly Film Bulletin, vol.43 no.507, April 1976. p78-79.
Variety, 28 May 1975, p.19.
Continental Film Review, vol.22 no.10, August 1975, p.11.
Continental Film Review, April 1976, p.9.
Wertenstein, Wanda. ***Polish Film Polonaise***, April 1975.
L'Avant-Scène du Cinéma, no. 317-318, December 1983, p.86, in French.

East German poster

LA MARGE [the margin]
AKA The Streetwalker / Emanuelle 77

France | 1976 | 88 min

Directed by	Walerian Borowczyk
from the novel by	André Pieyre de Mandiargues
adaptation by	Walerian Borowczyk

••••••••••••••••••CAST••••••••••••••••••

Sylvia Kristel	Diana
Joe Dallesandro	Sigimond Pons
André Falcon	Antonin Pons
Mireille Audibert	Sergine Pons
Denis Manuel	Le moustachu
Emmanuel Franval	
Dominique Marcas	
Norma Picadilly	The stripper
Camille Larivière	
Luz Laurent	
Louise Chevalier	Feline
Karin Albin	
Jean Lara	
Carlo Nell	
Dominique Erlanger	
Sylvaine Charlet	
Isabelle Mercanton	
Esther Farfan	
Régis Porte (uncredited)	
Rosette (uncredited)	Prostitute

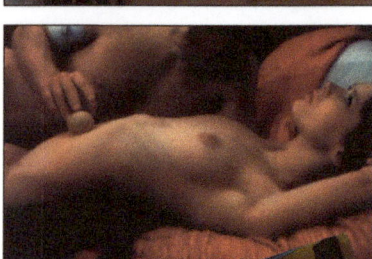

••••••••••••••••••CREW••••••••••••••••••

Raymond Hakim	producer
Robert Hakim	producer
Cinematography by	Bernard Daillencourt
Film Editing by	Louisette Hautecoeur
Production Design by	Jacques D'Ovidio
Costume Design by	Marie-Françoise Perochon
Jacky Douban	key makeup artist
Henri Baum	production manager
Jacques Perrier	unit manager
Jean Pieuchot	unit manager
Alain Cayrade	second assistant director
André Heinrich	first assistant director
Maurice Gilbert	sound mixer
Louis Hochet	sound

Bernard Baillon	assistant camera
Jean-Pierre Platel	assistant camera
Raymond Voinquel	still photographer
Noël Véry	camera operator
Khadicha Bariha	assistant editor
Eliane Baum	script supervisor

• JOE DALLESANDRO •

Famous for not having his face on the cover of two of the most influential rock albums of all-time, Joe Dallesandro's crotch appeared on the cover of The Rolling Stones 1971 LP **Sticky Fingers** and his torso on The Smiths' eponymous 1984 debut.

After a tough childhood in Harlem, Brooklyn and Queens, Dallesandro drifted into a life of crime and teenage gang life. After running away from a rehabilitation camp, he took up nude modelling and appeared in at least one gay porno short. He met Andy Warhol and Paul Morrissey whilst they were filming ******** (AKA **Four Stars**, USA, 1967) and was immediately cast as College Wrestler. He followed this with a role in **Flesh** (USA, 1968) which became a crossover hit after **Rolling Stone** named it their best film of the year. Dallesandro became the highest profile icon of the US underground and was, of course, immortalised in the Lou Reed song "Walk on the Wild Side". He went on to make other films for Morrisssey, **Lonesome Cowboys** (USA, 1968), **San Diego Surf** (USA, 1968), **Trash** (USA, 1970), **Heat** (USA, 1972), **Flesh for Frankenstein** (USA/Italy/France, 1973), and **Blood for Dracula** (Italy/France, 1974). The last two of these were filmed in Europe, where Dallesandro chose to remain after shooting was complete, making **Black Moon** (France/W. Germany, 1975, d. Louis Malle), **Je T'Aime Moi Non Plus** (France, 1976, d. Serge Gainsbourg) before being cast opposite Sylvia Kristel in Borowczyk's glumfest. Other than his role in **Suor Omicidi** [**Killer Nun**] (Italy, 1978, d. Giulio Berruti), most of his later film and tv work has been regarded as disappointing.

• SYLVIA KRISTEL •

Born in Utrecht in the Netherlands, Sylvia Kristel won Miss TV Europe in 1973 and made a few films in the Netherlands before getting the part of **Emmanuelle** (France, 1974, d. Just Jaeckin) that made her into an overnight star in France. Kristel followed up with roles in **Un Linceul n'a pas de Poches** [no pockets in a shroud] (France, 1974, d. Jean-Pierre Mocky) and **Jeu avec Le Feur** [**Playing with Fire**] (France, 1975, d. Alain Robbe-Grillet) before returning to **Emmanuelle II** (France, 1975, d. Just Jaeckin). **Une Femme Fidèle** [**A Faithful Woman**] (France, 1976, d. Roger Vadim) was based on **Les Liaisons Dangereuses** [**Dangerous Liaisons**] by Pierre Choderlos de Laclos, and now Kristel was typecast as the face of historical female sex icons, **Lady Chatterley's Lover** (UK/France/W.Germany, 1981, d. Just Jaeckin) and even **Mata Hari** (USA, 1985, d. Curtis Harrington). **La Marge** was retitled **Emanuelle 77** in West Germany to cash in on Sylvia Kristel's most famous role, and Boro would later be reduced to directing an official entry in the series, albeit one of the few in which she did not appear.

• FURTHER READING •

Monthly Film Bulletin, vol.44 no.523, August 1977, p.169.
Positif, no.187, November 1976, p.120, in French.
Continental Film Review, vol.23 no.4, February 1976, p.11.
Variety, 22 September 1976, p.19.
Sex Stars System, no.18, October 1976, p.41, in French.

French poster

German poster

Japanese poster

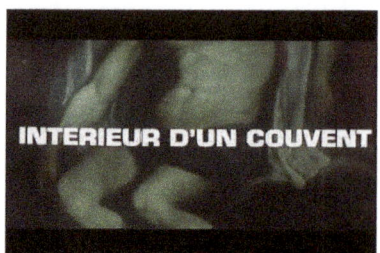

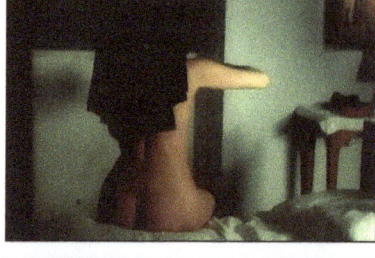

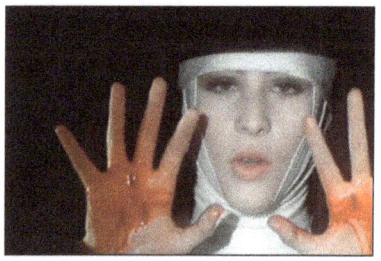

Interno di un Convento [inside a convent]

BEHIND CONVENT WALLS

AKA Sex Life in a Convent / Within a Cloister

Italy | 1978 | 95 min

Written and directed by Walerian Borowczyk
from motifs in **Walks in Rome** by Henri Stendhal

• **CAST** •

Ligia Branice	Sister Clara
Howard Ross	Rodrigo Landriani
Marina Pierro	Sister Veronica
Gabriella Giacobbe	Abbess Flavia Orsini
Rodolfo Dal Pra	Bishop
Loredana Martínez	Sister Martina
Mario Maranzana	Father Confessor
Alessandro Partexano	Silva
Olivia Pascal	
Gina Rovere	
Dora Calindri	
Francesca Balletta	
Maria Cumari Quasimodo	
Raymonde Carole Fouanon	
Miana Merisi	
Simona Villani	
Paola Arduini	
Silvano Bernabei	
Brid Cranitch	
Stefania D'Amario	
Elisabeth Jane Long	
Imelde Marani	
Patrizia Mauro	
Paola Morra	
Mike Morris	
Antonietta Patriarca	
Elisabetta Pedrazzi	
Rossella Pescatore	
Valeria Pescatore	
Paola Prosdogemi	
Romano Puppo	
Jole Rosa	
Romana Monti	
Greta Vayan	

• **CREW** •

Giuseppe Vezzani	producer
Music by	Sergio Montori
Cinematography by	Luciano Tovoli
Film Editing by	Walerian Borowczyk
Set Decoration by	Francesco Chianese
	Luciano Spadoni
Costume Design by	Maria Laura Zampacavallo
Maria-Luisa Fraticelli	hair stylist
Franco Rufini	key makeup artist
Andreina Ambrosini	assistant makeup artists
Mario Michisanti	
Carmelo Bianco	production manager
Raffaele Errigo	assistant director
Filippo Bufo	assistant set decorator
Carlo Palmieri	sound
Alberto Tinebra	sound mixer
Giulio Molinari	special effects
Maurizio Lucchini	assistant camera
Giuseppe Tinelli	still photographer
Roberto Olivieri	assistant editors
Elvira Zincone	
Anna Maria Bifarini	script supervisor
Mario Longardi	press attache
Bruno Bagella	production secretaries
Alessandrina Pellegrini	

French poster

• **NOTES** •

Never one to be less than scrupulously fair, Borowczyk's overt anti-clericism of **The Beast** found its gender balance in his contribution to the nunsploitation genre at the height of its popularity. Borowczyk's film was based on a short section from Stendhal's **Promenades dans Rome**, perhaps to lend the air of faux-couture that these films often sought, although his is a relatively restrained example the genre. The film is notable for bringing Ligia Branice and Marina Pierro together in the same film and as such marks a neat turning-point in Borowczyk's career for those disposed to such things.

Here Borowczyk minimises his pretentions to narrative to sketch out a series of vignettes of escalating weirdness, some of which are eerily precogniscient. We have nuns performing nude aerobics several decades before the craze took off, and DIY sex toys, still very much a fringe interest.

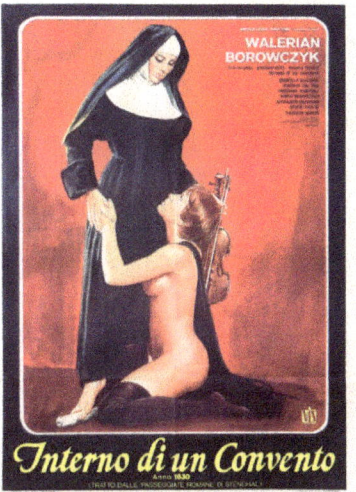

Italian poster

• • • • • • • • • • • • • • • **FURTHER READING** • • • • • • • • • • • • • • •

Monthly Film Bulletin, vol.46 no.539, December 1978, p.241-242.
Variety, 2 August 1978, p.14.
Ecran, no. 70, 15 June 1978, p.63-64, in French.

Belgian? poster

Nunsploitation

Prefigured by sequences in Benjamin Christensen's *Häxan* [the witch] (Sweden/Denmark, 1922) and Boro compatriot Jerzy Kawalerowicz's *Matka Joanna od Aniołów* [*Mother Joan of the Angels*] (Poland, 1961). Nunsploitation is an exploitation sub-genre that came to prominence in the mid-seventies, generally in strongly catholic countries, in the wake of the success of Ken Russell's *The Devils* (UK, 1971).

Drawing on the conventions of the WIP (women in prison) genre, the most archetypical examples of nunsploitation focus on deviant nuns, and sometimes other members of the clergy, who are overwhelmed by a mania arising from their social isolation, religious authoritarianism and/or sexual celibacy. They are characterised by themes of lesbianism, flagellation and anti-clericism.

As with the WIP film, it was the genius Jesús Franco who gave us the first true nunsploitation *Les Demons* [the demons] (France, 1972) and followed with the powerful *Die Liebesbriefe einer Portugiesischen Nonne* [*Love Letters of a Portuguese Nun*] (West Germany, 1976) which starred Romina Power.

It as in Italy, unsurprisingly, that the theme really took off, with Le Monache di Sant'Arcangelo [the nuns of St Arch-angel] (AKA *The Nun and the Devil*, Italy, 1973, d. Domenico Paolella), followed by *Flavia, la Monaca musulmana* [*Flavia the Heretic*] (Italy, 1974, d. Gianfranco Mingozzi), *Le Scomunicate di San Valentino* [*The Sinful Nuns of St Valentine*] (Italy, 1974, d. Sergio Grieco). *Suor Emmanuelle* [*Sister Emanuelle*] (Italy, 1977, d. Giuseppe Vari) was a nunsploitation/Emmanuelle cross-pollination, and *Suor Omicida* [*Killer Nun*] (Italy, 1978, d. Giulio Berruti) an anomalous giallo/nunsploit hybrid, set in the present day, staring Joe Dallesandro fresh from his role in *La Marge*. Joe D'Amato arrived here belatedly but gave us *Immagini di un Convento* [*Images in a Convent*] (Italy, 1979) and *La Monaca del Peccato* [*Convent of Sinners*] (Italy, 1986). Some of these films also circulated in versions with hardcore footage, usually via inserts, but sometimes contemporaneous footage, and the genre became popular, especially in Germany, as a staple of the hardcore market.

Outside of Europe, other Catholic countries got in on the act with *They Call Her Cleopatra Wong* (Philippines, 1978, d. Bobby A. Suarez), and *Satánico Pandemonium* (Mexico, 1975, d. Gilberto Martínez Solares) and *Alucarda* (AKA *Sisters of Satan*, Mexico, 1975, d. Juan López Moctezuma).

In Japan, where Christianity is a minority religion but the transgressive tropes of nunsploitation are familiar the genre caught on slightly later but proved surprisingly durable. The first pinku-nunsploitater was 聖獣学園 *Seijū Gakuen* [*School of the Holy Beast*] (Japan, 1974, d. Norifumi Suzuki), followed by 修道女ルナの告白 *Shudojo Runa no Kokuhaku* [*Cloistered Nun: Runa's Confession*] (Japan, 1976, d. Masaru Konuma) and even as late as 1995, Sachi Hamano gave us the blunt-but-accurately-titled 巨乳修道院 [*Big Tit Monastery*].

Outside of the European hardcore porno market, the genre was pretty much burned out by 1980 and later isolated examples adopted an ironic or parodic approach that offset or nullified their still controversial content.

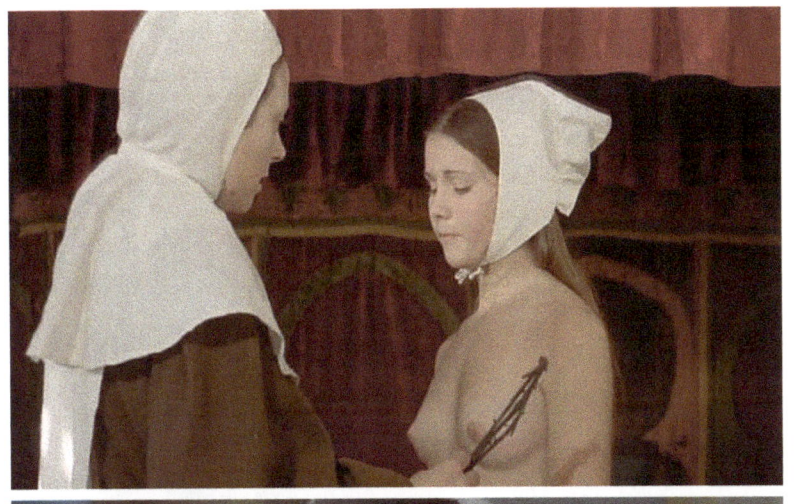

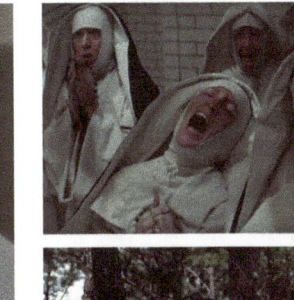

▼ The Demons
◄ Flavia, The Heretic

▲▲▲ Love Letters of a Portuguese Nun
▲▲ Sister Emmanuelle
▲ School of the Holy Beast

Top to bottom: Häxan / Mother Joan of the Angels / The Devils / They Call Her Cleopatra Wong / Satanico Pandemonium / Cloistered Nun: Runa's Confession

Les Héroïnes du Mal [heroines of evil]

THREE IMMORAL WOMEN

AKA Heroines of Pain / Immoral Women

France | 1979 | 109 min

Written and directed by	Walerian Borowczyk
"Marceline" based on a story by	André Pieyre de Mandiargues

•••••••••••••••••••• CAST ••••••••••••••••••••

Marina Pierro	Margherita Luti
Gaëlle Legrand	Marceline Cain
Pascale Christophe	Marie
François Guétary	Raphael Sanzio
Jean-Claude Dreyfus	Bini
Jean Martinelli	Pope
Pierre Benedetti	Mad Painter
Philippe Desboeuf	Doctor
Noël Simsolo	Julio Romano
Roger Lefrere	Michelangelo
Gérard Falconetti	Tomaso
Hassane Fall	Petrus
France Rumilly	Madame Cain
Yves Gourvil	Cain
Lisbeth Arno	Floka
Gérard Ismaël	Antoine
Henri Piégay	Husband
Mathieu Rivollier	
Robert Capia	
Daniel Marty	
Jacky Baudet	
Sylvain Ramsamy	
Jean Boullu	
Françoise Queré	
Mazouz Ould-Abderrahmane	
Bernard Hiard	

•••••••••••••••••••• CREW ••••••••••••••••••••

Gisèle Braunberger	associate producer
Pierre Braunberger	producer
Jean-Paul De Vidas Michel de Vidas	executive producers
Music by	Philippe d'Aram Olivier Dassault
Cinematography by	Bernard Daillencourt

Film Editing by	Khadicha Bariha
Art Direction by	Jacques D'Ovidio
Emilienne Pecqueur	production manager
Michel Champetier Michel Levy	assistant director
Guy Rophé	sound recordist
Éric Rophé	boom operator
Noël Véry	camera operator

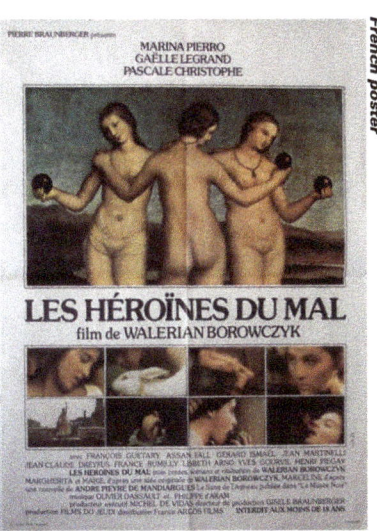

French poster

• • • • • • • • • • • • • • • • • • • **EPISODES** • • • • • • • • • • • • • • • • • • •

I. MARGHERITA. In the first episode, Marina Pierro plays the scheming mistress of the painter Raffaello Sanzio da Urbino (1483-1520), better known as Raphael, who stands alongside Michelangelo and Leonardo da Vinci in the traditional trinity of great masters of the High Renaissance. He produced a huge body of work, mostly for the Vatican palace, under the patronage of Pope Julius II and Leo X, who ruled just after the reign of Alexander VI (qv Boro's **Immoral Tales**). Although much of his work has biblical themes, his best-known work is the classical **Three Graces** (c. 1500) which Boro used as the title card for this film. Another well-known work is **La Fornarina**, [the baker] (c. 1518) which is considered to be a portrait of his mistress and later fiancé, Margherita Luti, who also sat for **La Donna Velata** [the veiled woman] (c. 1516). Raphael died at the early age of 37, on what was possibly his birthday, from a fever supposedly contracted after a night of frenzied sex with Margherita. Boro however, postulates his own hypothesis.

II. MARCELINE. The second episode is drawn from "Le Sang de l'Agneau" [blood of the lamb] by Mandiargues from his debut collection of stories, **Le Musée Noir** [the black museum] (Paris: Robert Laffont, 1946). Here we see Borowczyk returning to the theme of zoophilia between the eponymous heroine and her pet Souci, a rabbit rather than a lamb. The episode is notable as one of the most explicitly violent in Borowczyk's canon and holds its own in the bunsploitation genre alongside **Harvey** (USA, 1950, d. Henry Koster), **Night of the Lepus** (USA, 1972, d. William F. Claxton) and **Watership Down** (UK, 1978, d. Martin Rosen).

III. MARIE. Contemporary urban settings don't bode well when it comes to Boro action, and the third episode here doesn't fail to disappoint. The story of a beautiful gallery owner sexually menaced by a tramp and subsequently rescued by her faithful hound is a shaggy dog too far, with a series of twists in the tail that are all too foreseeable.

As a whole, the film appears intended as a sequel to his **Immoral Tales** but lacks the visual flair and generalised weirdness of the earlier film, substituting a more accessible and straightforward approach. Interested readers should check out Scott Murray's excellent in-depth essay on the film for a more generous appraisal.

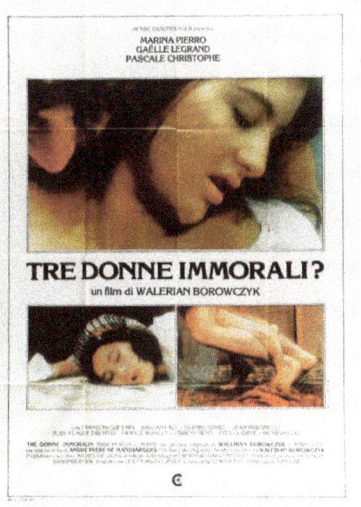

Italian poster

• • • • • • • • • • • • • • • **FURTHER READING** • • • • • • • • • • • • • • •

Monthly Film Bulletin, vol.48 no.570, July 1981, p.139.
Variety, 23 May 1979, p.27.
Cahiers du Cinema, no.299, April 1979, p.51, in French.
Positif, no. 218, May 1979 p.73, in French.
Murray, Scott. "Walerian Borowczyk's Heroines of Desire." **Senses of Cinema**, www.sensesofcinema.com, accessed 4 February 2007.

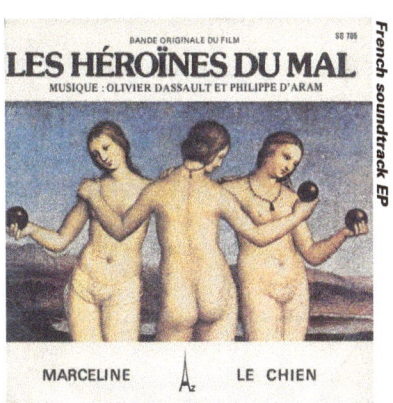

French soundtrack EP

7" EP 45rpm | Disc Az, France | SG 705

Music by Olivier Dassault and Philippe d'Aram. (2 tracks: "Marceline" b/w "Le Chien" [the dog])

MARINA PIERRO

Marina Pierro was born in 1960 in Boscotrecase, a small town twenty kilometres southeast of Naples, but spent her youth in Turin where her family had moved when she was young. She manifested an early talent for art and studied photography, theatre and French, maintaining an interest in astrology, esotericism and psychoanalysis and developing a passion for film and acting. Her favourite directors include Visconti, Bergman, Dreyer, Buñuel, Hitchcock, Fassbinder and Parajanov. After her studies, she moved to Rome where she met Coco Albino, assistant director to Visconti, who offered her a small role in his last film *The Innocent* (Italy, 1976). This was followed by a role in *Taxi Love* (Italy, 1976), directed by Sergio Bergonzelli, better known for *Nelle Pieghe della Carne* [*In the Folds of the Flesh*] (Italy/Spain, 1970), and a small role in Dario Argento's *Suspiria* (Italy, 1977).

Shortly afterwards she encountered Walerian Borowczyk, then enjoying celebrity for *Immoral Tales* and *The Beast*, and he wrote the part of Sister Veronica for her in *Behind Convent Walls*. Their artistic partnership would last more than a decade and she would appear in all his following features except *Lulu* and *Emmanuelle 5*. Beyond her work for Borowczyk, she would be acclaimed for her role for Jean Rollin in his *La Morte Vivante* [*The Living Dead Girl*] (France, 1982).

After some experience in experimental theatre in Rome, she wrote *La Memoria e Osaka* [memory and Osaka] for the stage and treatments for short films, including *Floaters* (Italy, 2006) about the artworks of her son, the painter Alessio Pierro, who had been a pupil of Borowczyk. Following publication of a volume of poetry, *Nubi Ardenti* [burning clouds] (Rome: Cupressus Edizioni, 2009), they collaborated on a short film, *Himorogi*, in tribute to the work of Borowczyk (Italy, 2012), and it premiered at the seventh International Film Festival of Rome.

▲▲ Marina's brief role in Dario Argento's "Suspiria"

▲ Marina and Francoise Blanchard in Jean Rollin's "The Living Dead Girl"

◄ Marina on the cover of "Photo" (France), February 1988.

► Marina in Visconti's "L'Innocente"

MARINA PIERRO
FILMOGRAPHY

1960   Born in Boscotrecase, Italy.

1976 — L'Innocente [the innocent] (Luchino Visconti)

— Taxi Love (Sergio Bergonzelli)

— I Prosseneti [the pimps] (Brunello Rondi)

— Sorbole... che romagnola! (Alfredo Rizzo)

1977 — Suspiria (Dario Argento)

1978 — Behind Convent Walls (Walerian Borowczyk)

1979 — Three Immoral Women (Walerian Borowczyk)

1981 — The Strange Case of Dr. Jekyll and Miss Osbourne (Walerian Borowczyk)

1982 — La Quinta Donna [the fifth woman] (TV movie by Alberto Negrin)

— The Living Dead Girl (Jean Rollin)

— La Smemorata (Giancarlo Soldi)

1983 — The Art of Love (Walerian Borowczyk)

1987 — Love Rites (Walerian Borowczyk)

1987 — La Parete della Stanza Accanto [the walls of the next room] (TV episode by Carlo Di Carlo)

1990 — A Justified Treatment (TV episode by Walerian Borowczyk)

1990 — La Scommessa [the bet] (Short by Pietro Santagada)

2006 — Floaters (short by by Marina Pierro)

2008 — In Versi (Short by Marina Pierro)

2012 — Himorogi (Short by Marina and Alessio Pierro)

L'ARMOIRE [the wardrobe]

France | 1979 | 49 min

Written and directed by — Walerian Borowczyk
Based on the short story by — Guy de Maupassant

•••••••••••••••••••• CAST ••••••••••••••••••••

Marie-Catherine Conti	the young woman
Yves-Marie Maurin	The client
Isabelle Jeannette	A dancer
Michel Lévy	
Alice Deneige	The old singer
Louis Lalanne	
Françoise Quéré	A dancer
Laurence Caubet	A dancer
Sophie Blanchard	A dancer
Brahim Bouillon	
Louis-Michel Colla	
Jean Rios	The child
Hubert Lassiat	The old man
Régis Le Rohellec	
Ari Arcadi	
Jean-Pierre Rambal (uncredited)	Audience member

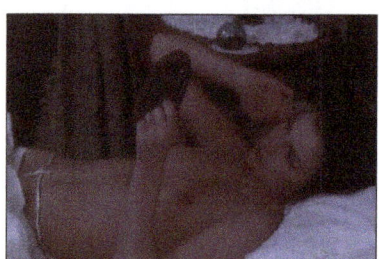

•••••••••••••••••••• CREW ••••••••••••••••••••

Pierre Braunberger	producer
Jean-Paul De Vidas	executive producer
music	Carlo Rustichelli
Cinematography by	Noël Véry
Film Editing by	Khadicha Bariha
Costume Design by	Piet Bolscher
Marc Blanchard	makeup artist
Gisèle Braunberger	production manager
Christophe Smith	assistant director
Joël Beldent	sound mixer
Jean-Pierre Platel	assistant camera
Bernard Ramel	key grip
Sarah Mallinson	assistant costume designer
Hamida Mekki	assistant editor
Véronique Cadet	script supervisor
Dominique Duvergé	collaborator
Marcelle Héron	production administrator
Jean-François Pignard	

•••••••••••••••• FURTHER READING ••••••••••••••••

Variety, 11 July 1979, p.19.
Variety, 7 March 1984, p. 369.
Positif, no.222, September 1979, p.69-70, in French.

Pierre "Boum-Boum" Braunberger started his production work in 1927 with Jean Renoir's *Sur un air de Charleston*, a bizarre sf short, and went on to an illustrious career bankrolling key works by Godard, Rouch, Marker, Resnais. By the time of his death in 1990 he had produced almost 100 features and 300 short films.

Braunberger was a close friend of Anatole Dauman (producer of *The Beast* and *Immoral Tales*). They were known as Castor and Pollux, the celestial twins, of high-class French cinema. Braunberger was therefore a natural choice to produce Borowczyk's *Three Immoral Women* following his works for Dauman, and that was followed by this curious portmanteau work.

Braunberger had long been interested in experimenting with form, having produced the first French talkie *La Route est Belle* (1929) and the first compilation film *Paris 1900* (d. Nicole Védrès, France, 1947). The anthology film had proved a popular draw in the sixties, the key examples of the genre being: *Les Sept Péchés Capitaux* [*The Seven Deadly Sins*] (France/Italy, 1961), *Les Plus Belles Escroqueries du Monde* [*The World's Most Beautiful Swindlers*] (France/Italy/Japan, 1963), *RoGoPaG* (France/Italy, 1963), *Paris vu Par...* [*Paris Seen by...*] (France, 1965), *Amore e Rabbia* [*Love and Anger*] (Italy/France, 1967). At the end of the seventies Braunberger thought to resurrect the form in a sexy fashion, and commissioned three eminent exponents of erotica to realise the project.

Before turning to film direction Just Jaekin had been a fashion photographer and art director for *Marie Claire*. His first film was an adaptation of Emmanuelle Arsan's bestselling eponymous novel, distinctively shot in a glossy soft-focus style. Previously the domain of dirty old men, *Emmanuelle* (France, 1974) expanded erotic cinema to the lucrative couples market and provided a "sophisticated"

Collections Privées

alternative (or hors d'oeuvre perhaps) to the hardcore productions that would soon flood Parisian cinemas. He followed up his monster success with a predictable choice of *The Story of O* (France, 1975), another bestselling pretentious porno novel, this time by Pauline Reagé, for his second hit. Attempting to widen his stylistic palette Jaekin produced three duds before taking on D.H. Lawrence's *Lady Chatterley's Lover* (France, 1981) and finished his directing career with *Gwendoline* (France, 1984) based on the drawings of John Willie from the influential bondage journal *Bizarre*.

Jaeckin's episode for *Private Collections* was *L'Ile aux Sirenes* [island of sirens], and starred Laura Gemser, famous for her role as "Black Emmannuelle" in a series of unofficial knock-offs.

The second episode, 草迷宮 [Kusa-Meikyû / *The Grass Labyrinth*] was directed by Shûji Terayama who had started directing for the influential Art Theatre Guild in 1971 with トマトケッチャップ皇帝 [Tomato Kecchappu Kotei/*Emperor Tomato Ketchup*] and 書を捨てよ町へ出よう [Sho Wo Suteyo Machi He Deyou/*Throw Away Your Books, Rally in the Streets*], both critically important works of the Japanese new wave. He followed up in 1974 with the brazenly psychedelic 田園に死す [Den-en Ni Shisu/*Pastoral: To Die in the Country*] which was nominated for the Palme d'Or at the 28th Cannes Film Festival. In 1977 he made his first and last commercial feature based on his lifelong love of pugilism and one of the classics of boxploitation, ボクサー [Bokusā/ *The Boxer*]. After *Private Collections*, Terayama made a film for Dauman, *Fruits of Passion* (France/Japan, 1981), an adaptation of *Return to the Chateau*, Pauline Reagé's sequel to *The Story of O*.

The first two episodes here clocked in at 29 minutes each, but Borowczyk rounded off the trilogy with a fifty minute segment based on an 1884 story by Guy de Maupassant. The story plays out like a precursor to his work on *Serie Rose*. A wealthy gent picks up a prostitute at the Folies Bergère and they repair to her hovel to do business, but are disturbed by a noise from the wardrobe.

▲ Laura Gemser and Roland Blanche in Just Jaeckin's *L'Ile aux Sirenes*.

▼ Representative strangeness from Shûji Terayama's *The Grass Labyrinth*.

LULU
AKA Los Amantes de Lulú [Lulu's lovers]

France/Italy/Germany | 1980 | 95 min

Written and directed by	Walerian Borowczyk
Screenplay by	Anton Giulio Majano
	Géza von Radványi
Based on the plays by	Frank Wedekind

•••••••••••••••••••••CAST•••••••••••••••••••

Anne Bennent	Lulu
Michele Placido	Schwarz
Jean-Jacques Delbo	Doctor Goll
Hans-Jürgen Schatz	Alwa Schoen
Bruno Hübner	Schigolch
Beate Kopp	Baroness Geschwitz
Carlo Enrici	Monsieur Hunidei
Pierre Saintons	Kungu Poti
Udo Kier	Jack the Ripper
Heinz Bennent	Dr. Schoen
Carla Angeloni	

••••••••••••••••••••• CREW •••••••••••••••••••

Robert Kuperberg	producer
Jean-Pierre Labrande	producer
Music by	Giancarlo Chiaramello
Cinematography by	Michael Steinke
Film Editing by	Khadicha Bariha
Production Design by	Walerian Borowczyk
Angelika Jendrusch	production coordinator

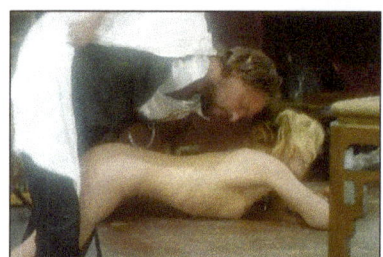

•••••••••••••• THE LULU PLAYS•••••••••••••••

Frank Wedekind (1864-1918) was a German playwright whose "Lulu" plays **Erdgeist** [earth spirit] (1895) and **Die Büchse der Pandora** [pandora's box] (1904) are critical works in the development of expressionism and of European theatre more generally. Conceived as a single play, they tell the story of a young dancer, an archetypal "gold-digger", who rises in society through her relationships with wealthy men, but who falls into poverty and prostitution and winds up being murdered by Jack the Ripper, who was played by Wedekind himself in the original production. The plays' violent and sexual content pushed the boundaries of acceptability on the stage at the time.

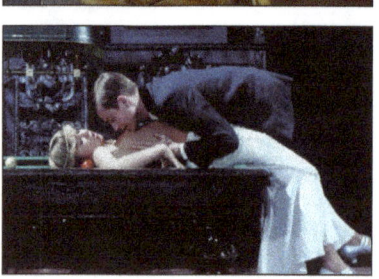

• • • • • • • • • • • • • • • I ♥ AUTO TRANSLATE • • • • • • • • • • • • • • •

French poster

The recent Lulu, who has ever seen, even the barest, and the quickest:

"I'm an animal," she says to Kess, and brings hush hush four husbands in succession into the grave and then slaughtered on the Babystrich of Jack the Ripper, the devil knows why. It is the last superlative, even the most harmless Lulu, ever.

The huge pictures of repressed eroticism and electrifying fear that the Pole Walerian Borowczyk has created in his early short films, nightmarish difficult and mysterious — that is long gone. Since meat in the cinema is cheap, his canvases which are full and empty. Borowczyk has blossomed in France as a confectioner erotomane delicacies that were in this country verschütt under titles like **Immoral Novices** or **Emanuela 77** is equal to the correct wrong cinemas: rosy curd.

And now, **Lulu**. The quick-fix version of Wedekind's "Monstre" which Borowczyk was executed with a smooth and nimble skill, is interested - even if it tastes from in fin-de-siecle decor — not a moment for the violence of repressed sexuality taboo for fractures, for the inner life of a society, which draws its broken pleasure from repression, concealment, denial of the meat.

If there (just because it is in the text) at the mere idea of "lingerie" or "negligees" begin to wheeze Men in Black, which seems bizarre, because jumping the obscure object of desire them so frequently as shower fresh small naked body in front of the nose around. Borowczyk's Lulu is to be a child-vamp.

Lulu's secret demonic Lulu, Lulu's afraid Lulu's desire — that like to imagine other; Lulu is here reduced to minor death elk. By touching seriousness of a hamster it sounds like the ramblings of men who claim to be in danger of her so wild and hopelessly, and not bad amazed how fast then everyone drops dead.

Spanish poster

Lively circus music accompanies the agonies, a prompt final marks the exitus, and the bodies' dedicated camera, which otherwise has little patience, the quiet close-up. This is Lulu only male desire, empty assertion that never came true. The only perfect record in Borowczyk's film are the death. Eros and death, I hear you galumph.

So the true story, this film tells that a frightened schoolgirl named Anne renames that because it goes so blithely to play the nymphet and so like to recite bulky Wedekind texts, is mauled in a film studio as Lulu, gently a director and evil by his own father, Heinz renames, which is always grumpy grimace with Lulu duration lover Dr. Schön.

"God bless Poland!" calls Lulu and the painter black skin of one of his pictures on the skull. God bless it. Sagittarius he Borowczyk, even Louise Brooks. And he protect especially the Bennent and us from them.

• • • • • • • • • • • • • • • • **FURTHER READING** • • • • • • • • • • • • • • • •

Variety, 23 July 1980.
Cahiers du Cinema, no.314, July 1980, p.54, in French.
Cinéma, no.259-260, July 1980, p.116, in French.
Von Jenny, Urs. "Todesengelchen" [angel of death]. **Der Spiegel**, no. 46, 10 November 1980, in German.
Positif, no.234, September 1980, p.70, in French.

Italian soundtrack LP

12" LP | Cetra Records, Italy | LPX 83

Music by the Orchestra of the Musicians' Union of Rome conducted by Giancarlo Chiaramello. (11 tracks, 45:20)

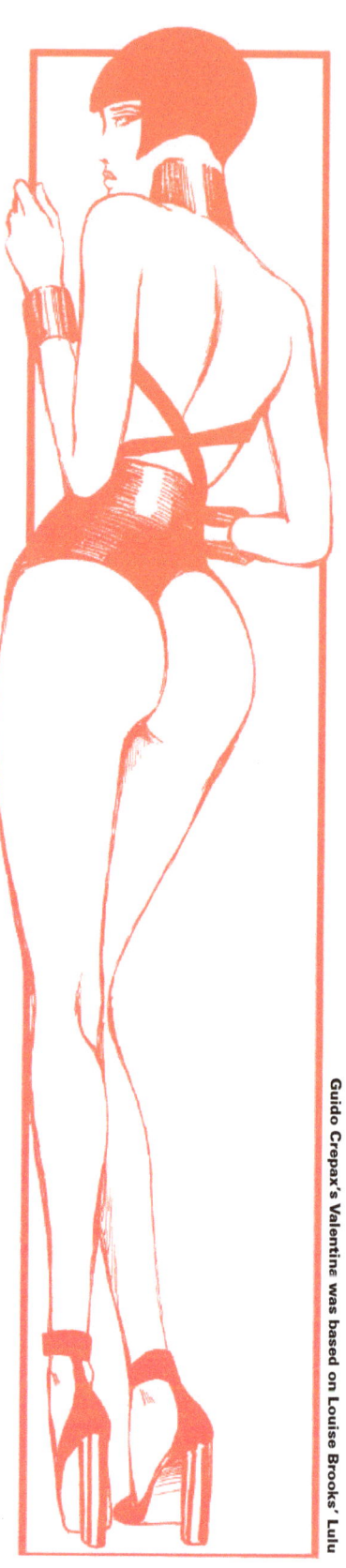

LULU

Wedekin's "Lulu" plays were first filmed as *Pandora's Box* (Germany, 1929, d. G.W. Pabst) starring Louise Brooks in the title role. Although poorly received at the time, it eventually made her a star and is now considered one of the classics of the Weimar film industry.

Less well-liked is the 1962 Austrian version, directed by Rolf Thiele entitled simply *Lulu* and starring former Miss Austria Nadja Tiller. The film was released in the UK under the James Hadley-Chase influenced title *No Orchids for Lulu* in the UK.

Louise Brooks' portrayal of Lulu inspired the look of Guido Crepax's heroine Valentina, who appeared in thirty comic books between 1965 and 1995. One of these, *Baba Yaga*, was made into a feature film (Italy/France, 1973, d. Corrado Farina) with French actress Isabelle De Funès playing Valentina.

Nadja Tiller in Rolf Thiele's *Lulu* (1962)

Guido Crepax's Valentine was based on Louise Brooks' Lulu

 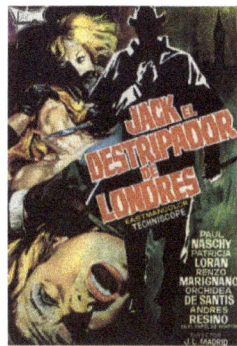 

Ripperology

By the end of the twentieth century the serial killer had almost entirely superseded traditional supernatural bogeymen in straight-faced scary cinema. The motif of the serial killer can be traced back through Jekyll and Hyde, itself an updating of the werewolf trope, to the "real life" career of Jack the Ripper.

It has been widely surmised that the ascendancy of the serial killer is attributable to an upsurge of rationalism in the salient demographics, and is linked to a supposed dwindling of religious power. Although these factors may have contributed, I would postulate that it is more likely due to a generalised suppression of the classical trinity (of vampire, werewolf, zombie) due to these creatures' historical association with elements of the class struggle. It should be noted that the Ripper's class is contradictory. He is commonly portrayed as upper class, but this is contradicted by his bestial nature. His anonymity conceals his class origins and adds social anxiety to physical threat.

There is little dispute that the Ripper constitutes the first modern serial killer as such. The Ripper murdered five prostitutes around the Whitechapel district of London between 31 August and 9 November 1888 and may have been responsible for a further eleven murders up until 1891, but police failed to conclusively link those. The murderer's deeds were reported in graphic detail in the media of the day and speculation on his identity was rife, although never conclusively attributed.

The first Ripper film came in 1924 from Germany, as an episode in a portmanteau film, although it conflated the Ripper with the earlier folk-devil Spring-Heeled Jack. This was followed by Alfred Hitchcock's first soundie The Lodger, based on a 1913 novel by Marie Belloc Lowndes and starring Ivor Novello as the murderer, who is probably meant to be the Ripper. The film was remade in 1932 (as *The Phantom Fiend*) and 1944.

Frank Wedekin's Lulu Plays, featuring a cameo by the Ripper, were realised in 1929 by G.W. Pabst, starring Louise Brooks as Lulu in an iconic performance. The plays were remade in 1962 by Rolf Thiele.

The liberalisation of cinema in the 1970s made the Ripper an appealing prospect for salacious producers, and a whole raft of films were produced, brazenly pandering to the anxieties and predilections of the times. It became customary to pit the Ripper against other Victorian icons such as Sherlock Holmes, Dr Jekyll, H.G. Wells., and to offer extravagant theories as to his identity.

Although no film can match the audaciousness of amateur ripperologist Richard Wallace, who in his 1996 book *Jack the Ripper, Light-Hearted Friend*, proposed an imaginative theory that Lewis Carroll, author of *Alice in Wonderland* etc., was responsible for the murders.

SELECTED RIPPER FILMS

- 1924 — Das Wachsfigurenkabinett [waxworks] (Paul Leni, Germany)
- 1926 — The Lodger: A Story of the London Fog (Alfred Hitchcock, UK)
- 1929 — Pandora's Box (G.W. Pabst, Germany)
- 1932 — The Phantom Fiend (Maurice Elvey, UK)
- 1944 — The Lodger (John Brahm, USA)
- 1950 — Room to Let (Godfrey Grayson, UK)
- 1953 — Man in the Attic (Hugo Fregonese, USA)
- 1959 — Jack the Ripper (Monty Berman & Robert S. Baker, UK)
- 1962 — Lulu (Rolf Thiele, Germany)
- 1965 — A Study in Terror (James Hill, UK)
- 1971 — Hands of the Ripper (Peter Sasdy, UK)
- 1971 — Dr. Jekyll and Sister Hyde (Roy Ward Baker, UK)
- 1971 — 7 Murders for Scotland Yard (José Luis Madrid, Spain/Italy)
- 1972 — The Ruling Class (Peter Medak, UK)
- 1975 — What the Swedish Butler Saw (Vernon P. Becker, Sweden/USA)
- 1976 — Jack the Ripper (Jesús Franco, Switzerland/West Germany)
- 1976 — Assault! Jack the Ripper (Yasuharu Hasebe, Japan)
- 1979 — Murder by Decree (Bob Clark, Canada/UK)
- 1979 — Time After Time (Nicholas Meyer, UK)
- 1989 — Edge of Sanity (Gérard Kikoïne, UK/USA/France/Hungary)

Docteur Jekyll et les Femmes

DR. JEKYLL AND THE WOMEN

AKA **The Strange Case of Dr. Jekyll and Miss Osbourne / The Blood of Doctor Jekyll / The Bloodbath of Doctor Jekyll / The Experiment / Bloodlust / Nel Profondo del Delirio [deep in delirium]**

France/West Germany | 1981 | 92mins

♛ Best director, Catalonian International Film Festival, Sitges

Directed by	Walerian Borowczyk
Screenplay by	Walerian Borowczyk
based on the novel by	Robert Louis Stevenson

•••••••••••••••••••• **CAST** ••••••••••••••••••••

Udo Kier	Dr. Henry Jekyll
Marina Pierro	Miss Fanny Osbourne
Patrick Magee	General
Gérard Zalcberg	Mr. Hyde
Howard Vernon	Dr. Lanyon
Clément Harari	Reverend Donald Regan
Jean Mylonas	
Eugene Braun Munk	
Louis Colla	
Catherine Coste	
Rita Maiden	
Michèle Maze	
Agnès Daems	
Magali Noaro	
Dominique Andersen	
Isabelle Cagnat	
Gisèle Préville	

•••••••••••••••••••• **CREW** ••••••••••••••••••••

Produced by	Ralph Baum
	Robert Kuperberg
	Jean-Pierre Labrande
Music by	Bernard Parmegiani
Cinematography by	Noël Véry
Film Editing by	Khadicha Bariha
Production Design by	Walerian Borowczyk
Costume Design by	Piet Bolscher
Christine Fornelli	makeup artist
Jacqueline Kofman	wardrober

Martine Alleton	production manager
Roland Fruytier	assistant director
Anny Bartanowski	production assistant
Gérard Barra	sound recordist
Alex Pront	sound re-recordist
Jean-Pierre Platel	camera operator

THE CAST

Borowczyk's take on one the most versioned stories in cinema is unusual in casting two different actors to play the titular characters. Dr Jekyll is played by the prolific Udo Kier, fresh from his role as Jack the Ripper in Boro's Lulu the previous year. Kier had appeared with Marina Pierro in **Suspiria** (Italy, 1977) and alongside Joe Dallesandro in **Flesh for Frankenstein** (USA/Italy/France, 1973), and **Blood for Dracula** (Italy/France, 1974) and worked with Just "Emmanuelle" Jaeckin on **The Story of O** (France/W.Germany/Canada, 1975). Mr Hyde is played by newcomer Gérard Zalcberg, who would go on to play the mute henchman Gordon in Jess Franco's classic **Faceless** (Spain/France, 1987). The supporting cast includes Jess Franco regular Howard Vernon, who had also played in Godard's **Alphaville** (France/Italy, 1965) and Patrick Magee, whose performance here steals the show!

BERNARD PARMEGIANI

The soundtrack for **Dr Jekyll and the Women** was provided by Bernard Parmegiani (1927-2013), a distinguished French composer of experimental electronic music. Parmegiani had commenced studies in mime under Jacques Lecoq before joining Groupe de Recherches Musicales (GRM) in 1959 shortly after its founding by Pierre Schaeffer. Parmegiani then moved on to the Music/Image unit of ORTF where he worked with Iannis Xenakis and others, but he continued to produce work for films including Jacques Baratier's **La Poupée** [the doll] (Italy/France, 1962), Jan Lenica's animation **'A'** (W.Germany, 1965) and Pierre Kast's **Les Soleils de l'île de Pâques** [**The Suns of Easter Island**] (France/Brazil/Chile, 1972).

He composed his first major work, **Violostries**, in 1964 and Borowczyk used some elements of this for his animation **Les Jeux des Anges**, other parts of the soundtrack would on appear Parmegiani's later works such as **L'Oeil Écoute** [the listening eye] 1970). Parmegiani also provided the soundtrack to Boro's shorts **Le Dictionnaire de Joachim** and **Scherzo Infernal** (1984) but his tour-de-force was his score for **Doctor Jekyll and the Women**, which reworked his 1972 composition, **Pour en Finir avec le Pouvoir d'Orphée** [to have done with the power of Orpheus].

FURTHER READING

L'Écran Fantastique, no.18, May 1981, p.36-37, in French.
Filmcritica, no.350, December 1984, p.554-556, in Italian.
Films and Filming, no.367, April 1985, p.30.
Monthly Film Bulletin vol.51 no.603, April,1984. p.114.
Positif, no.244/245, July 1981, p.122, in French.

French poster

Finnish poster

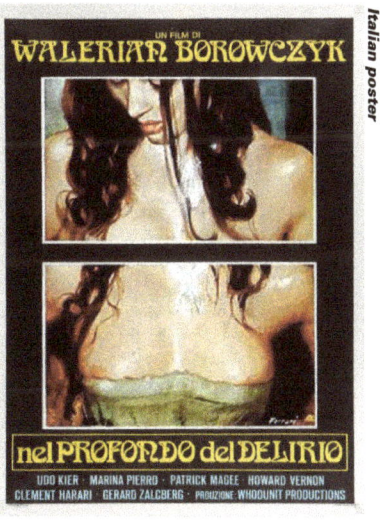

Italian poster

-- JEKSPLOITATION --

Robert Louis Stevenson's *Strange Case of Dr Jekyll and Mr Hyde* (1886) is one of classics of Scottish literature and one of the earliest examples of the literature of schizophrenia, dealing as it does with a form of dissociative identity disorder.

According to some accounts of the book's writing, Stevenson, or maybe his fiancé, burned the first version of the completed manuscript, either unsatisfied by its rendering or due its scandalous nature, and rewrote the story afresh from memory. The revised version was an immediate success upon publication, not hampered by the publicity around the Jack the Ripper murders that were then terrifying Londoners, and it went on to become one of the most adapted works in theatre and later in cinema.

The first serious theatrical adaptation premiered in Boston, USA, just a year after publication of the book, and was by Thomas Russell Sullivan with Richard Mansfield in the titles roles. Mansfield performed the role again in London in 1888 at the time of the Ripper murders, and his transformation was apparently so convincing that one terrified theatre-goer wrote to the police accusing him of the murders. Mansfield attempted to offset the bad publicity by giving a performance (i.e. of a different play) for the benefit of reformed prostitutes. Sullivan's version of Jekyll formed the basis of the most famous film version (USA, 1920, d. John S. Robertson) starring John Barrymore, which was remade in 1931 with Frederic March starring. This Pre-Code version is notable for its strong sexual content and had to be cut by eight minutes when it was re-released five years later. This version was itself remade ten years later, this time with Spencer Tracy as Jekyll.

Other notable adaptations include Hammer's *The Two Faces of Dr. Jekyll* (UK, 1960, d. Terence Fisher) and Amicus's version entitled *I, Monster* (UK, 1971, d. Stephen Weeks). Both feature Christopher Lee, the latter with him in the starring role(s). Parodies and spoofs also abound, including *Abbott and Costello Meet Dr. Jekyll and Mr. Hyde* (USA, 1953) and Jerry Lewis's *The Nutty Professor* (USA, 1963).

By the 1970s, the hoary story needed new twists, so we got the first gender-bending versions with Hammer's *Dr. Jekyll and Sister Hyde* (UK, 1971, d. Roy Ward Baker), updating the 1960 version and incorporating more elements of the Jack the Ripper mythos. It goes without saying that Jess Franco's *Les Maîtresses du Docteur Jekyll* [the mistresses of Dr. Jekyll] (Spain, 1964) includes no elements of the novel or its adaptations, to the extent it has been suggested that the protagonist in this version is actually a relative of the more famous doctor. The film was actually intended as a sequel to his *The Awful Dr. Orloff* (Spain/France, 1961) and was originally known as *The Secret of Dr. Orloff*.

Next there came blaxsploitation versions such as *Dr. Jekyll and Mr. Black* (USA, 1973, d. Slim Pecker) and *Dr. Black, Mr. Hyde* (USA, 1976, d. William Crain), which is not so well remembered as his 1972 *Blacula*.

Inevitably the porn industry entered the market with *The Adult Version of Dr. Jekyll and Mr. Hyde* (US. 1972, d. Byron Mabe), *Dirty Dr. Jekyll* (USA, 1973, d. unknown) and *The Erotic Dr. Jekyll* (USA, 1976, d. Victor Milt).

In animated versions the role of Jekyll has been taken by Daffy Duck, Bugs Bunny, both Tom and Jerry, Goofy and Alan (Brain) from *Arthur*, whose song "Jekyll and Hyde" is so towering genius that it has to be heard to be believed.

None of the numerous adaptations of the book remain very faithful to Stevenson's original story, with most omitting the narrator, Gabriel John Utterson, in favour of relating the story from Jekyll/Hyde's viewpoint, customarily with both roles being played by the same actor. This allows an emphasis on the transformation sequences with their attendant visual impact, but destroys the original's twist ending that the disclosure originally provided. Given that this disclosure has been in the public domain for generations, this tendency is understandable and, in a sense, Hitchcock's *Psycho* (USA, 1960) can be viewed as a updated and arguably more faithful version of the work. Additionally, whilst Hyde in the novel is simply an evil-looking man of short stature, many adaptations depict him with bestial or monstrous features, lending a zoophilic undercurrent to his crimes. Also, most adaptations also introduce a romantic element for Dr Jekyll that does not exist in the original story. Borowczyk offset any accusations of unfaithfulness by maintaining that he had based his adaptation on the destroyed first draft of Stevenson's manuscript.

Facing: Poster for Thomas Russell Sullivan's stage adaptation that opened in Boston in 1887 and ran Internationally for two decades.

This page: The changing faces of Jekyll and Hyde —

1. *Dr. Jekyll and Mr. Hyde* (USA, 1920) 2. *Dr. Jekyll and Mr. Hyde* (USA, 1931) 3. *Abbott and Costello Meet Dr. Jekyll and Mr. Hyde* (USA, 1953) 4. *The Two Faces of Dr. Jekyll* (UK, 1960) 5. *Dr. Jekyll and Sister Hyde* (UK, 1971) 6. *The Adult Version of Dr. Jekyll and Mr. Hyde* (USA, 1972) 7. *Dr. Jekyll Likes Them Hot* (Italy, 1979) 8. *Dr. Jekyll's Dungeon of Death* (USA, 1979)

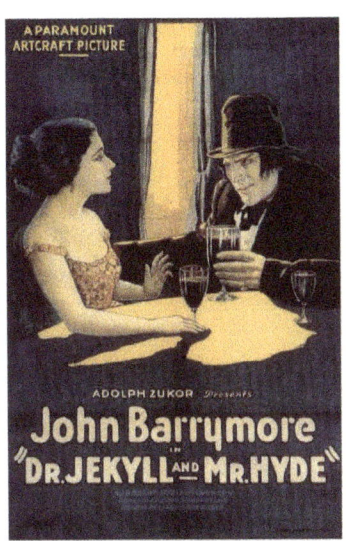
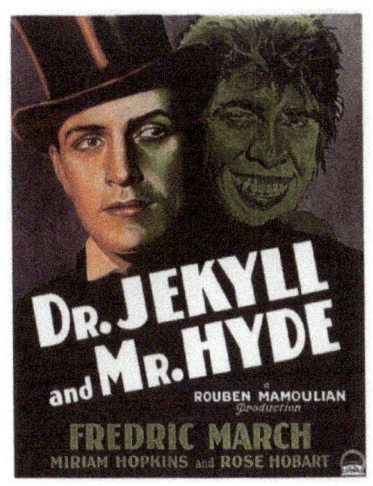

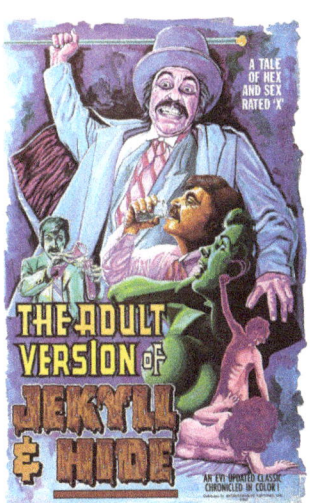

Ars Amandi / L'Arte d'Amare
THE ART OF LOVE
AKA L'Art d'Aimer

France/Italy | 1983 | 101 min

Directed by	Walerian Borowczyk
Story by	Walerian Borowczyk & Wilhelm Buchheim
Screenplay by	Walerian Borowczyk & Enzo Ungari
based on the book by	Ovid

•••••••••••••••• CAST ••••••••••••••••

Marina Pierro	Claudia
Michele Placido	Macarius
Massimo Girotti	Ovid
Laura Betti	Clio
Milena Vukotic	Modestina
Philippe Lemaire	General Laurentius
Mireille Pame	Sepora
Philippe Taccini	Cornelius
Simonetta Stefanelli	Widow
Antonio Orlando	Rufus
Pier Francesco Aiello	Flavius

•••••••••••••••• CREW ••••••••••••••••

Marcel Albertini	executive producer
Jacques Nahum	associate producer
Mario Lupi	producer
Camillo Teti	
Ugo Tucci	
Music by	Luis Bacalov
Cinematography by	Walerian Borowczyk Noël Véry
Film Editing by	Walerian Borowczyk
Costume Design by	Luciana Marinucci
Gianni Ricci	first assistant director
Claudio Oliviero	sound mixer
Noël Véry	camera operator
Elide Cortesi	continuity

• • • • • • • • • • • • • • • • TOGASPLOITATION • • • • • • • • • • • • • • • •

The togasploitation genre has its roots in the peplum (AKA "sword and sandal") genre that dates back to the silent Maciste series that ran from 1914. In the late fifties classical themes resurfaced, inspired by the success of Hollywood cinemascope epics shot in Italy such as **Quo Vadis** (USA, 1951, d. Mervyn LeRoy) and **Ben Hur** (USA, 1959, d. William Wyler). A spate of locally-produced cash-ins and spin-offs appeared, again featuring Maciste (25 films, 1960–1965), or Hercules (19 films 1957–1965), Ursus, sometimes son of Hercules, (9 films, 1961–1964), Samson (5 films, 1961–1964), and Goliath (5 films, 1960–1964). The genre then span-off into gladiator movies, barbarian films, Viking films, swashbucklers/pirate films, Biblical and Babylonian epics, as well as ancient Egyptian and Greek mythological topics. Even Jess Franco turned out two Maciste films, back-to-back, in 1973.

After a relative hiatus, Bob Guccione of Playboy hired Gore Vidal and Tinto Brass to make **Caligula** (Italy/USA, 1979, d. Bob Guccione, Tinto Brass). about the controversial Roman emperor. The upshot of that was a handful of unofficial sequels, the best known of which are **Caligola: La storia mai raccontata** [**Caligula: The Untold Story**] (AKA **Caligula 2**, Italy, 1982, d. Joe D'Amato) with Laura Gemser and David Brandon, and **Caligula and Messalina** (Italy/France, 1981, d. Bruno Mattei). Such were the conditions for Borowczyk to raise finance on his adaptation of Ovid, but sadly for him, the murderous exploits of a tyrannical sex-crazed emperor made better commercial sense than the wisdom of an erudite and witty classical poet.

• • • • • • • • • • • • • • • I KNOW IT'S OVID • • • • • • • • • • • • • • •

Ars Amatoria was written in 2AD by Roman poet Publius Ovidius Naso, better known as Ovid in the English-speaking world, who is also remembered for his fifteen-volume **Metamorphoses**, an epic mythological narrative that forms one of the most important sources of classical mythology. Written in three volumes, **Ars Amatoria** is an early example of the relationship counselling manual, and Ovid draws on mythology, everyday life and general observation to instruct readers in courtly behaviour between the sexes. Although sexual matters are covered, they are treated with restraint and a humour that is ironic rather than bawdy.

• • • • • • • • • • • • • • • • • • NOTES • • • • • • • • • • • • • • • • • •

This film is sometimes described as the third instalment of Boro's "Immoral Trilogy", which supposedly comprises also **Immoral Tales** and **Three Immoral Women**. There appears to be no legitimate provenance for such a taxonomy as **The Art of Love** displays none of the distinguishing characteristics of either of those films. It isn't a time-hopping portmanteau film and doesn't feature input from Mandiargues.

According to Variety, the film played in Paris at 101 minutes, but most versions in circulation are 89-93 minutes long. In an effort to boost the film's Italian box-office, distributors spiced it up with out-takes from Joe D'Amato's **Caligula: The Untold Story** including an unsimulated horse masturbation footage. So be careful which version you get hold of, and in no circumstances get it confused with the 1965 British comedy of the same name, directed by Norman Jewison and starring James Garner and Dick Van Dyke.

• • • • • • • • • • • • • • • FURTHER READING • • • • • • • • • • • • • • •

Variety, 21 December 1983, p.14.
Positif, no.276, February 1984, p.58-9. in French.

French poster

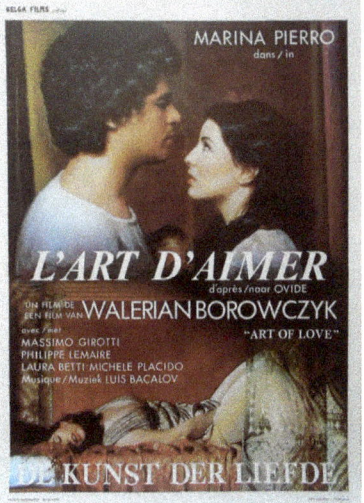

Belgian poster

Distribution ad from Variety, 12 May 1982.

EMMANUELLE 5
AKA Emmanuelle V

France | 1987 | 85min

Directed by	Walerian Borowczyk
	Steve Barnett (US version)
Written by	Walerian Borowczyk
	Alex Cunningham
	Howard R. Cohen (US version)
based on the novel by	Emmanuelle Arsan

••••••••••••••••••••• **CAST** •••••••••••••••••••••

Monique Gabrielle	Emmanuelle
Crofton Hardester	Eric
Dana Burns Westburg	Charles Foster
Bryan Shane	(US version)
Yaseen Khan	Rajid
Julie Miklas	Linda
Pamm Vlastas	Suvi
Max Strom	Talking Soldier
Heidi Paine	Girl No. 1
Roxanna Michaels	Girl No. 2
Michele Burger	Girl No. 3
Marie Chocolat	
Marie Vanille	
Isabelle Strawa	
Muriel Catau	
Jessica Stehl	
Michael Rogers	
Peter Lowell	
Noelle Fabiani	
François Clavier	
Paul Ricci	
Katia Valys	
André Kay	
Claude Bruna	
Martine Coudeville	

••••••••••••••••••••• **CREW** •••••••••••••••••••••

Alain Siritzky	executive producer
Music by	Pierre Bachelet
	Bernard Levitte
Cinematography by	Zoran Hochstätter
	Max Monteillet
Film Editing by	Nina Gilberti
	Kevin Tent
	Steve Barnett (US version)
Production Design by	Steve Greenberg

Costume Design by	A.C. Lathuilliere
	Kimberly Love
	Sophie Maret
Bruno Boucher	unit manager
Pierre Dufour	assistant unit manager
Jacques Monge	steadicam operator
Camilla Mauritzson	sound re-recording mixer
Luis Clos	music engineer
Jim Wynorski	assistant to Ms. Gabrielle

• • • • • • • • • • • • • • A MODEST PROPOSAL • • • • • • • • • • • • • •

Borowczyk's feature film career started and ended with consensus. In the beginning **Goto** and **Blanche** were universally praised as he was heralded as a major new talent, but the confronting content of **Immoral Tales** split his audience like an outsized courgette and viewers, in dwindling numbers, would henceforth argue his relative merit until the premiere of **Emmanuelle 5**, which was taken as undeniable proof of the exhaustion of his skills. After this, **Love Rites** was seen, if at all, as a fundamentally flawed work. Whilst there may be some debate as to Borowczyk's finest work, there are no reports of any dissent with respect to **Emmanuelle 5**, which is widely regarded as his creative nadir.

Simplistic and reductionist appraisals such as these are always worse than useless. There can be no definitive summary of an oeuvre when every element is recontextualised with each new viewing. This is the game that moves as you play. A bug documented is a feature. How much of the opprobrium heaped on the film is the product of received wisdom or conditioned misreading? It could easily be contended that the film is a spectacular attempt to break free of the conventions of, not just the Emmanuelle series and euro-erotica in particular, but of cinema and filmed entertainment entirely. In some ways, it is Borowczyk's (or anyone's) most radical work.

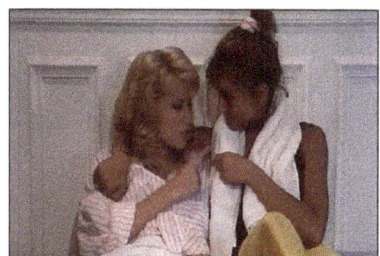

Consider, just for starters, that there exists no definitive version of the film, or perhaps several. Timothy Taylor's article for **Video Watchdog** provides a comprehensive overview of the differences, summarised here.

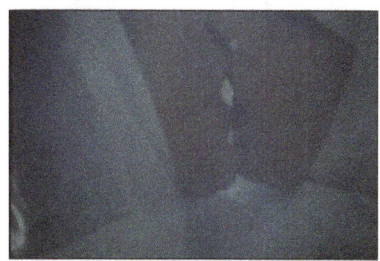

1. The European theatrical version (~78 mins) shot in English and dubbed into French, Italian and German. This was the basis for most subsequent European video releases.

2. The French hardcore edit (~85 mins) which was released on VHS in France only and never reissued. This version omits some footage from the theatrical version (including the long **Love Express** sequence at the start) but substitutes hardcore sex scenes, albeit featuring different actors to the rest of the film. Shorn of its hardcore scenes, this served as the basis for a UK DVD in 2006.

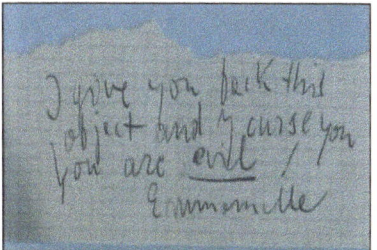

3. The US version (~74 mins), produced by Roger Corman. This version also includes some of Borowczyk's out-takes from the European release and new sequences shot in LA by Borowczyk's assistant Steve Barnett. It was edited together on video and never released theatrically, appearing belatedly in the USA on home video in 1992. This version substitutes inept action footage for most of the sex sequences and, in an apparently racist move, replaces most of the black and creole actresses with white counterparts in the short sequences that remain.

The European version opens with seven minutes of footage from **Love Express**, a fictional film starring Emmanuelle, played for the first time here by American former Penthouse Pet Monique Gabrielle rather than Sylvia Kristel who had made the role her own in the prior four films.

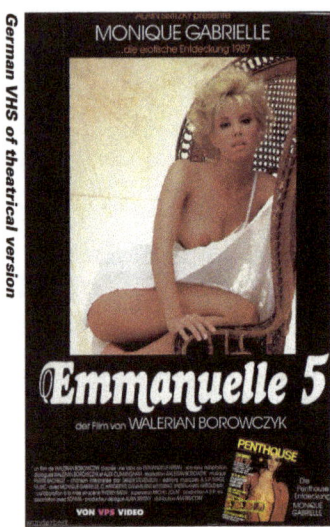

German VHS of theatrical version

French hardcore VHS

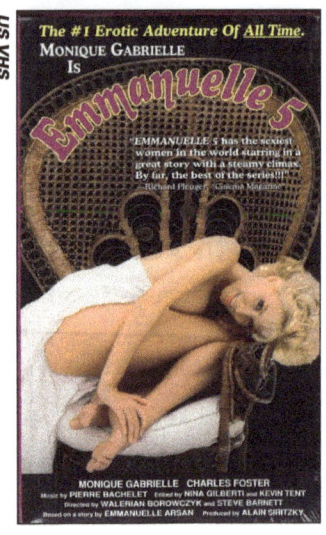

US VHS

Monique's suitability for the role has been questioned on the grounds that she doesn't look French and that her dramatic skills are inadequate. However, if these attributes are viewed as Brechtian alienation techniques, her performance is less troubling.

Borowczyk has claimed that the "Love Express" sequence was the only footage that he filmed, but the film is a virtual anthology of his motifs: the stripping of Emmanuelle as she flees through Cannes inevitably recalls Romilde in **The Beast**, and the striking harem scene's nods to both **Behind Convent Walls** and the Erzebet Báthory sequence of **Immoral Tales**. There are also shots of documents and drawings that are common throughout his oeuvre, and even the hardcore sequences appear to bear his distinctive composition and lighting. The grainy nature of these inserts contrast with the conflicting styles of the **Love Express** and Barnett-directed sequences and add to the rhapsodic feel of the film. The disparate material and its apparently haphazard arrangement of some of the sequences evoke Borowczyk's earlier animations.

Notwithstanding questions of definition, verisimilitude and authorship, the "inept" scenes and "jarring" editing only serve to underscore the formal beauty and inexplicability of much of the material. Seemingly invoking Robbe-Grillet's compositional methods, a pungent air of mystery and novelty pervades the entire enterprise, as if Borowczyk was attempting to produce a new kind of entertainment in the margin between his auteur's vision and a branded franchise. This is alluded to as Emmanuelle hears a radio blare an ad for **Love Express** listing its antecedents (such as Mandiargues, Ovid and Maupassant alongside other faves like Henry Miller, Georges Bataille, Pierre Louys, The Marquis de Sade and Rabelais). The climax of the film provides it own denunciation, and is spectacular in precisely the "wrong" way. Alluding to **Citizen Kane** (USA, 1941, d. Orson Welles) via Howard Hughes (i.e. rather than William Randolph Hearst), the final flight of Charles Foster's plane features a number of obviously different aircraft (including some stock footage and models) and culminates in what must surely be the lamest plane crash effect ever committed to film — an ultimate scene of casual disregard bordering on contempt, not for the audience, nor the producers, nor the medium itself, but for all the conventions thereof.

In the final analysis, **Emmanuelle 5** can be (partially) redeemed as one of the most striking gestures of defiance ever committed to celluloid (or ¾" U-matic in the case of the US version).

• • • • • • • • • • • • • • • • • • • YES WE CANNES • • • • • • • • • • • • • • • • • • •

The general level of confusion around **Emmanuelle 5** is exacerbated by the fact that seven years earlier there had been an unofficial entry in the franchise entitled **Emmanuelle à Cannes** [Emmanuelle in Cannes] France/Hong Kong, 1980, d. Jean-Marie Pallardy). Pallardy had also released his **Le Journal Érotique d'une Thailandaise** [**Erotic Diary of Woman of Thailand**] (France/Italy/Hong Kong, 1980) as **Emmanuelle 3** that same year, presumably retitled to capitalise on the non-sequential title of the third official film.

Emmanuelle at Cannes featured the flexible hardcore (in some cuts) stylings of Olinka Hardiman, playing a stripper who flees to the Cannes Film festival to make the big time but comes unstuck. It is widely regarded as nominally less terrible than Borowczyk's later effort.

• • • • • • • • • • • • • • • • • FURTHER READING • • • • • • • • • • • • • • • • •

Taylor, Timothy. "Defiling the Version." **Video Watchdog Special Edition**, no.1, 1994, p. 102.
Cinéma, no.382, 7 January 1987, p.4, in French.
Variety, 21 January 1987, p.17.

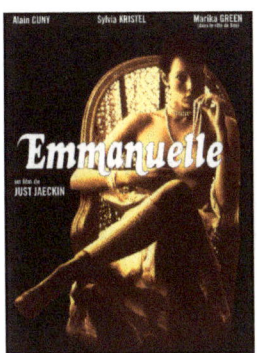

Emmanuelle

The erotic novel *Emmanuelle: The Joys of a Woman*, was first published and distributed clandestinely in France in 1959. By 1967 it had surfaced overground under the name of Emmanuelle Arsan, first revealed as a pseudonym for Marayat Rollet-Andriane, wife of a french diplomat in Bangkok, and then as the husband, Louis-Jacques, himself. It's widely believed that the book could have been joint authored. It was translated into English in 1971 and filmed in 1974 by Just Jaeckin. The film became an huge international smash, spawning sequels and imitators. Only films produced by the original producer Alain Siritzky are considered "official" but unofficial adaptations simply needed to omit an 'm' from the name to offset litigation risk.

The first four official films all star Sylvia Kristel and draw heavily on the novel and its 1976 sequel *Emmanuelle 2*. By the time of filming *Emmanuelle 5* Kristel handed over to Monique Gabrielle, a former *Penthouse* Pet of the Month (December 1982) who had small roles in films including *Flashdance* (USA, 1983, d. Adrian Lyne) and *Bachelor Party* (USA, 1983, d. Neal Israel). No. 6 (written and co-directed by Jean Rollin) starred Natalie Uher who never made anything afterwards. The belated no. 7 ("in the virtual world, nothing is true, everything is permitted" — !) was a spin-off of the first TV series and a throwback to no. 4 with Sylvia Kristel returning as Emmanuelle and Francis Leroi returning as director.

Of the unofficial entries, the most lauded are the Italian "Black Emanuelle" series starring Laura Gemser and the least lauded is the British spoof *Carry On Emmanuelle* (UK, 1978, d. Gerald Thomas).

Further spin-offs included Italian artist Guido Crepax's 1978 graphic adaptation of the novel, and an officially licensed Emmanuelle video game.

FILTHOGRAPHY
Official ASP releases in bold

- 1974 — **Emmanuelle** (d. Just Jaeckin)
- 1975 — **Emmanuelle 2** (d. Francis Giacobetti) AKA "Emmanuelle: The Joys of a Woman" (US) "Emmanuelle l'antivierge" [Emmanuelle the anti-virgin] (Fr)
- 1975 — Black Emanuelle (It., d. Bitto Albertini)
- 1976 — Laure (It./Fr. d. Emmanuelle Arsan) AKA "Forever Emmanuelle"
- 1977 — **Goodbye Emmanuelle** (d. François Leterrier)
- 1978 — Carry On Emmanuelle (UK, d. Gerald Thomas)
- 1980 — Emmanuelle Goes to Cannes (Fr./HK, d. Jean-Marie Pallardy)
- 1984 — **Emmanuelle 4** (d. Francis Leroi & Iris Letans)
- 1986 — **Emmanuelle 5** (d. Walerian Borowczyk)
- 1988 — **Emmanuelle 6** (d. Bruno Zincone & Jean Rollin (uncredited)
- 1992-93 — **Emmanuelle** (Fr., 7 tv eps plus film "Emmanuelle's Seventh Heaven" AKA "Emmanuelle 7"
- 1994 — **Emmanuelle in Space** (USA 7 tv eps)
- 2000 — Emmanuelle: A Hard Look (UK documentary, d. Alex Cox)
- 2000-02 — **Emmanuelle 2000** (USA, 7 tv eps plus film "Emmanuelle Pie")
- 2003 — **Emmanuelle in Rio** (USA, tv film d. Kevin Alber)
- 2004-06 — **Emmanuelle Private Collection** (USA, 7 tv eps plus film "Emmanuelle Tango")
- 2011-12 — **Emmanuelle Through Time** (USA, 7 tv eps plus film "Emmanuelle in Wonderland")

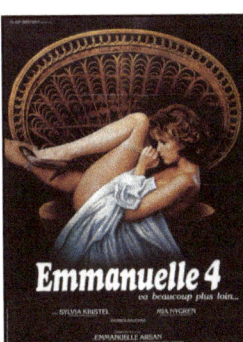
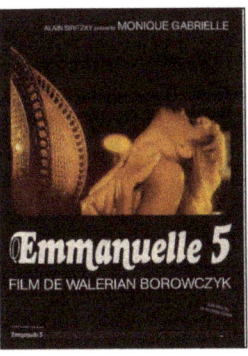
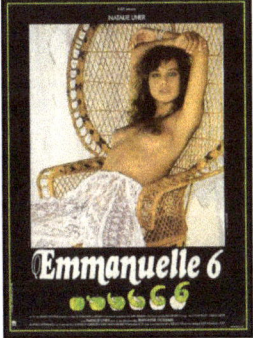

Cérémonie d'Amour
LOVE RITES
AKA Queen of the Night / Rites of Love

France | 1988 | 100 mins

Directed by	Walerian Borowczyk
Written by	Walerian Borowczyk
Based on **Tout Disparaitra** by	André Pieyre de Mandiargues

•••••••••••••••••••• **CAST** ••••••••••••••••••••

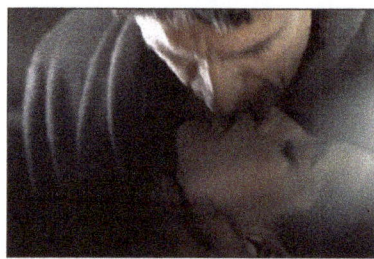

Marina Pierro	Myriam
Mathieu Carrière	Hugo Arnold
Josy Bernard	Mériem Ben Saada
Isabelle Tinard	Nora Nix
Jacques Couderc	
Guy Bonnafoux	
Claudine Berg	
Lucette Gill	
Julian Lee	
Jennifer Ford	
Sabrina Belleval	
Jean-Raphael Sessa	
Jean Négroni	Narrator

•••••••••••••••••••• **CREW** ••••••••••••••••••••

Philippe Guez	producer
Alain Sarde	executive producer
Cinematography by	Gérard Monceau
	Jean-Paul Sergent
	Michel Zolat
Film Editing by	Florence Poulain
	Guila Salama
	Lili Sonnet
	Marie-Hélène Zirisch
Costume Design by	Valérie Adda
Hair stylist	Nathalie Blanc
Daniel Delume	unit production manager
Catherine Mazières	production manager
Michel Loro	unit manager
Jean-Jacques Tabali	unit manager
Isabelle Vinke	unit manager
Gérard Grégory	assistant director
Alain Jacques Adiba	second assistant director
Odile Huhardeux	
Thierry Godard	sound
Joël Beldent	sound: auditorium
Dominique Dalmasso	
Guy Rophé	

Marc-Antoine Beldent	sound assistants: auditorium
Michel Kharat	sound assistant: auditorium
Jean-Louis Lebras	sound assistant: auditorium
Guy Maillet	sound assistant: auditorium
Bruno Langiano	foley artist
Julien Naudin	foley artist
Fred Mays	post-synchronization
Alain Muslin	sound mixer
Michel Dalmet	electrician
Patrice Guillou	assistant camera
David Koskas	still photographer
Frédéric Lacoste	key grip
Jean-Paul Imbert	musician: organ
Nelly Niay	production administrator
Isabelle Poisson	production secretary
André-Paul Ricci	press attache

NOTES

Having progressed from Anatole Dauman via Pierre Braunberger, it was perhaps inevitable that Boro would end up produced by Alain Sarde, who had kicked off his producing career with the odd **Touche pas la Femme Blanc** [**Don't Touch the White Woman**] (France, 1974, d. Marco Ferreri) and wasn't afraid of idiosyncratic works. Sarde had gone on to produce many of Jean-Luc Godard's features following his eighties comeback, and many of Roman Polanski's better-received films.

It is a convention that elderly idiosyncratic directors who have operated on the margins should end their careers with films that are heavily redundant, as if running through their tropes one last time to reassure their dwindling audience that they have exhausted their vocabulary and no novelty will be lost by their passing. This seems consistently the case for "eurotica" directors, demonstrated by Jean Rollin's **Le Masque de la Méduse** [**Mask of Medusa**] (France, 2010), Jess Franco's **Al Pereira vs. the Alligator Ladies** (Spain, 2012) and Alain Robbe-Grillet's **Gradiva** (France, 2006). All these films offer little novel, but rather provide a summarised reiteration of their directors' motifs as a sort of coda for their career. This phenomenon is consistent with the Serialist perspective that supposes that "the creative act" is nothing more nor less than a precognition of the completed artefact, and that the artist is simply running out of living. Hence, the effect is most prominent in the work of film-makers operating as auteurs and effecting (sic) the outcome of their works more significantly than would be the case had they been influenced by a higher degree of consensus.

FURTHER READING

Positif, no.332, October 1988, p. 74, in French.
La Revue du Cinéma/Image et Son, no. 441, September 1988, p.30, in French.
Variety, 31 August 1988, p.40.

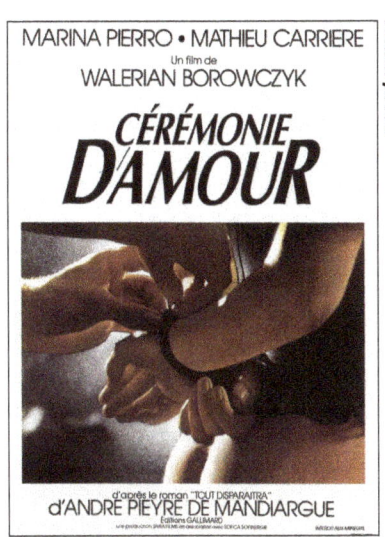

French poster

Italian poster

German poster

André Pieyre de Mandiargues

APDM on Les Fêtes du Corps TV show ▶
Marianne Faithfull in The Girl on a Motorcycle ▶▶
APDM demonstrates the dildo mirror (as seen in Behind Convent Walls) in A Private Collection ◀
Carole André in Violentata sulla Sabbia ▶◢

André Pieyre de Mandiargues (1909-1991) was a French author of fiction, poetry, drama and literary and art criticism. His work was acclaimed by critics in France, but he was little known in his lifetime, especially outside France, despite the best efforts of his friend Borowczyk to bring his work to a wider audience.

His fiction is unlike anyone else's, sharing characteristics with nouveau-romanciers (such as Robbe-Grillet) with whom he shared English publishers and translators, but Mandiargue's work expresses a sensuality and quality of introspection that is personal and unique, a hybrid of baroque fantasy and minute detail, usually with a dreamlike or fantastic aspect or a cruel eroticism.

His first openly published work, a collection of short stories, came out in 1946, the year of Borowczyk's first film. *Le Musée Noir* [the black museum] included "Le Sang de l'Agneau" [blood of the lamb] on which the episode "Marceline" in *Three Immoral Women* was based. After several more volumes of stories he pseudonymously published the overtly pornographic *L'Anglais Décrit dans le Château Fermé* [The Englishman described in his closed castle] in 1953. This was his attempt to produce "as erotic, sadistic and scandalous a story as possible", and it remains shocking to this day, although the scope and degree of its excesses may appear parodic to today's cynical readers. It was belatedly translated into English as *Portrait of an Englishman in his Chateau* in 1998.

Mandiargues' first openly-published novel was *Le Lis de Mer* [the sea-lily] in 1956, translated as *The Girl Beneath the Lion* a couple of years later. If that retitling appears rather liberal, it pales beneath the filmed version (Italy/France, 1969, d. Renzo Cerrato) which was also known as *Violentata Sulla Sabbia* [*Raped on the Beach*]. In 1963 came Mandiargues' best-known work, *La Motorcyclette* [the motorcycle girl], translated as *The Girl on the Motorcycle* by the ever-busy Alex Trocchi. This was filmed in 1968, starring Marianne Faithfull and Alain Delon and directed by Jack Cardiff, better known as a cinematographer. The film was known in the USA as *Naked Under Leather*, which is very misleading since in the final circus sequence, wherein Miss Faithfull is stripped by a whip-cracking ringmaster, she is patently wearing a body stocking.

Mandiargues moved closer to Borowczyk's milieu when he wrote the commentary for *La Femme Fleur* [the woman flower] (France, 1965), an animated short by Jan Lenica, and produced by Argos Films.

Borowczyk used Mandiargues and a collection of erotic curiosa for *A Private Collection* and his books became one of Borowczyk's primary well-springs of material. The story *La Marée* [the tide] (from *Mascarets* [tidal bores], a 1971 collection) opened *Immoral Tales* after *A Private Collection* had been excised. His 1967 novel *La Marge* [The margin], which had been critically lauded and won the Prix Goncourt, France's greatest literary prize, was filmed by Borowczyk in 1976.

In addition to his novels and stories, Mandiargues produced many essays and annotated several art monographs. In the seventies the polymath produced several works for theatre and translated Octavio Paz, W.B. Yeats, Filippo de Pisis and Yukio Mishima.

Fittingly Mandiargues' final novel *Tout Disparaitra* [everything must go] became Borowczyk's last feature, *Love Rites*, in 1987, the same year it was published.

Mandiargues died 13 December 1991 and was buried in Père-Lachaise, division 35. He still is. On 6 December 1999 a walkway located in quartier de la Maison-Blanche, in the 13th arrondissement of Paris was named after him and in 2000, his daughter Sibylle Pieyre de Mandiargues produced a 48 minute documentary on her father.

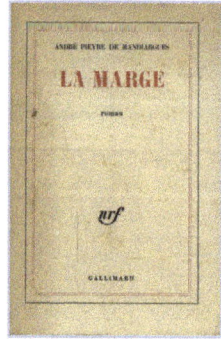

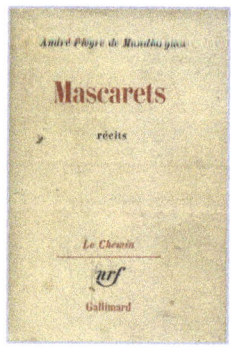
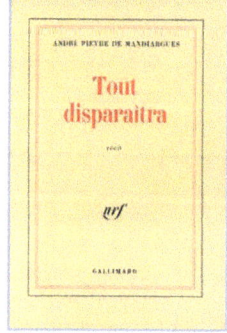

BIBLIOGRAPHY

Novels and story collections only.

1909   Born 14 March in Paris.
1946 — Le Musée Noir [the black museum] (stories)
1951 — Soleil des loups [wolves' sun] (stories)
1953 — Marbre [marble] (novel)
1953 — L'Anglais Décrit dans le Château Fermé [Portrait of an Englishman in his castle] (novel)
1956 — Le Lis de Mer [the sea-lily] (novel translated as "The Girl Beneath the Lion")
1959 — Feu de Braise [charcoal fire] (stories translated as "Blaze of Embers")
1963 — La Motocyclette [the motorcycle girl] (novel translated as "The Girl on the Motorcycle")
1965 — Porte dévergondée [shameless door] (stories)
1967 — La Marge [the margin] (novel)
1970 — La Nuit de mil neuf cent quatorze [Night of 1914] (stories)
1971 — Mascarets [tidal bores] (stories)
1976 — Sous la Lame [under the lame] (stories)
1983 — Le Deuil des roses [funeral roses] (stories)
1987 — Tout Disparaîtra [everything must go] (novel)
1991 — Died 13 December in Paris.

FILMOGRAPHY

1965 — La Femme Fleur (Short by Jan Lenica)
1968 — The Girl on a Motorcycle (Jack Cardiff)
1969 — Violentata sulla Sabbia [raped on the beach] (film of "Le Lis de Mer" by Renzo Cerrato)
1973 — A Private Collection (Walerian Borowczyk)
1974 — Immoral Tales (Walerian Borowczyk)
1976 — La Marge (Walerian Borowczyk)
1979 — Immoral Women (Walerian Borowczyk)
1987 — Les fêtes du corps [feasts of the body] (TV documentary by Jean-Louis Cap)
1987 — Love Rites (Walerian Borowczyk)

ZOOPHILMOGRAPHY
SIMULATIONS OF BESTIALITY IN (NOT VERY) MAINSTREAM CINEMA

Tarzan the Ape Man
USA | 1932 | 100 min   d. W. S. Van Dyke

Considered the ninth cinematic adaptation of Edgar Rice Burroughs' bestselling novel but the first to introduce the character of Cheetah the Chimp. As a pre-Code film, it and its immediate sequel were more daring than subsequent issues in the thirteen-part series, although they still stopped short of implying inter-species relationships. Paradoxically, attempts to sanitise the films only served to emphasise any unsavoury imputations and gave the game away by putting Cheetah the Chimp in a body stocking. Perhaps the fact that Disney produced their version of *Tarzan* (USA, 1999) soon after their *Beauty and the Beast* (USA, 1991) implies something too.

In the US during 1973-75, the hardcore porno boom was seeking to expand beyond its traditional repertoire and the bloke in a moth-eaten gorilla suit became a fixture of films such as *The Sexualist* (USA, 1973, d. Kemal Horulu), *Sexcula* (Canada, 1974, d. John Holbrook), *Tarz and Jane and Cheeta* (USA, 1975, d. Itza Fine) and *Thundercrack!* (USA, 1975, d. Curt McDowell). Only the last of these is (currently) considered a cinematic classic.

Stuck as we are now at the limits of association, we may as well recollect the gorilla suit of Marlene Dietrich in *The Blue Angel* (Germany, 1930). Apparently her compatriot Greta Garbo encountered Aristotle Onassis on a boat that had previously belonged to King Farouk. The bar-stools they sat on were upholstered in white whale foreskin, and Ari told her "Madam, you are now sitting on the largest penis in the world". Class.

King Kong
USA | 1933 | 100 min
d. Merian Cooper & Ernest Schoedsack

One may expect *King Kong* to be mentioned here by virtue of the famous sequence where the gorilla strips Fay Wray halfway up the Empire State Building. Although the monkey in question is unfeasibly large, the same cannot be said for the penis of most unimaginary gorillas, which resemble a human's but measure approximately three quarters of an inch long and an inch in diameter. The question of the practicalities of the consummation of this relationship is addressed in Jean Ferry's essay first published in the surrealist journal *Minotaur* (1934) where he points out the oft-overlooked fact that Kong possesses the ability to change size: "One minute his hand is big enough to seize an underground train, the next it only goes round the torso of a woman we see waving her arms and legs about."

It's notable that the implied bestiality in *King Kong* was admissible at a time when an implied inter-racial relationship would have been taboo in a mainstream film, and it is interesting to speculate on the use of bestiality as a covert metaphor for interracial sex. This metaphor can be cynically defended on the basis that any accusation of such could be counter-argued as predicated on racist principals.

The Wolf Man
USA | 1941 | 70 min   d. George Waggner

Reduced to absurdity, the Marxist typology of horror archetypes sees the vampire representing the capitalist class, the aristocracy, ruling by fear and deceit, and existing only so long as they can drain life from the masses. The proletariat is represented by zombies, collectivized, un-individuated and with no agenda beyond subsistence. The bourgeois, in contrast, will shift his political allegiance to the aristocracy or the proletariat dependent on the state of their interests at the time. This vacillatory and mutable nature is expressed by the werewolf, whose status is not fixed and may be aligned contingent on external forces as uncontrollable as the phase of the moon. The unwilled, externally-ordained nature of the werewolf's transformations distinguishes it from the character of Jekyll/Hyde.

Tarzan

King Kong

The Wolf Man

These tropes arose autonomously from cultures of the underclasses around the world. This is evident from the absence of documentation surrounding their genesis. Their characteristics were unformalised until their adoption by Hollywood, particularly Universal Studios, respectively: *Dracula* (USA, 1931, d. Tod Browning), *White Zombie* (USA, 1932, d. Victor Halperin), *The Wolf Man* (USA, 1941 (d. George Waggner).

It is notable that the class characteristics of each of these tropes resisted revisionism, usually in the form of parody, until the mid-eighties when attempts to neutralise their subversive and progressive aspects entailed sympathetic renderings of vampires and, less commonly, werewolves. As representatives of the working class, it goes without saying that zombies were not invited to the rehabilitation party.

Likewise, in the newly-respectable academic-style horror criticism, we saw a return to Freudianism, a discredited sex-and-drug cult that had been promoted during the depression to provide the upper classes with an alternative worldview than radical socialism. Freud's essays, *The Wolf Man* (1918) and *The Uncanny* (1919), which both took as their starting points the dreams of the mentally ill, were established as the cornerstones of critical analysis of the genre. Despite the intrinsic funty laff-value of these exercises in extruded credulity, it is self-evident to anyone lacking a vested interest or a covert agenda that their only relevance is in providing some insight into the intellectual milieu of their own, and hence these films', times.

This academic mission of neutralisation (recuperation if you prefer) was complemented by attempts to supersede these popular characters with a trope more palatable to the interests of the newly re-empowered ruling classes: the serial killer, i.e. Jack the Ripper relieved of his aristocratic lineage.

Popular intermediate tropes that had evolved in the progressive seventies (e.g. sex-crazed nuns and nazis) were now subject to extreme sanction and, in the UK were suppressed by news laws. Little humour follows from the irony of subjecting people to the true horrors of the prison industry on the pretext of their predilections for fictional horror.

Cat People

USA | 1942 | 73 min   d. Jacques Tourneur

The story of a young Serbian woman who believes herself to be a descendant of a race of people who turn into cats when sexually aroused, potentially fatally mauling their partner. This is essentially a double-reversal of the werewolf trope, switching genders and substituting feline for canine characteristics, perhaps due to the fact that during Code-era Hollywood, the word "bitch" was proscribed. The film was remade in 1982 by Paul Schrader.

La Belle et la Bête
[Beauty and the Beast]

France | 1946 | 96 min   d. Jean Cocteau

Given the arbitrary nature of social relations, be they inter-sexual, inter-generational, or inter-species, it should come as no surprise that bestiality is only deemed socially acceptable when produced specifically for an audience of children. It seems likely that the survival of this tale is due to the fact that overt sexuality used to be excluded from children's stories. Many versions of this tale have been filmed: the most commercially successful being the Disney cartoon of 1991 and the most critically acclaimed being this one.

Borowczyk's film *The Beast* is not a direct adaptation of any variant of the tale, but rather fuses its subtext with diverse other references (e.g. *Little Red Riding Hood*, *Bo Peep*) to produce a new work.

Horse

USA | 1965 | 105 min   d. Andy Warhol

Filmed in March 1965, this was the precursor of Warhol's better known *Lonesome Cowboys* (USA, 1968). The action, such as it is entirely shot in The Factory and centres around a horse, which had been transported to the artist's studio by elevator with no little effort. The four hunky young men in vaguely western outfits spout generic western dialogue as various technicians, onlookers and hangers-on (most notably Edie Sedgwick in her first Warhol appearance) wander around. The cowboys gleefully subvert western clichés and emphasise the homoerotic subtexts of the genre: a poker game becomes a strip poker game, and the cowboy's legendary love of his horse becomes manifest in a quasi-zoophilic romp as our boys suggestively caress the poor animal. The sudden intrusion of a cheesy aria that's wildly dramatized by one of the boys takes the concept of "horse opera" to its literal extreme. Warhol was as sadistic toward his audience (assuming he had one) as he was toward his players. This film is feature length and the first third is mostly an extended shot of the horse eating.

Futz!

USA | 1969 | 92 min   d. Tom O'Horgan

This oft-overlooked attempt at a countercultural musical concerns a young farmer who showers love and affection upon his

Cat People

La Belle et La Bete

Horse

pet pig, named Amanda. Their ensuing marriage causes a scandal so complete that even the neighbouring hillbillies are up in arms. Having not viewed it, we must assume that the love scenes are not graphic. Joseph Stefano had previously written for *The Twilight Zone*, and the screenplay for *Psycho* (USA, 1960), so he should have known better.

The Devil in Miss Jones

USA | 1973 | 67 min   d. Gerard Damiano

No sooner had mechanical cinema been invented then it was put to the service of the sex industry. The 1890s onwards saw brothels in major cities installing this latest porno-technology. To our modern eyes, the content produced in these times appears simultaneously quaint and shocking. Given that the existence of any kind of pornographic film was in those days a crime so serious as to be unlegislated, there was little to deter producers from including scenes depicting acts that were then criminal such as homosexuality or bestiality. It was only when pornography gained a degree of social acceptability in the 1970s that the negotiation of its "socially acceptable bounds" could be begun. Given the rarified conditions of capitalism that new markets engender, pornographers embarked on a programme of content escalation to get the edge on their competitors. Just about every form of exotic behaviour was market-tested, culminating in the snuff movie hoax that signalled the start of a backlash against unfettered filth.

In this period animal abuse porn made some incursions into relative prominence, the best-known examples being Linda Lovelace's "dogarama" loops, the Kronhausens' *Hvorfor gør de det?* [why do they do it?] (Denmark, 1971) which featured Bodil Joensen who attained star status for her antics but came to a predictable sticky end, and the loop comp known as *Animal Farm*, which attained cult status during the UK home video explosion of the early eighties. I haven't viewed any of these works and there are any number of other good reasons to exclude them from this overview.

The Devil in Miss Jones was Gerard Damiano's follow-up to his smash-hit *Deep Throat* (USA, 1972). It remains one of the most lauded porno movies. It includes a scene of a nude Georgina Spelvin cavorts with a snake. Although no actual ophidicism (snake sex) takes place, it was implied on some advertising for the film, acknowledging an audience for films pushing the envelope beyond vanilla hardcore. Conversely, in *Spooky Kama Sutra* (AKA Beautiful Dead Body) (Hong Kong, 1987, d. Xin Ren.) a patently fake snake engages in unsimulated sex.

Snakes have been associated with sex since the Garden of Eden and the snake biting its own tail has symbolised sex since it appeared in ancient Egypt: the snake representing the male organ and the circle representing the female organ. A one (1) and a zero (0) play the same role in binary logic, upon which the foundations of modern computing are lain, but more on that in a few pages.

Vase de Noces
[The Wedding Trough]

Aka: The Pig Fucking Movie

Belgium | 1974 | 79 min   d. Thierry Zéno

An art-house black and white film without dialogue but with a growing cult reputation. It's about a man who lives alone on a farm putting dolls' heads on pigeons. He rapes a sow on his farm, and we hope that this is simulated, although the film's scatological excursions are not. Confronted by the offspring of this coupling, he hangs the hideous progeny, then kills the sow before collecting his aggregated excreta (from a bathtub he has been cultivating), boiling and eating it, and then hanging himself.

The film-makers had previously made *Of the Dead* (France/Belgium, 1972, with Jean-Pol Ferbus), an idiosyncratic documentary that seriously examines rituals surrounding death presenting harrowing footage without commentary.

Τα παιδιά του Διαβόλου
[Island of Death]

Greece | 1975 | 110 min   d. Nico Mastorakis

In the mid-seventies bestiality briefly came into vogue in European exploitation cinema, especially in Greece and Italy, perhaps due to the influence of the Classics.

Island of Death was filmed on the quaint Greek island of Mykonos. To summarise, a young couple rent a house for the Winter holidays. They seem normal enough and enjoy having sex in a phone booth. First impressions are upturned when Chris goes for a morning stroll and encounters a lost lamb. He has sex with it then kills it. Meanwhile, Celia seduces a local house painter, before they torture him by nailing his hands to the ground, pissing on him and making him drink a bucket of paint. Later they combust an ageing lesbian who winds up decapitated by a bulldozer. At one point Chris invades a party with a sword, chasing one of the guests through the middle of town with a sword, not that anyone seems to notice. The couple justify all this on the grounds that they are helping God punish devi-

The Devil in Miss Jones

Vase de Noces   *Island of Death*

ants by torturing and killing them. As Christopher memorably asserts "I am his angel, with a flaming sword, sent to kill dirty worms", but the strap-line put it more bluntly: "The lucky ones simply got their brains blown out". This film made the UK DPP's list of video nasties.

Bestialità [Bestiality]

AKA Dog Lay Afternoon

Italy | 1976 | 85 min   d. Peter Skerl

Although *491* (Sweden, 1964, d. Vilgot Sjoman) features an off-screen rape by a dog (if such a thing is possible) *Bestialità* is notable as the first generally released film that I have discovered that takes the topic as its primary subject.

This is a typical low-rent seventies Italian giallo that starts with a, thankfully simulated, scene of a woman and a rottweiler. Her daughter observes and her husband intercedes. Violently! He ties up the dog and torches the house with the pooch inside. Then the credits start and things get out of hand...

Padre Padrone
[Father and Master]

Italy | 1977 | 113 min   d. P. & V. Taviani

If Italy seems disproportionately well represented in this genre, it may be attributable to the fact that the country resembles the penis of the beast of mainland Europe, but since the map of Europe resembles no actual creature, such discussion cannot be accommodated here.

Padre Padrone won the Palme D'Or at Cannes, making it the most feted example of the genre to feature the topic. Based on the autobiography of the son of a Sardinian shepherd, and filmed in their distinctive documentary style, the Tavianis' treatment of the book is un-flinching, and notable for its approach to bestiality, in the form of chicken abuse, which is presented unsensationally and sensitively.

La Bella e la Bestia
[Beauty and the Beast]

Italy | 1977 | 105 min   d. Luigi Russo

It seems safe to assume that this portmanteau film was strongly influenced by Borowczyk's *Immoral Tales*. It likewise comprises four segments: "La Schiava" [the slave], "Zooerastia" [zoophilia], "La Fustigazione" [The Whipping] and "La Promessa" [The Promise]. Lisbeth Hummel (Lucy Broadhurst from *The Beast*) stars in the first two of these. This isn't entirely surprising as the director is her husband, Luigi Russo, who had also cast Hummel in his *Dolly il sesso biondo* [Dolly the blonde sex] (Italy, 1979), *Una donna senza nome* [woman without a name] (Italy, 1987) and *Le Diaboliche* [diabolical] (Italy, 1989), and she barely worked beyond these. Lisbeth now concentrates on art, detailed pencil sketches and her pictures have something of Bona des Mandiargues about them.

Tanya's Island

Canada | 1980 | 82 min   d. Alfred Sole

Canadian softcores tend to be less mean-spirited than their US counterparts and, despite its generous flesh quota, this tale of a love triangle between a man, a woman and some kind of ape-man is more likely to offend due its overwrought earnestness than anything else. It stars Vanity, who had started as a model and was recruited into the Prince-sponsored group Vanity 6 afterwards. In 1994 she became a Christian evangelist following a bad experience with crack cocaine and reverted to her birth name Denise K. Matthews.

Bigfoot-themed erotica had enjoyed an early start with *The Geek* (USA, 1971, d. unknown), an example of anthropological field-trip porn that plays like an inept fore-runner of *The Beast*, but after *Tanya's Island* the theme would not recur until the 21st century.

Hokusai Manga

Japan | 1981 | 119 min | d. Kaneto Shindô

The prolific and versatile Kaneto Shindô (1912-2012) was director of many acclaimed films, including *Onibaba* (Japan, 1964) and *Kuroneko* (Japan, 1968). He also gave us this, probably the first graphic example of cephaphiliac cinema, fittingly based on one of the earliest and best known graphic instances. *The Dream of the Fisherman's Wife*, a woodcut by Katsushika Hokusai, depicts a woman entwined by a pair of octopuses that has been reworked by a number of artists. The prototype in the classical world is the legend of Andromeda, naked and chained to the rocks, sacrificed to the monster, a recurring motif in romantic and classical art.

Examples of cephaphiliac cinema are relatively rare in mainstream cinema, and convention dictates that the sex scenes are sublimated into violent confrontations. The mushroom cloud of anti-communist hysteria of the mid-fifties netted a bumper catch, most notably: *The Beast from 20,000 Fathoms* (USA, 1953, d. Eugène Lourié). Disney's *20,000 Leagues Under the Sea* (USA, 1954, d. Richard Fleischer) with Kirk Douglas, James Mason, *It Came from Beneath the Sea* (USA, 1955, d. Robert Gordon), and *Bride of the Monster* (USA, 1955, d. Ed Wood), although

Bestialità

La Bella e la Bestia

Tanya's Island

strictly speaking that one features only tentacles. Later came the Beatles most psychedelic spin-off in *Yellow Submarine* (UK, 1968, d. George Dunning) which includes a number of hippified octopuses but oddly no gardening. The success of Steven Spielberg's *Jaws* (USA, 1975) encouraged a number of cash-ins about the dangers of aquatic life, one of the least appealing being *Tentacles* (Italy/USA, 1977, d. Ovidio G. Assonitis) with John Huston, Shelley Winters, Henry Fonda, which is redeemed by a sequence where a giant squid goes up against a naked swimmer, female naturally. It can be argued that any film of this genre could be included in this book on the grounds that the phalluses are so numerous as to transform quantity (of tentacles) into the quality of pornography. But it won't be.

More explicit cephalophiliac material has been available for centuries in Japan, and "tentacle rape" is common in "hentai" titles where various (usually imaginary, or specifically alien) creatures rape or otherwise impale young women and, less commonly, men. The genre exploits the controversial realms of bodice ripper and rape fantasy genres, ostensibly mitigated by the fact that the scenes are so absurd or fanciful that they could have no parallel in the real world. Toshio Maeda reinvented the genre with his *Urotsukidoji: Legend of the Overfiend* (Japan, 1989) circumventing Japanese censorship regulations that prohibit the depiction of penises but allow sexual penetration by a tentacle or similar appendage. It is tempting to speculate that organised groups of cine-cephalophiles traffic in this kind of material, forming squid rings.

It is believed that Borowczyk's film *The Beast* is the only bestiality-themed film to feature molluscs of the gastropod class, although they take no active part in the sex acts. The eels in the aforementioned *Animal Farm* are of course vertebrates (phylum: chordata) of the class acteropterygii and thus completely irrelevant.

Sadomania

Spain/W. Germany | 1981 | 103 min
d. Jesús Franco

Jesús Franco is often cited as the most prolific director of fiction features of all time so the law of averages dictates that he must eventually have featured the theme of bestiality in one of his films, not least since virtually all his works feature some perverted sleaziness of one kind or another. It's surprising perhaps that, after reviewing perhaps sixty of his films (admittedly less than a quarter of his oeuvre) this is the only film of his to feature here. The nasty scene in question has a shackled prisoner assaulted by an Alsatian in order to sexually arouse the otherwise impotent prison governor. Oddly, the room is filled mechanical dolls in a possible nod to Borowczyk himself.

Animales Racionales
[Human Animals]

Spain | 1983 | 91 min   d. Eligio Herrero

This is possibly the most idiosyncratic example of post-nuclear apocalypse cinema, a genre that includes *A Boy and his Dog* (USA, 1975, d. L.Q. Jones) which has Don Johnson in it, so that's going some. The film kicks off with stock footage of mushroom clouds, and as they're from several different eras it gives the impression that World War III must have lasted a long time, maybe jumping backwards and forwards too. Then we cut to a slag heap. Two guys, a woman and a dog have survived. The woman (Carole Kirkham's only film) loves to wander round nude so the guys inevitably fight over her and all take part in customary eurosleaze softcore action. Things get weird when the dog gets in on the action, and the climax is so trite as to be completely unexpected. Throughout the whole film, there's no dialogue, just grunting, which thankfully make the nonexistent subtitles easier on the eye.

Café Flesh

USA | 1983 | min   d. Rinse Dream

Post-apocalypse zoophilia also occurs in what is considered the classiest of eighties pornos. The action centres around grotty nightclub where impotent punters of both genders observe elaborate dance cum sex numbers in mounting frustration. The first number opens with a bored housewife menaced by a weird rat/milkman hybrid. The guy's outfit is purely representative and he's endowed with a long tail that he puts to predictable use against a surreal backdrop. In the second number, a girl gets it from a guy wearing a giant pencil head, but films about sex with office supplies lie outside the scope of this work.

Noi e l'Amore: comportamento sessuale deviante
[Us and Love: Deviant Sexual Behaviour]

Italy | 1986 | 83 min   d. Antonio D'Agostino

Generally categorised as a mondo film, despite being simulated (with an exception outlined below) and naming its cast, this example illustrates the difficulties that films dealing with bestiality seem to experience in conforming to conventions of form as well as content. The films opens with shades of Hitchcock as a man observes various pervy antics

Hokusai Manga

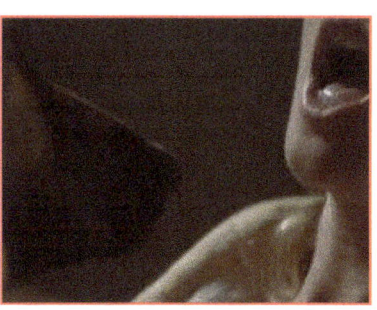

Sadomania

Animales Racionales

in a block of flats opposite through binoculars. The film is punctuated by a sombre deskbound psychoanalyst then a woman is raped by a gang of men, others indulge in sadomasochism, watersports, envelope adhesive fetishism, and there's a man who abuses a woman's shoe by shoving it down his trousers. The episode most relevant here concerns woman so aroused by seeing two horses mating that she lets a dog give her oral sex. Like the rest of the picture, it's explicit though not hardcore, which doesn't do anything useful to prepare the viewer for what comes next. They do give you a warning though: ATTENZIONE ATTENZIONE ATTENZIONE fills the screen before a graphic sex-change footage rolls. Similar footage being a staple of more orthodox mondo films.

Max Mon Amour

France/USA/Japan | 1986 | 92 min
d. Nagisa Oshima

Oshima has pushed the envelope in several directions with his hit *In the Realm of the Senses* (France/Japan, 1976) which featured restrained though hardcore sex action plus a bloody castrating conclusion. Perverts expecting a similarly frank approach here will be disappointed. Charlotte Rampling plays a diplomat's uptight wife who falls for a gorilla with a bloody frustrating conclusion. There's no on-screen action to speak of, making it even less explicit than the remake of *Tarzan, The Ape Man* (USA, 1981, d. John Derek) that had Bo Derek cavorting with a gibbon over the end credits.

N.B. If I had made this film it would have probably been called *I am Curious (George)*.

The Revenge of Billy the Kid

UK | 1991 | 87 min
d. Jim Groom

At the start of the nineties, the obvious comic potential of bestiality has been exploited with increasing frequency, culminating at the turn of the millennium in such mundane Hollywood slop as *Nutty Professor II: The Klumps* (USA, 2000, d. Peter Segal), *Super Troopers* (USA, 2001, d. Jay Chandrasekhar), *Freddy Got Fingered* (USA, 2001, d. Tom Green) *American Pie: The Wedding* (USA, 2003, d. Jesse Dylan). These films cannot be discussed here due to their overwhelming mediocrity. It is hard to assess whether the higher visibility of the topic in mainstream comedy is due to a corresponding decrease in its shock value, or whether the latter is a function of the former.

The Revenge of Billy the Kid was perhaps influenced by the early work of Peter Jackson, was made with a budget of £50,000 raised from a house sale and supplemented by investment generated from an advert in *Private Eye*. This very independently produced oddity introduces us to the antics of the McDonald Family. As the strap-line puts it: "Old McDonald had a farm... and on that farm he *had* a goat."

The offspring is a hideous goat-headed baby that is adopted by the family but is eventually tied into a sack and thrown in the river after wrecking the farmer's beer stash. Needless to say, it returns to wreak a revenge as ghastly as it is predictable.

It Came from the Deep

USA | 2000 | 30 min
d. Jim Powers (?)

Episode 25 of the *Perverted Stories* series demonstrates that pornography is always at the vanguard of human experience. Although there is no recorded sighting of a living giant (or colossal) squid, the erotic possibilities of such a union have already been postulated.

Perverted Stories is a successful porno franchise specialising in extremely bizarre and frequently blackly humorous scenarios. Each feature length tape includes four stories in a portmanteau format and the treatments are sometimes quite elaborate: alien abductions, ventriloquist dolls and quadruple amputees are all grist to this gristly mill. One episode even has a (female) Prof. Challenger in a threesome with a couple of guys done up as pterodactyls, making it the only example I have discovered of ptero-porn. Although admittedly I haven't looked very hard, and to be completely honest I haven't even seen that one, or indeed this one, or for that matter many of the films in this section at all.

Regardless of that, these films still demonstrate that this manner of artefact is viable, so we may be certain that as soon as physical time travel is realised pornographers will be amongst its first users and that prehistoric zoophilia will soon follow, as inevitable as anything else that may be conceived of by the poisoned well-springs of human endeavour.

Max Mon Amour

The Revenge of Billy the Kid

It Came from the Deep

THE BIGGEST SCREEN

In pre-technological times, cinema was the sole prerogative of the natural world, perhaps under the direction of a supreme auteur or as the product of an arcane bureaucratic system. Since the development of artificial cinema during the industrial age, however, the constellations of night sky are now of interest only to professional scientists, enthusiasts and lovers.

These prototype films are projected simultaneously and, as in a drive-in multiplex, the viewer must merely shift their gaze to watch a different film. One soundtrack fits all.

The action unfolds slowly of course, over the course of the year as the constellations traverse the heavens. This slowness is only perceived by contemporary audiences, their attention spans stunted by industrialised media. Primitive audiences had no precedents for comparison.

Narratives are interrupted by the regular coming of day, prefiguring the concept of the intermission, wherein refreshments could be procured and necessary obligations of life could be fulfilled.

Although directed by the laws of physics, the screenwriters remain anonymous, plagiarising from urban legends, conspiracy theories and extreme gossip. The whole shithouse is produced by G-d themselves. The actors are the stars of course. Giant distant balls of flaming probably toxic gas, projecting their image across the empty vastness of space. These first stars are still there, of course, and still burn just as bright even though they appear dimmed by artificial illumination in industrialised areas. These actors appear stationery but the motion of the earth makes a tracking shot, or a slow pan over the action.

The configuration of actors relative to each other makes the shape of the constellation that implies its story. The degree of imagination required by the viewer to impute an artefact's intrinsic properties from its extrinsic form varies in inverse proportion to the resolution of the medium.

In those days, the shapes of the constellations were not a function of contemporary mores, overt and covert agendas, or economies of sex and money. They were organised by conjunctions of what we think of as order and chance. Arcane forces described by science and magick and esoteric shit. So the heavenly films all play every night. The programme alters as they migrate across the sky. Never exactly the same twice. Not till next year anyway, and not exactly the same then either. Every nation gets the same version. No dubbing or localised product placement. No region restriction or copy protection. Censorship, however, is still with us. Arbitrary alterations to the materials may be demanded by agents of the weather bureau. Meteorological interventions during projections vary in their frequency, nature and severity dependent on the time of year and geographic location. Sometimes the cuts or optical censoring contribute aesthetically to the experience of the films: thunder and lightning like some kind of cgi response perhaps? In any case, the vicissitudes of the weather system seem less obscure to me than the judgements of earthly censors.

Albrecht Dürer's hemispheres of 1515 were the first European printed star charts. This polymorphously perverse clusterfuck looks like nothing so much as the traditional climax of generic pornographic films, a convention thankfully eschewed by the director of The Beast.

▶ The Abduction of Europa by Gustave Moreau (c.1869)
◀ Jupiter und Asteria by Marco Liberi (c.1690)
▼ Leda and the Swan by Peter Paul Rubens (1601)

Taurus The Bull

Considered by many to be the oldest constellation identified, **Zeus** (Jupiter to the Romans) abducted and enjoyed **Europa** under the form of a bull. A complimentary story has Zeus transform his mistress Io into a heifer to hide her from his wife.

Other Greek bull stories concern **Neptune**, transformed into a fierce bull, to rape **Canace**, and more elaborately **Pasiphaë**, wife of **King Minos**, who burned with desire for a snow-white bull, she had the artificer **Daedalus** to construct for her a wooden image of a cow, in which she placed herself in such a posture that her vagina was presented to the amorous attack of the bull, without fear of any hurt from the animal's hoofs or weight. The fruit of this embrace was **the Minotaur**, half bull, half man, slain by **Theseus**. The constellation Corona Borealis (AKA The Northern Crown/Cross) represents the crown of King Minos, who kept the Minotaur.

According to Suetonius, Nero caused this spectacle to be enacted at the public shows. Borowczyk provides us with a cinematic rendering in **The Art of Love** although the sequence is clumsily executed and the details of the episode unclear.

Aquila The Eagle

Although there are more widely accepted precedents for the constellation, Zeus ravished Asterie under the shape of an eagle, and afterwards changed her into a quail; According to some, he also changed himself into an eagle to seduce Aegina, though others say a fire. Zeus also lay with Medusa under the form of a bird and, according to some she bore the winged horse Pegasus (and its associated constellation) by him.

Cygnus The Swan

Leda lent herself to Zeus's embraces whilst he was disguised as a swan. Helen and Polydeuces resulted from that sexual union. The motif became popular in Italian painting and sculpture of the 16th Century. The most familiar examples are the copies of Leonardo da Vinci's lost painting, with the two sets of infant twins; Correggio's elaborate composition of c. 1530 (Berlin); and two versions of a lost Michelangelo [Leda and the Swan, 1530, copy after a lost original by Michelangelo] that is also known from an engraving by Cornelis de Bos, c. 1563; the marble sculpture by Bartolomeo Ammanati in the Bargello, Florence; and the painting after Michelangelo, c. 1530, in the National Gallery, London. Leda and the Swan went on to be a common motif for the visual arts into the 19th century, and in 1924 a poem by W.B. Yeats revived what had become an insipid classical cliché by combining psychological realism with a mystic vision.

The motif was exploited by Kurt Kren in **7/64: Leda mit dem Schwan** [Leda and the swan] (Austria, 1964) and Peter Greenaway's **A Zed and Two Noughts** (UK/Netherlands, 1985) and by Borowczyk in **The Art of Love**, and later in the advertising for **The Story of a Sin**.

The extent to which the audience was responsible for their role in the formation of these narratives can only be postulated. Did they assume their stories to have a divine authority? Or was this a function of those seeking to control the dissemination of these tales? Whichever is the case, it seems likely that the notion that people could invent their own tales post-dated the relation of these stories that were considered to be dictated by the whim of the heavens. The invention of writing was instrumental in fixing these legends. The first stories most likely concerned the formation of the world that these people knew and their relation to it, but progressed onto describing social relations between people.

Modern science can now calculate the distance of many stars from our planet, but in ancient times it was not obvious that the stars occupied a third spatial dimension. They were most often conceived as points equidistant from the earth of varying brightness. That is, occupying two spatial dimensions and a fixed dimension of time in which to relate their story. As time passed the stellar legends became predominantly related through their telling, rather than their observation, and the story came to be related through one spatial dimension and a variable (although sequential) temporal dimension as is generally the case with written texts.

Most ancient societies developed their own systems of classifying different configurations of stars, forming a kind of prehistoric "World Cinema". These differing constellations provided variant readings of the heavens and, prior to the dominance of the Greco-Roman typology, little consensus existed, or was indeed necessary. However, one characteristic that is common to almost all, and strikingly frequent in some, seems shocking to our contemporary morality: sex between humans and animals. Around half of the traditional western constellations have a sexual basis, and half of those involve zoophilia. Those odds are worse than the internet.

The "Flammarion" engraving (1888), by an unknown artist.

Sex technology has come a long way since Cleopatra (allegedly) used a gourd filled with bees as a prototype vibrator. Virtual reality can already present an immersive three-dimensional environment when special viewing apparatus are worn. These are sometimes complemented by gloves or suits that can communicate tactile sensations. Motorised artificial genitals (and sundry orifices) that mimic their organic counterparts are already being manufactured by a burgeoning teledildonics industry. We can postulate a technology that will connect such devices to future interactive videos, and perhaps retrospectively interface to already existent pornos, responsive to soundtrack cues. In this instance the exaggerations of most pornographic soundtracks will simplify the task. Fantastically realistic sex dolls are already available, and it is only a matter of time before they are mechanically animated to provide the first erotomatons. How long will it be before manufacturers receive orders for simulated animals for sexual purposes? It has already happened.

So, having tracked these phenomena from the aeons-old constellations in the furthest reaches of visible space to the tiniest electronic discharge in a modern computer network, we can now foresee a not distant time when cinema will be as obsolete as the constellations. We will we have no use for the dreams of others, no matter they be so more beautiful and wise than our own. From the most base depths of degradation to the pinnacles of human achievement, the forces of reaction will not be able to suppress these dreams until they find a way to extinguish the stars. As indicated earlier, they are working on it.

✦

If I have to choose an epoch and an identity, it would be Leda's swan in antiquity, if she really was as beautiful as the artists represent her.

— **Borowczyk**

FURTHER READING

There are few full-length works on Borowczyk and his films but the following books and magazines provided useful information on the cinematic environment in which he was working. Whilst they may not offer much in the way of background information, they are rich in future avenues of exploration.

Immoral Tales: Sex and Horror Cinema in Europe 1956-1984.
Cathal Tohill & Pete Tombs
(London: Primitive Press, 1994)
Tohill and Tombs gave us the first comprehensive overview of the golden years of continental European sleaze. They understood that readers wanted hard data and context for films rather than subjective blathering and reactionary obfuscation.

The scale of the job a hand should not be underestimated - and the accessible writing makes sense out of some extremely convoluted filmographies. The authors provide useful guides to the Italian, German, French and Spanish contexts before moving onto detailed accounts of the careers of prime movers Jess Franco, Jean Rollin, José Larraz, José Bénazéraf, Walerian Borowczyk and Alain Robbe-Grillet, then appendices on other prominent figures in the industry, and a bonus article on the influence of comic books on the genre.

Anatomie du Diable
Walerian Borowczyk
(Paris : P. Belfond, 1992)
Borowczyk's book of short stories was somewhat predictably influenced by the work of Mandiargues. Unfortunately I have not been able to find a copy (either in French or English) to review.

Cinéaste Onirique: le cas étrange du Dr Jekyll et Miss Osbourne.
(Paris : La Vue, 1981).
Apparently a promotional tie-in with **Dr Jekyll et Les Femmes,** this profusely illustrated booklet has a foreword by Andre Pieyre de Mandiargues and an article by Robert Benayoun and quotes by Borowczyk, followed by a colour insert from the movie, then b/w photos to illustrate his career, plus a filmography of shorts and features.

Walerian Borowczyk: Cinema of Erotic Dreams
by Jeremy Mark Robinson
(Maidstone: Crescent Moon Pubs, 2008)
The author deserves credit for getting out the first full-length

treatment of Boro's oeuvre, but sadly the amateurish production emphasises the shortcomings of the work. The tone oscillates unevenly from pseudo-scholarly to fannish without establishing any kind of credibility and although omissions are noted, there are rather more than seem warranted. The book filled useful gap for a time, but is compromised but the relative shallowness of its research, admittedly much easier now than when this book was compiled.

The Ambiguous Image.
Roy Armes
(London: Secker & Warburg, 1976).
Roy Armes book examines unconventional approaches to narrative, from its roots in surrealism and antecedents such as Tati, Bresson and Bergman through Resnais, Robbe-Grillet, Pasolini and Borowczyk (shorts, **Goto** and **Blanche**) before addressing the more overtly political implications via Godard and Makavejev. As a time capsule of a period when film-makers were striving to make their works interesting rather than tedious, this book is unsurpassed at tying

together disparate but related works and provides an unmatched guide to European cinema of the period, albeit focussing on the more cerebral end of the spectrum.

Anatole Dauman: Pictures of a Producer
Jacques Gerber
(London: British Film Inst, 1992)
Originally published by the Centres Georges Pompidou to tie in with their Dauman exhibition and retrospective, the expanded English translation of the catalogue covers the most eminent names from the Argos roster. Most of the material is taken from notes or interviews by Dauman or his directors, and there are many previously unseen photos and enclosures including a detailed interview with Borowczyk about **The Beast**.

Cut! The Unseen Cinema
Baxter Philips
(London: Lorrimer Pub, 1975)
Baxter Philips' account of screen censorship was highly prized in English playgrounds in the 1970s. With much in common with Continental Film

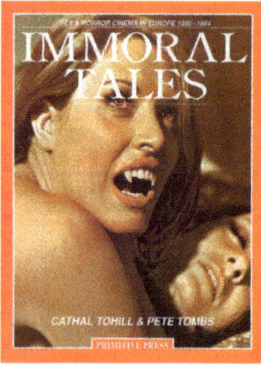
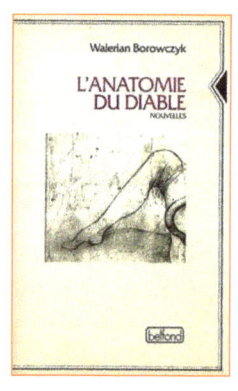

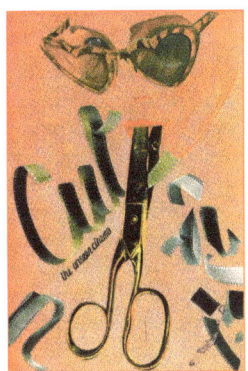

Review, it provides a vivid overview of the cinematic context of the times. Borowczyk scores a couple of mentions on the closing pages.

Film as a Subversive Art. Amos Vogel
(London Weidenfeld & Nicholson, 1974).

Although Borowczyk only scores a couple of mentions here for his shorts, this is nevertheless a crucial work. Vogel was an instigator of the Cinema 16 film club in New York and compiled this guide from notes for his programmes of obscure and ephemeral film. Running from the dawn of cinema, his enthusiasm for novel cinematic forms and methods makes this an essential checklist to the most bizarre films up till that time.

Sex Stars System
This French mag ran monthly from April 1975 till September 1976 (#18), changing to Stars System and broadening its coverage for a further two issues. Written largely by the multitalented Jean-Pierre Bouyxou, it covered most of the territory currently defined as Eurotica: Rollin, Franco, Eurociné, Alpha France etc. Some of Boro's later films made occasional appearances.

Continental Film Review
Edited by Gordon Reid
(London: Eurap Pubs)
This much-loved British film journal ran from November 1952 (#1) until March 1984 (#372). Although it emphasised continental European cinema (including Scandinavia and then-Communist countries), it also covered British, Asian and occasionally US material. As well as Reid himself, writers included Jean-Pierre Bouyxou, Peter Cowie and Antony Balch.

As the sixties progressed, the mag's photographic illustrations became racier and more prominent, usefully expanding its readership to the Raincoat Brigade, but despite this, the writing continued to be erudite and comprehensive to the point that the magazine now provides the single most useful resource for studying popular cinema in the UK through the sixties and seventies.

GENERAL ARTICLES ON BOROWCZYK

Cinema Papers, no.50, February 1985, p.22-27.
Cinématographe, no.21, October 1976, p.30-31, in French.
Davis, Colin. "True to his Obsessions: the Films of Walerian Borowczyk". in Stefan Jaworzyn ed ***Shock Xpress 2*** London: Titan Books, 1994. p.106-114.
Image et Son, no.322, November 1977, p.34-48, in French.
Krogius, Toffo. "The Immoral Tales of Walerian Borowczyk." ***Divinity***, no.1, 1992.
Murray, Scott. "Desire that Dares: the Films of Walerian Borowczyk, part 2." ***Cinema Papers***, no.129, January 1999, p.44-50.
Murray, Scott. "Museum of the Rare: the Films of Walerian Borowczyk." ***Cinema Papers***, no.128, December 1998, p.18-21.
Positif, no.316, June 1987, p.54-55, in French.
Jacques Rivette, Michel Delahaye, Sylvie Pierre. Interview. ***Cahiers du Cinéma***, no.209, February 1969, p.30-42,58-61, in French.
Strick, Philip. "The Theatre of Walerian Borowczyk." ***Sight and Sound***, vol.38 no.4, October 1969, p.166-200.

OBITUARIES & MEMORIALS

Bird, Daniel. "The Ghost of Goto: Walerian Borowczyk remembered." ***Vertigo***, vol.3 no.1, July 2006, p.57-59.
Brooke, Michael. "One of film's irreplaceable originals." ***Sight and Sound***, vol.16 no.4, April 2006.
Kurz, Iwona. "Powrot Borowczyka: Ozywic ducha." ***Kino***, vol.42 no.1, January 2008, p.22-25, Polish.
Pagliano, Jean-Pierre. "Hommage: Walerian Borowczyk 1923-2006." ***Positif***, no.542, April 2006, p.69, in French.
"Pozegnania - Walerian Borowczyk 83." ***Kino***, vol.40 no.3, March 2006, p.88, Polish.
Salas, André. "Tales of Perversion." ***Filmmaker***, vol.14 no.3, April 2006, p.20.

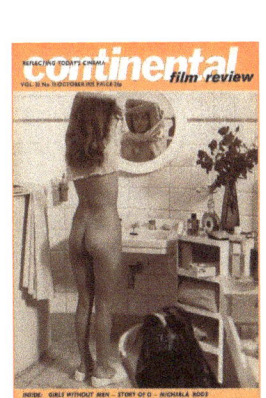

Full page ad from *Pariscope: Une semaine de Paris*, no. 585, 8 August 1979, p.39.

"Lovers of fantasy who do not fear sexual audacity will be seduced by this 'Beast'".

I kept this copy of *Pariscope* as a souvenir of a my first visit to France, on a school exchange, aged fifteen.

ADDENDA

The Actual Facts about the Beast of Gevaudan

Beauty and the Beast
by Marie Leprince de Beaumont

Lokis — from the ms. of Professor Wittembach
by Prosper Mérimée

Studio 5-6-7

Index

FIGURE
DE LA BÊTE
FAROUCHE

ET EXTRAORDINAIRE, QUI DÉVORE LES FILLES
Dans la Province de Gévaudan, & qui s'échappe avec tant de vitesse, qu'en très-peu de tems on la voit à deux ou trois lieues de distance, & qu'on ne peut l'attraper ni la tuer.

EXPLICATION.

On écrit de Marvejols, dans la Province de Gévaudan, par une Lettre en date du premier Novembre mil sept cent soixante-quatre, que depuis deux mois il paroît aux environs de Langogne, & de la Forêt du Mercoire une Bête farouche qui répand la consternation dans toutes les Campagnes. Elle a déja dévoré une vingtaine de Personnes sur-tout des Enfans & particulièrement des Filles. Il n'y a guère de jours qui ne soient marqués par quelques nouveaux désastres. La frayeur qu'elle inspire empêche les Bucherons d'aller dans les Forêts, ce qui rend le bois fort rare & fort cher.

Ce n'est que depuis huit jours qu'on a pû parvenir à voir de près cet Animal redoutable. Il est beaucoup plus haut qu'un Loup; il est bas du devant, & ses pattes sont armées de griffes. Il a le poil rougeâtre; la tête fort grosse, longue, & finissant en museau de Lévrier; les oreilles petites, droites comme des cornes; le poitrail large & d'un gris blanc, sur lequel on voit une grande étendue ou raie de dents si tranchantes, qu'il a séparé plusieurs têtes du corps, comme pourroit le faire un rasoir. Il n'a pas allez lent, & il court en bondissant. Il est d'une agilité & d'une vitesse extrêmes: dans un intervalle de tems fort court on le voit à deux ou trois lieues de distance. Il se dresse sur ses pieds de derrière & s'élance sur sa proie, qu'il attaque toujours au cou, par derrière, ou par le côté. Il craint les Bœufs, qui le mettent en fuite. L'alarme est universelle dans ce Canton; on vient de faire des Prières publiques; on a rassemblé quatre cens Paysans pour donner la chasse à cet Animal féroce, mais on n'a pû encore l'atteindre.

Vû par nous Censeur pour la Police.
Vû l'Approbation, permis d'imprimer à la charge d'enregistrement à la Chambre Syndicale. Ce 24 Novembre 1764.
DE SARTINE.
Registré sur le Registre N°. 12. de la Communauté des Libraires & Imprimeurs, page 191.

Se vend AUX ASSOCIÉS, Chez P. G. Desnos &c, Libraire, rue Saint-Jacques.

THE ACTUAL FACTS ABOUT THE BEAST OF GÉVAUDAN

Although little known in the anglophone world, the Beast of Gévaudan is still a household name in France, and with characteristic chauvinism they call her The Greatest Enigma of History. Over three years between 1764 and 1767 the Beast devoured one hundred or so people, mostly women and children, and generally in bizarre and especially ghastly circumstances. There is little doubt that the Beast existed, but its true nature remains a mystery despite ongoing interest that constitutes a virtual Beast industry.

Despite the personal interest of King Louis XV, and the massive resources deployed against it, the Beast resisted most of the many attempts to track and destroy it, Its attacks had come at a time of political and religious turmoil, and conspiracy theories — often implicating the king's anti-Jesuit policies — quickly sprang up and endure to this day.

The first documented sighting of the Beast was in June of 1764 in the forest of Mercoire, near Langogne. A young woman was tending a herd of cows when she was suddenly charged by a horrendous beast. Her dogs fled, but her cows turned on the Beast with their horns and she was lucky to escape with minor injuries, although deeply traumatized. When she regained her composure she described the Beast as about the same size as her cows, with a huge head and neck, short straight ears, two long fangs, and a long nose from which ran a black stripe to the tip of its long and very thin tail. She maintained that it could leap up to thirty feet in one bound.

After that, it wasn't long before the corpses started to pile up. To start with, the Beast showed a preference for children in their early teens, and typically attacked at dusk, known locally as "the hour between dog and wolf".

The attacks were grisly and almost always fatal. Body parts and entrails commonly littered the autumnal fields, and it wasn't unusual to find disembodied organs hanging from branches, or the occasional decapitated head bouncing jauntily down a hill.

The tables might have been turned in October, when two hunters shot the Beast at point blank range, but it seemed to have no effect other than to enrage the Beast and increase the number and ferocity of attacks in the coming months.

As the terrible year closed, Captain Duhamel was appointed to the case and organised the peasants to flush out the creature so that his dragoons, forty on foot and seventeen mounted, could corner and kill the Beast. Despite all the planning it was not to be, and despite several close shaves the Beast escaped.

The next step was to offer a large reward, bringing hunters from all over France. Pictures of the Beast were circulated, including some from the most elegant of Paris art houses. Prints of many are still sold, principally from bookshops in Mende, which is the centre of Beast tourism despite there being no killings there.

Meanwhile, back in the 18th century, the peasants were became disgruntled with the outsiders consuming their food and disturbing their crops. Frustrated by the Beast, Duhamel responded harshly, by imprisoning one man whose only crime was to belatedly report an attack while attending to his child whose throat had been torn open by the Beast. Many other attacks went unreported due to the peasants reticence to engage the ponderous bureaucracy.

It was then that the Beast launched into a killing spree more terrible than ever before, and in February the following year King Louis XV despatched M. Denneval and his faithful bloodhounds that were reputed to have killed more than 1,200 wolves.

Then, in March, Jacques, Jeanne and Julienne Denis were watching their livestock near Malzieu when the Beast suddenly attacked, seizing Jeanne by the head. Jacques managed to throw the Beast onto their campfire and it fled howling. Jeanne had gaping wounds behind each ear and a torn shoulder. Her fleshly wounds soon healed but her mind was lost and she never recovered her senses. Her uninjured sister was overcome with guilt and took to wandering the slopes of Malzieu in the hope that she might tempt the Beast out of hiding. Jacques swore to avenge his sister and joined Denneval on his elaborate hunts which always came to naught but the Beast leaving a trail of slaughter behind it.

The following month, a nobleman named de la Chaumette sighted the Beast near his home in Saint-Chey. He and his two brothers pursued and shot it but it escaped into the woods leaving a trail of its blood. Everyone assumed the Beast was done for and had crawled away to die so when the village Spring Fair kicked off a few days later it became a celebration of deliverance from the Beast. Unfortunately, at the height of the festivities,

97

GÉVAUDAN FILMS

The first filmed adaptation of the story of the Beast of Gevaudan was broadcast on 3 October 1967 by ORTF as the first episode in the series **Le Tribunal de l'impossible** [court of the impossible], produced by Michel Subiela and directed by Yves-André Hubert. Weirdly, the film featured Guy Tréjan as Dr. Antoine de Beauterne, who would later play Pierre de l'Esperance in **The Beast**.

Le Tribunal de l'impossible

The broadcast was followed by a lively debate featuring the director with Francis Peter (Deputy Director of the Museum of Natural History), Mr Saint-Aubin (hunting specialist), Georges-Henri Riviere (founder of Museum of Arts and Popular Traditions), Ms. Elise Seguin (historian) and Mr Francis Lacassin (author of several studies on witchcraft). ORTF followed up on 17 July 1972 with an episode of the popular tv show **Alain Decaux Raconte** [Alain Deccaux recounts] devoted to the topic. Then it was a long wait until a self-produced documentary, entitled **La Bête du Gévaudan** (France, 2001, d. Philippe Bordier) turned up, just in time to capitalise on the interest generated by Christopher Gans' blockbuster.

Christopher Gans struck box-office gold with his **Le Pacte de Loups** [**Brotherhood of the Wolf**] (France, 2001) which gleefully skips through just about every movie genre other than porno. The film riffs on the conspiracy aspects of the myth

a rider galloped into the village square declaring the Beast had struck again. Jacques Denis was gobsmacked when he discovered that the victim was Marguerite Martin, a friend of his. He found her on the outskirts of the village with her throat ripped out. There were many corpses that day, but the Beast left them undevoured, as they were reprisals for its being wounded. The villagers were overcome with disappointment at this reappearance and set out as a Frankenstein-style mob, with Jacques at the head. They were armed with pikes, pitchforks, bayonets, cudgels, pointy sticks, burning torches and pieces of 2×4 with nails hammered in. There are no coincidences, only sometimes the pattern is more obvious, and so Jacques soon found himself confronting the Beast once more. Gamely, he counter-attacked with his bayonet, but the Beast leapt onto him and it was only the timely arrival of the angry mob that saved him, but once more the fortunate Beast escaped. GAH! Denneval gave up the game in June and the Beast went on another spree, now killing and partly devouring mostly preteen children.

By this time, the Church were exploiting the problem, declaring the Beast to be a "messenger of evil" punishing the population for their sins as rumours of witchcraft and terrible rites started to spread. The Beast had generally avoided clerics and limited its attacks on the clergy to one convent near Grèzes in 1766. The Beast's predilection for women and children might have been simply due to the fact that they were simply more easily available, tending their flocks in pairs or alone while their men worked the fields in groups, armed with spades and scythes and skilled at driving off wolves.

Meanwhile, the King was becoming impatient at the lack of a result. He had already commissioned a nude rocking horse ready for the arrival of the Beast's hide. He ordered Antoine de Beauterne, his chief trouble-shooter to the province but for three months he appeared to do very little but draw up maps of the Beast's hunting grounds. Finally, on 21 September, a hunt with forty local hunters and twelve dogs set off. The beaters soon

encircled a ravine in the woods of Pommier. Suddenly the dogs started barking. Unleashed, they rushed into the woods and the Beast sprang out, flushed into the open. Surrounded, it twisted around, searching for an escape before lumbering off towards the hunt. De Beauterne fired and one of his shots went right on target into its right eye. The Beast stumbled and fell. The horn of triumph was sounded, but amazingly the Beast stumbled to its feet and lunged toward De Beauterne. Another hunter fired and hit, but the Beast just turned and made off through the cordon into a neighbouring pasture. There it collapsed and finally expired.

The carcass measured six feet from nose to tail and weighed 143lb, it was stuffed and taken at last to the King, ending up in the Museum of Natural History. And so, on 3 November, the victorious De Beauterne departed the province.

*

That wasn't to be the end of the Beast though... the killings went on! The King issued a proclamation forbidding anyone to speak of the Beast, for now the peasants were in a state of complete terror. They spent the winter barricaded in their homes, except for Jacques Denis's sister Jacqueline who continued to wander the countryside, crazed with despair, until she disappeared on Christmas Eve. A week later some unidentifiable human remains were found in a ravine. It is hard to know how many killings occurred in this period as the King's proclamation meant many of the Beast's victims were not attributed as such, and many families did not even admit the deaths, so fearful were they of the King's wrath. Nevertheless, it is thought that in the first half of the year there were at least fourteen victims in one small area around Paulhac.

Aided by terrible weather and a downturn the local cloth industry, the Beast dragged the entire region down to a state of poverty and famine. Peasants were too scared to tend their livestock and were constantly being called away from the fields to hunt the Beast. The neglect of their farms teetered the fragile local economy towards utter collapse.

As the summer came, peasants began to make pilgrimages and pray for relief from the Beast. One of these was Jean Chastel, who returned from his devotions with three blessed cartridges. He didn't have long to wait to use them! In June another hunt was organised with 300 hunters and beaters. Jean joined in, positioning himself on the Sogne d'Aubert as de Beauterne had positioned himself in the Beal Ravine to slay the previous Beast. Jean read his book of prayer and waited. Suddenly, the Beast, fleeing the dogs and beaters, appeared right before him. Chastel calmly finished praying, then stowed his holy book and his spectacles, before raising his gun and firing. The Beast fell stone dead. It is said that to this day no grass will grow on the ground where it fell. In a postscript as grisly as it is gratuitous, some sources say that when it was gutted the remains of a small girl were found inside its entrails.

*

With two carcasses to choose from, it might seem that the case of the Beast was closed, but the mystery had endured too long to be ended by so mundane a thing as death. The strength, cunning and invulnerability of the Beast gave it a supernatural resonance.

A century after the attacks, Robert Louis Stevenson wrote about the Beast in his *Travels with a Donkey in the Cévennes* (1879). "If all wolves had been this wolf they would have changed the history of man". Perhaps the great writer and drug fiend was thinking of the Beast when he wrote *Strange Case of Dr Jekyll and Mr Hyde*, with his hairy hands and all that prefiguring both Freud and Jack the Ripper.

Ten years later L'abbé Pourcher (1831-1915), curate of the village of Saint Martin-de-Boubaux in les Cévennes, published his book *La Bête du Gévaudan, véritable fléau de Dieu* [the Beast of Gévaudan, God's true plague] (1889). The Abbé Pierre Pourcher was the most meticulous of the many chroniclers of the Beast — and the only to have their work personally approved by Pope Léon XIII, maintained that the wolf-like creature had been aided by God as a scourge on the region to punish the villagers' sins. Its powers sprang from divine assistance.

The remaining myriad works on the Beast are pretty evenly split between conventional explanations, such as large wolves and crossbred hyenas, and more outrageous suggestions such as aliens, mutants, or prehistoric creatures.

Some sources postulate an organised conspiracy. The Jesuits may have used her to bring their flock back to the church, which was under pressure from the King. Huguenots, persecuted by the Jesuits, welcomed the pretext to arm themselves. The King might have exploited the chance to send his troops into the region.

And what of the case of the three women from Pompeyrac and their encounter with a man with a fur-covered hand? Or the two women of Escures, accosted by a man whose shirt blew open to reveal a fur-covered chest? Or the werewolf aristocrat who was hidden by nuns of the Cistercian abbey of Mercoire?

But the scores of victims and the hundreds of sightings tell us that there was a real beast, and it comes as no surprise that its atrocities were exploited for intrigue or sensation.

*

The vicinity of the Village of Paulhac endured fourteen attacks by the Beast in the spring of 1766 but met an even more terrible fate at the hands of a non-supernatural (?) enemy when she was razed by the German army in 1944 as a reprisal for partisan activity. Consider the maquis striking from their forest hide-outs at the Wermacht on their missions of sabotage and assassination. These heroes must have seemed to the invaders as a latter day manifestation of the terrible legend that they had heard third-hand in their foxholes and mess halls.

And we can reflect on the final lesson of the Beast, here to remind us that humanity's self-proclaimed position at the peak of the evolutionary cycle is no contest for being at the top of the food chain.

and adeptly veers from wuxia to steampunk. It's just a shame that they couldn't wheel in Duran Duran to do a tune called "Hungry Like the Snake", on the soundtrack. Some copies of the DVD came with discs carrying the 1967 ORTF telemovie as a bonus, whilst other versions carried different, later produced, docos, of which there have been quite a few. Appropriately enough, Gans' most recent release is a critically acclaimed traditional retelling of **Beauty and the Beast** (France, 2014).

Le Pacte de Loups

In the vein of the original 1967 broadcast, the next dramatised reconstruction came in 2003, directed by Patrick Volson and imaginatively entitled **La Bête du Gévaudan**. Although it can claim to be the most accurate of dramatisations, one must remember that it's mainly up against Gans' kung-fu stylings and Borowczyk's sleazefest, which may damn it with faint praise. On the several occasions that the film deviates from the historical record, it is for no reason better than dramatic license.

La Bête du Gévaudan (2003)

After that, what with the coming of the internet and everything, it was open season on Beast docos and the flood-gates were opened.

Poster for Cocteau's 1946 adaptation by Jean-Denis Malclès

BEAUTY AND THE BEAST

BY
Marie Leprince de Beaumont

There was once a very rich merchant, who had six children, three sons, and three daughters; being a man of sense, he spared no cost for their education, but gave them all kinds of masters. His daughters were extremely handsome, especially the youngest; when she was little, every body admired her, and called her *The little Beauty*; so that, as she grew up, she still went by the name of *Beauty*, which made her sisters very jealous. The youngest, as she was handsome, was also better than her sisters. The two eldest had a great deal of pride, because they were rich. They gave themselves ridiculous airs, and would not visit other merchants' daughters, nor keep company with any but persons of quality. They went out every day upon parties of pleasure, balls, plays, concerts, etc. and laughed at their youngest sister, because she spent the greatest part of her time in reading good books. As it was known that they were to have great fortunes, several eminent merchants made their addresses to them; but the two eldest said they would never marry, unless they could meet with a Duke, or an Earl at least. Beauty very civilly thanked them that courted her, and told them she was too young yet to marry, but chose to stay with her father a few years longer.

All at once the merchant lost his whole fortune, excepting a small country-house at a great distance from town, and told his children, with tears in his eyes, they most go there and work for their living. The two eldest answered, that they would not leave the town, for they had several lovers, who they were sure would be glad to have them, though they had no fortune; but in this they were mistaken, for their lovers slighted and forsook them in their poverty. As they were not beloved on account of their pride, every body said, "they do not deserve to be pitied, we are glad to see their pride humbled, let them go and give themselves quality airs in milking the cows and minding their dairy. But," added they, "we are extremely concerned for Beauty, she was such a charming, sweet-tempered creature, spoke so kindly to poor people, and was of such an affable, obliging disposition." Nay, several gentlemen would have married her, though they knew she had not a penny; but she told them she could not think of leaving her poor father in his misfortunes, but was determined to go along with him into the country to comfort and attend him. Poor Beauty at first was sadly grieved at the loss of her fortune; "but," she said to herself, "were I to cry ever so much, that would not make things better, I must try to make myself happy without a fortune." When they came to their country-house, the merchant and his three sons applied themselves to husbandry and tillage; and Beauty rose at four in the morning, and made haste to have the house clean, and breakfast ready for the family. In the beginning she found it very difficult, for she had not been used to work as a servant; but in less than two months she grew stronger and healthier than ever. After she had done her work, she read, played on the harpsichord, or else sung whilst she spun. On the contrary, her two sisters did not know how to spend their time; they got up at ten, and did nothing but saunter about the whole day, lamenting the loss of their fine clothes and acquaintance.

"Do but see our youngest sister," said they one to the other, "what a poor, stupid mean-spirited creature she is, to be contented with such an unhappy situation." The good merchant was of a quite different opinion; he knew very well that Beauty out-shone her sisters, in her person as well as her mind, and admired her humility, industry, and patience; for her sisters not only left her all the work of the house to do, but insulted her every moment.

The family had lived about a year in this retirement, when the merchant received a letter, with an account that a vessel, on board of which he had effects, was safely arrived. This news had liked to have turned the heads of the two eldest daughters, who immediately flattered themselves with the hopes of returning to town; for they were quite weary of a country life; and when they saw their father ready to set out, they begged of him to buy them new gowns, caps, rings, and all manner of trifles; but Beauty asked for nothing, for she thought to herself, that all the money her father was going to receive would scarce be sufficient to purchase every thing her sisters wanted.

"What will you have, Beauty?" said her father.

"Since you are so kind as to think of me," answered she, "be so kind as to bring me a rose, for as none grow hereabouts, they are a kind of rarity." Not that Beauty cared for a rose, but she asked for something, lest she should seem by her example to condemn her sisters' conduct, who would have said she did it only to look particular. The good man went on his journey; but when he came there, they went to law with him about the merchandize, and after a great deal of trouble and pains to no purpose, he came back as poor as before.

He was within thirty miles of his own house, thinking on the pleasure he should have in seeing his children again, when going through a large forest he lost himself. It rained and snowed terribly, besides, the wind was so high, that it threw him twice off his horse; and night coming on, he began to apprehend being either starved to death with cold and hunger, or else devoured by the wolves, whom he heard howling all around him, when, on a sudden, looking through a long walk of trees, he saw a light at some distance, and going on a little farther, perceived it came from a palace illuminated from top to bottom. The merchant returned God thanks for this happy discovery, and hasted to the palace; but was greatly surprised at not meeting with anyone in the out-courts. His horse followed him, and seeing a large stable open, went in, and finding both hay and oats, the poor beast, who was almost famished, fell to eating very heartily. The merchant tied him up to the manger, and walked towards the house, where he saw no one, but entering into a large hall, he found a good fire, and a table plentifully set out, with but one cover laid. As he was wet quite through with the rain and snow, he drew near the fire to dry himself.

"I hope," said he, "the master of the house, or his servants, will excuse the liberty I take; I suppose it will not be long before some of them appear."

He waited a considerable time, till it struck eleven, and still nobody came: at last he was so hungry that he could stay no longer, but took a chicken and ate it in two mouthfuls, trembling all the while. After this, he drank a few glasses of wine, and growing more courageous, he went out of the hall, and crossed through several grand apartments with magnificent furniture, till he came into a chamber, which had an exceeding good bed in it, and as he was very much fatigued, and it was past midnight, he concluded it was best to shut the door, and go to bed.

It was ten the next morning before the merchant waked, and as he was going to rise, he was astonished to see a good suit of clothes in the room of his own, which were quite spoiled.

"Certainly," said he, "this palace belongs to some kind fairy, who has seen and pitied my distress." He looked through a window, but instead of snow saw the most delightful arbours, interwoven with the most beautiful flowers that ever were beheld. He then returned to the great hall, where he had supped the night before, and found some chocolate ready made on a little table.

"Thank you, good Madam Fairy," said he aloud, "for being so careful as to provide me a breakfast; I am extremely obliged to you for all your favours."

The good man drank his chocolate, and then went to look for his horse; but passing through an arbour of roses, he remembered Beauty's request to him, and gathered a branch on which were several; immediately he heard a great noise, and saw such a frightful beast coming towards him, that he was ready to faint away.

"You are very ungrateful," said the beast to him, in a terrible voice "I have saved your life by receiving you into my castle, and, in return, you steal my roses, which I value beyond any thing in the universe; but you shall die for it; I give you but a quarter of an hour to prepare

yourself, to say your prayers." The merchant fell on his knees, and lifted up both his hands:

"My Lord" said he, "I beseech you to forgive me, indeed I had no intention to offend in gathering a rose for one of my daughters, who desired me to bring her one."

"My name is not My Lord," replied the monster, "but Beast; I don't love compliments, not I; I like people should speak as they think; and so do not imagine I am to be moved by any of your flattering speeches; but you say you have got daughters; I will forgive you, on condition that one of them come willingly, and suffer for you. Let me have no words, but go about your business, and swear that if your daughter refuse to die in your stead, you will return within three months." The merchant had no mind to sacrifice his daughters to the ugly monster, but he thought, in obtaining this respite, he should have the satisfaction of seeing them once more; so he promised upon oath, he would return, and the Beast told him he might set out when he pleased;

"but," added he, "you shall not depart empty handed; go back to the room where you lay, and you will see a great empty chest; fill it with whatever you like best, and I will send it to your home," and at the same time Beast withdrew.

"Well" said the good man to himself "if I must die, I shall have the comfort, at least, of leaving something to my poor children."

He returned to the bed-chamber, and finding a great quantity of broad pieces of gold, he filled the great chest the Beast had mentioned, locked it, and afterwards took his horse out of the stable, leaving the palace with as much grief as he had entered it with joy. The horse, of his own accord, took one of the roads of the forest; and in a few hours the good man was at home. His children came around him, but, instead of receiving their embraces with pleasure, he looked on them, and, holding up the branch he had in his hands, he burst into tears.

"Here, Beauty," said he, "take these roses; but little do you think how dear they are like to cost your unhappy father; and then related his fatal adventure: immediately the two eldest set up lamentable outcries, and said all manner of ill-natured things to Beauty, who did not cry at all.

"Do but see the pride of that little wretch," said they); she would not ask for fine clothes, as we did; but no, truly, Miss wanted to distinguish herself; so now she will be the death of our poor father, and yet she does not so much as shed a tear."

"Why should I," answered Beauty, "it would be very needless, for my father shall not suffer upon my account, since the monster will accept of one of his daughters, I will deliver myself up to all his fury, and I am very happy in thinking that my death will save my father's life, and be a proof of my tender love for him."

"No, sister," said her three brothers, "that shall not be, we will go find the monster, and either kill him, or perish in the attempt."

"Do not imagine any such thing, my sons," said the merchant, "Beast's power is so great, that I have no hopes of your overcoming him; I am charmed with Beauty's kind and generous offer, but I cannot yield to it; I am old, and have not long to live, so can only lose a few years, which I regret for your sakes alone, my dear children."

"Indeed, father" said Beauty), you shall not go to the palace without me, you cannot hinder me from following you." It was to no purpose all they could say, Beauty still insisted on setting out for the fine palace; and her sisters were delighted at it, for her virtue and amiable qualities made them envious and jealous.

The merchant was so afflicted at the thoughts of losing his daughter, that he had quite forgot the chest full of gold; but at night, when he retired to rest, no sooner had he shut his chamber-door, than, to his great astonishment, he found it by his bedside; he was determined, however, not to tell his children that he was grown rich, because they would have wanted to return to town, and he was resolved not to leave the country; but he trusted Beauty with the secret: who informed him, that two gentlemen came in his absence, and courted her sisters; she begged her father to consent to their marriage, and give them fortunes; for she was so good, that she loved them, and forgave them heartily all their ill-usage. These wicked creatures rubbed their eyes with an onion, to force some tears when they parted with their sister; but her brothers were really concerned. Beauty was the only one who did not shed tears at parting, because she would not increase their uneasiness.

The horse took the direct road to the palace; and towards evening they perceived it illuminated as at first: the horse went of himself into the stable, and the good man and his daughter came into the great hall, where they found a table splendidly served up, and two covers. The merchant had no heart to eat; but Beauty endeavoured to appear cheerful, sat down to table, and helped him. Afterwards, thought she to herself,

"Beast surely has a mind to fatten me before he eats me, since he provides such a plentiful entertainment." When they had supped, they heard a great noise, and the merchant, all in tears, bid his poor child farewell; for he thought Beast was coming. Beauty was sadly terrified at his horrid form, but she took courage as well as she could, and the monster having asked her if she came willingly; "y—e—s," said she, trembling.

"You are very good, and I am greatly obliged to you; honest man, go your ways tomorrow morning, but never think of returning here again. Farewell, Beauty."

"Farewell, Beast," answered she; and immediately the monster withdrew.

"Oh, daughter," said the merchant, embracing Beauty, "I am almost frightened to death; believe me, you had better go back, and let me stay here."

"No, father," said Beauty, in a resolute tone, "you shall set out tomorrow morning, and leave me to the care and protection of Providence." They went to bed, and thought they should not close their eyes all night; but scarce were they laid down, than they fell fast asleep; and Beauty dreamed, a fine lady came, and said to her,

"I am content, Beauty, with your good will; this good action of yours, in giving up your own life to save your father's, shall not go unrewarded." Beauty waked, and told her father her dream, and though it helped to comfort him a little, yet he could not help crying bitterly, when he took leave of his dear child.

As soon as he was gone, Beauty sat down in the great hall, and fell a crying likewise; but as she was mistress of a great deal of resolution, she recommended herself to God, and resolved not to be uneasy the little time she had to live; for she firmly believed Beast would eat her up that night.

However, she thought she might as well walk about till then, and view this fine castle, which she could not help admiring; it was a delightful pleasant place, and she was extremely surprised at seeing a door, over which was wrote,

BEAUTY'S APARTMENT.

She opened it hastily, and was quite dazzled with the magnificence that reigned throughout; but what chiefly took up her attention, was a large library, a harpsichord, and several music books.

"Well," said she to herself, "I see they will not let my time hang heavy on my hands for want of amusement." Then she reflected,

"Were I but to stay here a day, there would not have been all these preparations." This consideration inspired her with fresh courage; and opening the library, she took a book, and read these words in letters of gold:–

Welcome, Beauty, banish fear,
You are queen and mistress here;
Speak your wishes, speak your will,
Swift obedience meets them still.

"Alas," said she, with a sigh, "there is nothing I desire so much as to see my poor father, and to know what he is doing." She had no sooner said this, when casting her eyes on a great looking-glass, to her great amazement she saw her own home, where her father arrived with a very dejected countenance; her sisters went to meet him, and, notwithstanding their endeavours to appear sorrowful, their joy, felt for having got rid of their sister, was visible in every feature: a moment after, every thing disappeared, and Beauty's apprehensions at this proof of Beast's complaisance.

At noon she found dinner ready, and while at table, was entertained with an excellent concert of music, though without seeing any body: but at night, as she was going to sit down to supper, she heard the noise Beast made; and could not help being sadly terrified.

"Beauty," said the monster, "will you give me leave to see you sup?"

"That is as you please," answered Beauty, trembling.

"No," replied the Beast, "you alone are mistress here; you need only bid me be gone, if my presence is troublesome, and I will immediately withdraw: but tell me, do not you think me very ugly?"

"That is true," said Beauty, "for I cannot tell a lie; but I believe you are very good-natured."

"So I am," said the monster, "but then, besides my ugliness, I have no sense; I know very well that I am a poor, silly, stupid creature."

"'Tis no sign of folly to think so," replied Beauty, "for never did fool know this, or had so humble a conceit of his own understanding."

"Eat then, Beauty," said the monster, "and endeavour to amuse yourself in your palace; for every thing here is yours, and I should be very uneasy if you were not happy."

"You are very obliging," answered Beauty; "I own I am pleased with your kindness, and when I consider that, your deformity scarce appears."

"Yes, yes," said the Beast, "my heart is good, but still I am a monster."

"Among mankind," says Beauty, "there are many that deserve that name more than you, and I prefer you, just as your are, to those, who, under a human form, hide a treacherous, corrupt, and ungrateful heart."

"If I had sense enough," replied the Beast, "I would make a fine compliment to thank you, but I am so dull, that I can only say, I am greatly obliged to you." Beauty ate a hearty supper, and had almost conquered her dread of the monster; but she had liked to have fainted away, when he said to her,

"Beauty, will you be my wife?" She was some time before she durst answer; for she was afraid of making him angry, if she refused. At last, however, she said, trembling,

"No, Beast." Immediately the poor monster began to sigh, and hissed so frightfully, that the whole palace echoed. But Beauty soon recovered her fright, for Beast having said, in a mournful voice,

"then farewell, Beauty," left the room; and only turned back, now and then, to look at her as he went out.

When Beauty was alone, she felt a great deal of compassion for poor Beast.

"Alas," said she, "'tis a thousand pities any thing so good-natured should be so ugly."

Beauty spent three months very contentedly in the palace: every evening Beast paid her a visit, and talked to her during supper, very rationally, with plain good common sense, but never with what the world calls wit;

and Beauty daily discovered some valuable qualifications in the monster; and seeing him often, had so accustomed her to his deformity, that, far from dreading the time of his visit, she would often look on her watch to see when it would be nine; for the Beast never missed coming at that hour. There was but one thing that gave Beauty any concern, which was, that every night, before she went to bed, the monster always asked her, if she would be his wife. One day she said to him,

"Beast, you make me very uneasy, I wish I could consent to marry you, but I am too sincere to make you believe that will ever happen: I shall always esteem you as a friend; endeavour to be satisfied with this."

"I must, said the Beast, for, alas! I know too well my own misfortune; but then I love you with the tenderest affection: however, I ought to think myself happy that you will stay here; promise me never to leave me." Beauty blushed at these words; she had seen in her glass, that her father had pined himself sick for the loss of her, and she longed to see him again.

"I could," answered she), indeed promise never to leave you entirely, but I have so great a desire to see my father, that I shall fret to death, if you refuse me that satisfaction."

"I had rather die myself," said the monster, "than give you the least uneasiness: I will send you to your father, you shall remain with him, and poor Beast will die with grief."

"No," said Beauty, weeping, "I love you too well to be the cause of your death: I give you my promise to return in a week: you have shewn me that my sisters are married, and my brothers gone to the army; only let me stay a week with my father, as he is alone."

"You shall be there tomorrow morning," said the Beast, "but remember your promise: you need only lay your ring on the table before you go to bed, when you have a mind to come back: farewell, Beauty." Beast sighed as usual, bidding her good night; and Beauty went to bed very sad at seeing him so afflicted. When she waked the next morning, she found herself at her father's, and having rang a little bell, that was by her bed-side, she saw the maid come; who, the moment she saw her, gave a loud shriek; at which the good man ran up stairs, and thought he should have died with joy to see his dear daughter again. He held her fast locked in his arms above a quarter of an hour. As soon as the first transports were over, Beauty began to think of rising, and was afraid she had no clothes to put on; but the maid told her, that she had just found, in the next room, a large trunk full of gowns, covered with gold and diamonds. Beauty thanked good Beast for his kind care, and taking one of the plainest of them, she intended to make a present of the others to her sisters. She scarce had said so, when the trunk disappeared. Her father told her, that Beast insisted on her keeping them herself; and immediately both gowns and trunk came back again.

Beauty dressed herself; and in the mean time they sent to her sisters, who hasted thither with their husbands. They were both of them very unhappy. The eldest had married a gentleman, extremely handsome indeed, but so fond of his own person, that he was full of nothing but his own dear self, and neglected his wife. The second had married a man of wit, but he only made use of it to plague and torment every body, and his wife most of all. Beauty's sisters sickened with envy, when they saw her dressed like a Princess, and more beautiful than ever; nor could all her obliging affectionate behaviour stifle their jealousy, which was ready to burst when she told them how happy she was. They went down into the garden to vent it in tears; and said one to the other,

"In what is this little creature better than us, that she should be so much happier?"

"Sister, said the eldest, a thought just strikes my mind; let us endeavour to detain her above a week, and perhaps the silly monster will be so enraged at her for breaking her word, that he will devour her."

"Right, sister, answered the other, therefore we must shew her as much kindness as possible." After they had taken this resolution, they went up, and behaved so affectionately to their sister, that poor Beauty wept for joy. When the week was expired, they cried and tore their hair, and seemed so sorry to part with her, that she promised to stay a week longer.

In the mean time, Beauty could not help reflecting on herself for the uneasiness she was likely to cause poor Beast, whom she sincerely loved, and really longed to see again. The tenth night she spent at her father's, she dreamed she was in the palace garden, and that she saw Beast extended on the grass-plot, who seemed just expiring, and, in a dying voice, reproached her with her ingratitude. Beauty started out of her sleep and bursting into tears,

"Am not I very wicked," said she "to act so unkindly to Beast, that has studied so much to please me in every thing? Is it his fault that he is so ugly, and has so little sense? He is kind and good, and that is sufficient. Why did I refuse to marry him? I should be happier with the monster than my sisters are with their husbands; it is neither wit nor a fine person in a husband, that makes a woman happy; but virtue, sweetness of temper, and complaisance: and Beast has all these valuable qualifications. It is true, I do not feel the tenderness of affection for him, but I find I have the highest gratitude, esteem, and friendship; and I will not make him miserable; were I to be so ungrateful, I should never forgive myself." Beauty having said this, rose, put her ring on the table, and then laid down again; scarce was she in bed before she fell asleep; and when she waked the next morning, she was overjoyed to find herself in the Beast's palace. She put on one of her richest suits to please him, and waited for evening with the utmost impatience; at last the wished-for hour came, the clock struck nine, yet no Beast appeared. Beauty then feared she had been the cause of his death; she ran crying and wringing her hands all about the palace, like one in despair; after having sought for him every where, she recollected her dream, and flew to the canal in the garden, where she dreamed she saw him. There she found poor Beast stretched out, quite senseless, and, as she

imagined, dead. She threw herself upon him without any dread, and finding his heart beat still, she fetched some water from the canal, and poured it on his head. Beast opened his eyes, and said to Beauty,

"You forgot your promise, and I was so afflicted for having lost you, that I resolved to starve myself; but since I have the happiness of seeing you once more, I die satisfied."

"No, dear Beast," said Beauty, "you must not die; live to be my husband; from this moment I give you my hand, and swear to be none but yours. Alas! I thought I had only a friendship for you, but, the grief I now feel convinces me, that I cannot live without you." Beauty scarcely had pronounced these words, when she saw the palace sparkle with light; and fireworks, instruments of music, every thing, seemed to give notice of some great event: but nothing could fix her attention; she turned to her dear Beast, for whom she trembled with fear; but how great was her surprise! Beast had disappeared, and she saw, at her feet, one of the loveliest Princes that eye ever beheld, who returned her thanks for having put an end to the charm, under which he had so long resembled a Beast. Though this Prince was worthy of all her attention, she could not forbear asking where Beast was.

"You see him at your feet," said the Prince): a wicked fairy had condemned me to remain under that shape till a beautiful virgin should consent to marry me: the fairy likewise enjoined me to conceal my understanding; there was only you in the world generous enough to be won by the goodness of my temper; and in offering you my crown, I can't discharge the obligations I have to you." Beauty, agreeably surprised, gave the charming Prince her hand to rise; they went together into the castle, and Beauty was overjoyed to find, in the great hall, her father and his whole family, whom the beautiful lady, that appeared to her in her dream, had conveyed thither.

"Beauty," said this lady, "come and receive the reward of your judicious choice; you have preferred virtue before either wit or beauty, and deserve to find a person in whom all these qualifications are united: you are going to be a great Queen; I hope the throne will not lessen your virtue, or make you forget yourself. As to you, ladies," said the Fairy to Beauty's two sisters, "I know your hearts, and all the malice they contain: become two statues; but, under this transformation, still retain your reason. You shall stand before your sister's palace gate, and be it your punishment to behold her happiness; and it will not be in your power to return to your former state till you own your faults; but I am very much afraid that you will always remain statues. Pride, anger, gluttony, and idleness, are sometimes conquered, but the conversion of a malicious and envious mind is a kind of miracle." Immediately the fairy gave a stroke with her wand, and in a moment all that were in the hall were transported into the Prince's palace. His subjects received him with joy; he married Beauty, and lived with her many years; and their happiness, as it was founded on virtue, was complete.

FINIS

*Illustrations by
W. Heath Robinson*

LOKIS

from the ms. of Professor Wittembach

by Prosper Mérimée

> Prosper Mérimée's 1869 story was filmed in Poland in 1970, directed by Janusz Majewski. It earned Majewski the "Best feature film director ex-aequo" award at the 14th International Festival of Science Fiction and Horror Films, Sitges, Spain and a number of Polish film awards.
>
> ◀ This striking Cuban poster is by Eduardo Muñoz Bachs.

I

"Théodore," said Professor Wittembach, "please give me that manuscript-book, bound in parchment, which is laid on the second shelf above my writing-desk—no, not that one, but the small octavo volume. I copied all the notes of my journal of 1866 in it—at least those that relate to Count Szémioth."

The Professor put on his glasses, and, amid profound silence, read the following:—

LOKIS

with this Lithuanian proverb as a motto:

*Miszka su Lokiu,
Abu du tokiu.*[1]

* * *

When the first translation of the Holy Scriptures into the Lithuanian language appeared in London, I published in the *Scientific and Literary Gazette* of Koenigsberg, an article wherein, while rendering full justice to the efforts of the learned interpreter and to the pious motives of the Bible Society, I pointed out several slight errors, and showed, moreover, that this version could only be useful to one portion of the Lithuanian people.

Indeed, the dialect from which they translated is hardly intelligible to the inhabitants of the districts where the *Jomaïtic* tongue, commonly called *Jmoude*, is spoken, namely, in the Palatinate of Samogitia. This language is, perhaps, nearer akin to the Sanskrit than to High Lithuanian. In spite of the furious criticisms which this observation drew down upon me from a certain well-known professor of the Dorpat University, it so far enlightened the members of the Committee of the Bible Society that they lost no time in making me a flattering offer to direct and supervise an edition of the Gospel of St. Matthew into Samogitian. I was too much occupied at the time with my researches in Trans-Uralian dialects to undertake a more extended work comprising all four of the Gospels. Deferring my marriage with Mlle. Gertrude Weber, I went to Kowno (Kaunas) for the purpose of collecting all the linguistic records, whether printed or in MSS., of Jmoude, that I could lay hands on. I did not overlook, of course, old ballads (*daïnos*), tales, or legends (*pasakos*) which would furnish me with material for a Jomaïtic vocabulary, a work which must necessarily precede that of translation.

I had been given a letter of introduction to the young Count Michel Szémioth, whose father, I was told, had come into the possession of the famous *Catechismus Samogiticus* of Father Lawiçki. It was so rare that its very existence had been disputed, particularly by the Dorpat professor to whom allusion has been already made. In his library I should find, according to the information given me, an old collection of *daïnos*, besides ballads in old Prussian. Having written to Count Szémioth to lay the object of my visit before him, I received a most courteous invitation to spend as much time at his Castle of Médintiltas as my researches might need. He ended his letter by very gracefully saying that he prided himself upon speaking Jmoude almost as well as his peasants, and would be only too pleased to help me in what he termed so important and interesting an undertaking. Besides being one of the wealthiest landowners in Lithuania, he was of the same evangelical faith of which I had the honour to be a minister. I had been warned that the Count was not without a certain peculiarity of character, but he was very hospitable, especially towards all who had intellectual tastes. So I set out on my journey to Médintiltas.

At the Castle steps I was met by the Count's steward, who immediately led me to the rooms prepared for me.

"M. le Comte," he said, "is most sorry not to be able to dine with you to-day. He has a bad headache, a malady he is unfortunately subject to. If you do not prefer to dine in your room you can dine with the Countess's doctor, Dr. Froeber. Dinner will be ready in an hour; do not trouble to dress for it. If you have any orders to give, there is the bell."

He withdrew, making me a profound salute.

The room was of immense size, comfortably furnished, and decorated with mirrors and gilding. One side of it looked out upon a garden, or rather the park belonging to the Castle, and the other upon the principal entrance. Notwithstanding the statement that there was no need to dress, I felt obliged to get my black coat out of my trunk, and was in my shirt-sleeves busy unpacking my simple luggage when the sound of carriage wheels attracted me to the window which looked on the court. A handsome barouche had just come in. It contained a lady in black, a gentleman, and a woman dressed in the Lithuanian peasant costume, but so tall and strong-looking that at first I took her for a man in disguise. She stepped out first; two other women, not less robust in appearance, were already standing on the steps. The gentleman leant over the lady dressed in black, and, to my great surprise, unbuckled a broad leather belt which held her to her seat in the carriage. I noticed that this lady had long white hair, very much dishevelled, and that her large, wide-opened eyes were vacant in expression. She looked like a waxen figure. After

---

1 "The two together make a pair"; word for word, Michon (Michael) with Lokis, both are the same. **Michaelium cum Lokide, ambo [duo] ipsissimi.**

having untied her, her companion spoke to her very respectfully, hat in hand; but she appeared not to pay the slightest attention to him. He then turned to the servants and made a slight sign with his head. Immediately the three women took hold of the lady in black, lifted her out as though she were a feather, and carried her into the Castle, in spite of her efforts to cling to the carriage. The scene was witnessed by several of the house servants, who did not appear to think it anything extraordinary.

The gentleman who had directed the proceedings drew out his watch, and asked how soon dinner would be ready.

"In a quarter of an hour, doctor," was the reply.

I guessed at once that this was Dr. Froeber, and that the lady in black was the Countess. From her age I concluded she was the mother of Count Szémioth, and the precautionary measures taken concerning her told me clearly enough that her reason was affected.

Some moments later the doctor himself came to my room.

"As the Count is indisposed," he said to me, "I must introduce myself to you. I am Dr. Froeber, at your service, and I am delighted to make the acquaintance of a savant known to all readers of the *Scientific and Literary Gazette* of Koenigsberg. Have you been properly waited on?"

I replied to his compliments as well as I could, and told him that if it was time to go down to dinner I was ready to accompany him.

When we were in the dining-hall, a major-domo brought us liqueurs and several piquant and highly spiced dishes on a silver salver to induce appetite, after a northern custom.

"Allow me, sir, in my office as doctor, to recommend a glass of that *Starka*, a true Cognac brandy casked forty years ago. It is a queen of liqueurs. Take a Drontheim anchovy; nothing is better for opening and preparing the digestive organs, the most important functions of the body.... And now to table. Why do we not speak in German? You come from Koenigsberg, I from Memel; but I took my degree at Jéna. We shall be more at ease in that way, and the servants, who only know Polish and Russian, will not understand us."

We ate at first in silence; then, after having taken our first glass of Madeira, I inquired of the doctor if the Count were often inconvenienced by the indisposition which deprived us of his presence that night.

"Yes and no," was the doctor's answer. "It depends upon what expeditions he takes."

"How so?"

"When he takes the road to Rosienie, for instance, he comes back with headache, and in a savage temper."

"I have been to Rosienie myself without such an experience."

"It depends, Professor," he replied, laughing, "on whether you are in love."

I sighed, thinking of Mlle. Gertrude Weber.

"Does the Count's *fiancée*, then, live at Rosienie?" I said.

"Yes, in that neighbourhood; but I cannot say whether she is affianced to him. She is a real flirt, and will drive him off his head, so that he will be in his mother's state."

"Indeed, then her ladyship is ... an invalid?"

"She is mad, my dear sir, mad; and I was even madder to come here!"

"Let us hope that your able attentions will restore her to reason."

The doctor shook his head, and looked attentively at the colour of the glass of Bordeaux which he held in his hand.

"The man you see before you, Professor, was once surgeon-major in the Kalouga regiment. At Sevastopol we cut off arms and legs from morning till night; not to speak of bombs which came down among us as thick as flies on a galled horse. But, though I was then ill-lodged and ill-fed, I was not so bored as I am here, where I eat and drink of the best, am lodged like a prince, and paid like a Court physician.... But liberty, my dear sir!... As you can guess, with this she-dragon I have not a moment to call my own."

"Has she been under your care for long?"

"Less than two years; but she has been insane at least twenty-seven, since before the birth of the Count. Did no one tell you this either at Rosienie or Kowno? Listen, then, for it is a case on which I should like some day to write an article for the *Medical Journal* of St. Petersburg. She went mad from fear...."

"From fear? How was such a thing possible?"

"She had a fright. She is of the house of Keystut.... Oh, there are no *mésalliances* in this house. We descend from the Gédymin.... Well, Professor, two or three days after her marriage, which took place in the castle where we are dining (I drink to your health ...), the Count, the father of the present one, went out hunting. Our Lithuanian ladies are regular amazons, you know. The Countess accompanied him to the hunt.... She stayed behind, or got in advance of the huntsmen,... I do not know which,... when, all at once, the Count saw the Countess's little Cossack, a lad of twelve or fourteen, come up at full gallop.

"'Master!' he said, 'a bear has carried off the Countess.'

"'Where?' cried the Count.

"'Over there,' replied the boy-Cossack.

"All the hunt ran towards the spot he pointed out, but no Countess was to be seen. Her strangled horse lay on one side, and on the other her lambs-wool cloak. They searched and beat the wood on all sides. At last a huntsman cried out, 'There is the bear!' and, sure enough, the bear crossed a clearing, dragging the Countess, no doubt for the purpose of devouring her undisturbed, into a thicket, for these beasts are great gourmands; they like to dine at ease, as the monks. Married but a couple of days, the Count was most chivalrous. He tried to fling himself upon the bear, hunting knife in his fist; but, my dear sir, a Lithuanian bear does not let himself be run through like a stag. By good fortune the Count's gun-bearer, a queer, low fellow, so drunk that morning as to be unable to tell a rabbit from a hare, fired his rifle, more than a hundred paces off, without taking care whether the bullet hit the beast or the lady...."

"And he killed the bear?"

"Stone dead. It takes a tipsy man to hit like that. There are also predestined bullets, Professor. There are sorcerers here who sell them at a moderate price.... The Countess was terribly torn, unconscious, of course, and had one leg broken. They carried her home, and she recovered consciousness, but her reason had gone. They took her to St. Petersburg for a special consultation of four doctors, who glittered with orders. They said that Madam was *enceinte*, and that a favourable turn might be expected after her delivery. She was to be kept in fresh air in the country, and given whey and codéine. Each physician received about a hundred roubles. Nine months later the Countess gave birth to a fine, healthy boy, but where was the 'favourable turn'? Ah, yes, indeed ... there was nothing but redoubled frenzy. The Count showed her her son. In novels that never fails to produce a good effect. 'Kill it! kill the beast!' she yelled; a little longer, and she would have wrung his neck. Ever since there have been phases of stupid imbecility, alternating with violent mania. There is a strong suicidal tendency. We are obliged to strap her down to make her take fresh air, and it takes three strong servants to hold her in. Nevertheless, Professor, I ask you to note this fact, when I have exhausted my Latin on her without making her obey me, I have a resort that quietens her. I threaten to cut off her hair. I fancy she must have had very beautiful hair at one time. Vanity! It is the sole human feeling left. Is it not odd? If I could experiment upon her as I chose, I might perhaps be able to cure her."

"By what method?"

"By thrashing her. I cured in that way twenty peasant women in a village where the terrible Russian madness (the *hurlement*[2]) had broken out. One woman begins to howl, then her companion follows, and in three days' time the whole village is howling mad. I put an end to it by flogging them. (Take a little chicken, it is very tender.) The Count would never allow me to try the experiment."

"What! you wanted him to consent to your atrocious treatment?"

"Oh, he had known his mother so little, and besides it was for her good; but tell me, Professor, have you ever held that fear could drive anyone mad?"

"The Countess's situation was frightful ... to find herself in the claws of a savage beast!"

"All the same, her son does not take after her. A year ago he was in exactly the same predicament, but, thanks to his coolness, he had a marvellous escape."

"From the claws of a bear?"

"A she-bear, the largest seen for some time. The Count wanted to attack her, boar-spear in hand, but with one back stroke she parried the blade, clutched the Count, and felled him to the ground as easily as I could upset this bottle. He cunningly feigned death.... The bear smelt and sniffed him, then, instead of tearing him to pieces, she gave him a lick with her tongue. He had the presence of mind not to move, and she went on her way."

"She thought that he was dead. I have been told that these animals will not eat a dead body."

"We will endeavour to believe that is so, and abstain from making personal investigation of the question. But, apropos of fear, let me tell you what happened at Sevastopol. Five or six of us were sitting behind the ambulance of the famous bastion No. 5, round a pot of beer which had been brought us. The sentry cried, 'A shell!' and we all lay flat on our stomachs. No, not all of us: a fellow named ... but it is not necessary to give his name ... a young officer who had just come to us, remained standing up, holding his glass full, just when the shell burst. It carried off the head of my poor comrade André Speranski, a brave lad, and broke the pitcher, which, fortunately, was nearly empty. When we got up after the explosion we saw, in the midst of the smoke, that our friend had swallowed his last mouthful of beer just as though nothing had happened. We dubbed him a hero. The following day I met Captain Ghédéonof coming out of the hospital. 'I dine with you fellows to-day,' he said, 'and to celebrate my return I will stand the champagne.' We sat down to the table, and the young officer of the beer was there. He did not wait for the champagne. A bottle was being uncorked near him, and fizz! the cork hit him on the temple. He uttered a cry and fainted away. Believe me, my hero had been devilishly afraid the first time, and his drinking the beer instead of getting out of the way showed that he had lost the control of his mind, and only unconscious mechanical movements remained to him. Indeed, Professor, the human mechanism—"

"Sir," said a servant who had just come into the room, "Jdanova says that the Countess will not take her food."

"Devil take her!" growled the doctor. "I must go to her. When I have made my she-dragon eat, Professor, if agreeable to you, we will take a hand at *préférence* or at *douratchki*."

---

[2] The Russian for one possessed is "a howler"; **klikoucha**, the root of which is **klik**, clamour, howling.

I expressed my regret that I was ignorant of the games, and, when he had gone to see the invalid, I went up to my room and wrote to Mlle. Gertrude.

II

It was a warm night, and I had left open the window overlooking the park. I did not feel ready for sleep after I finished my letter, so I set to work to rehearse the irregular Lithuanian verbs, and to look into Sanskrit to find the origins of their different irregularities. In the middle of my absorbing labours a tree close to my window shook violently. I could hear the dead branches creak, and it seemed as though some heavy animal were trying to climb it. Still engrossed with the bear stories that the doctor had told me, I got up, feeling rather uneasy, and saw, only a few feet from my window, a human head among the leaves of the tree, lit up plainly by the light from my lamp. The vision only lasted a second, but the singular brilliance of the eyes which met my gaze struck me more than I could say. Involuntarily I took a step backwards; then I ran to the window and demanded in severe tones what the intruder wanted. Meanwhile he climbed down quickly, and, seizing a large branch between both hands, he swung himself off, jumped to the ground, and was soon out of sight. I rang the bell and told the adventure to a servant who answered it.

"Sir," he said, "you must be mistaken."

"I am certain of what I tell you," I replied. "I am afraid there is a burglar in the park."

"It is impossible, sir."

"Well, then, is it someone out of the house?" The servant opened his eyes wide without replying, and in the end asked me if I wanted anything. I told him to fasten my window, and I went to bed.

I slept soundly, neither dreaming of bears nor of thieves. In the morning, while I was dressing, someone knocked at my door. I opened it and found myself face to face with a very tall and finely built young man in a Bokhara dressing-gown, holding in his hand a long Turkish pipe.

"I come to beg your pardon, Professor," he said, "for having welcomed such a distinguished guest so badly. I am Count Szémioth."

I hastened to say that, on the contrary, my humble thanks were due to him for his most courteous hospitality, and inquired if he had lost his headache.

"Very nearly," he said. "At all events, until the next crisis," he added, with a melancholy expression. "Are you comfortable here? You must not forget that you are among barbarians; it would be difficult to think otherwise in Samogitia."

I assured him I was most comfortably entertained. All the time I was speaking I could not prevent myself from studying him with a very impolite curiosity; there was something strange in his look which reminded me, in spite of myself, of the man whom I had seen climbing the tree the night before....

"But what probability," I said to myself, "is there that Count Szémioth would climb trees by night?"

His forehead was high and well—developed, although rather narrow. His features were large and regular, but his eyes were too close together, and I did not think that, measured from one lacrymal gland to the other, there was the width of an eye, the canon of Greek sculptors. His glance was piercing. Our eyes met several times, in spite of ourselves, and we looked at each other with some embarrassment. All at once the Count burst out laughing.

"You recognise me!" he said.

"Recognise you?"

"Yes, you detected me yesterday playing a scoundrelly part."

"Oh! Monsieur le Comte!"

"I had passed a suffering day shut up in my bedroom. As I was somewhat better at night I went for a walk in the garden. I saw your light and yielded to curiosity.... I ought to have told you who I was, and introduced myself properly, but I was in such a ridiculous situation.... I was ashamed, and so I fled.... Will you excuse me for having disturbed you in the midst of your work?"

He said all this with a would-be playful air; but he blushed, and was evidently confused. I did my best to reassure him that I did not retain any unpleasant impression from our first interview, and, to change the subject, I asked him if he really possessed the Samogitic Catechism of Father Lawiçki.

"It may be so; but, to tell you the truth, I do not know much about my father's library. He loved old and rare books. I hardly read anything beyond modern works; but we will look for it, Professor. You wish us, then, to read the Gospel in Jmoudic?"

"Do you not consider, M. le Comte, that a translation of the Scriptures into the language of this country is very desirable?"

"Certainly; nevertheless, if you will permit me a slight remark, I can tell you that amongst the people who know no other language than the Jmoudic, there is not a single person who can read."

"Perhaps so, but I ask permission of Your Excellency[3] to point out that the greatest obstacle in the way of learning to read is the absence of books. When the Samogitic countries have a printed text they will wish to read it, and will learn to read. This has already happened in the case of many savage races ... not that I wish to apply such a term to the people of this country.... Furthermore," I went on, "is it not a deplorable thing that a language should disappear, leaving no trace behind? Prussian became a dead language thirty years ago, and the last person who knew Cornic died the other day."

"Sad," interrupted the Count. "Alexander Humboldt told my father he had met with a parrot in America that was the only living thing which knew several words of the language of a tribe now entirely wiped out by small-pox. Will you allow me to order our tea here?"

While we drank tea the conversation turned upon the Jmoudic tongue. The Count found fault with the way Germans print Lithuanian, and he was right.

"Your alphabet," he said, "does not lend itself to our language. You have neither our J, nor our L, V, or Ë. I have a collection of *daïnos* published last year at Koenigsberg, and I had immense trouble to understand the words, they are so queerly formed."

"Your Excellency probably speaks of Lessner's *daïnos*?"

"Yes, it is very vapid poetry, do you not think?"

"He might perhaps have selected better. I admit that, as it is, this collection has but a purely philological interest; but I believe if careful search were made one would succeed in collecting the most perfect flowers of your folk-poetry."

"Alas! I doubt it very much, in spite of my patriotic desires."

"A few weeks ago a very fine ballad was given me at Wilno—an historical one.... It is a most remarkable poem.... May I read it? I have it in my bag."

"With the greatest pleasure."

He buried himself in an armchair, after asking permission to smoke.

"I can't understand poetry unless I smoke," he said.

"It is called *The Three Sons of Boudrys*."

"*The Three Sons of Boudrys*?" exclaimed the Count, with a gesture of surprise.

"Yes, Boudrys, as Your Excellency knows better than I, is an historic character."

The Count looked at me fixedly with that odd gaze of his. It was almost indefinable, both timid and ferocious, and produced an almost painful impression until one grew accustomed to it. I hurriedly began to read to escape it.

THE THREE SONS OF BOUDRYS

"In the courtyard of his castle old Boudrys called together his three sons—three genuine Lithuanians like himself.

"'My children,' he said to them, 'feed your war horses, and get ready your saddles; sharpen your swords and your javelins. It is said that at Wilno war has broken out between the three quarters of the globe. Olgerd will march against Russia; Skirghello against our neighbours, the Poles; Keystut will fall upon the Teutons.[4] You are young, strong and bold; go and fight; and may the gods of Lithuania protect you! This year I shall not go to war, but I wish to counsel you. There are three of you, and three roads are open to you.

"'One of you must accompany Olgerd to Russia, to the borders of Lake Ilmen, under the walls of Novgorod. Ermine skins and embroidered stuffs you will find there in plenty, and among the merchants as many roubles as there are blocks of ice in the river.

"'The second must follow Keystut in his incursion. May he scatter the cross-bearing rabble! Amber is there as common as is the sea sand; their cloths are without equal for sheen and colour; their priests' vestments are ornamented with rubies.

"'The third shall cross the Niémen with Skirghello. On the other side he will find base implements of toil. He must choose good lances and strong buckles to oppose them, and he will bear away a daughter-in-law.

"'The women of Poland, my sons, are the most beautiful of all our captives—sportive as kittens and as white as cream. Under their black brows their eyes sparkle like stars. When I was young, half a century ago, I brought away captive from Poland a beautiful girl who became my wife. She has long been dead, but I can never look at her side of the hearth without remembering her.'

"He blessed the youths, who already were armed and in the saddle. They set out. Autumn came, then winter ... but they did not come back, and the old Boudrys believed them to be dead.

"There came a snowstorm, and a horseman drew near, who bore under his black bourka[5] a precious burden.

"'Is it a sackful of roubles from Novgorod?' asked Boudrys.

"'No, father. I am bringing you a daughter-in-law from Poland.'

"In the midst of the snowstorm another horseman appeared. His bourka was also distended with a precious burden.

"'What have you, my child; yellow amber from Germany?'

"'No, father. I bring you a daughter-in-law from Poland.'

"The snow fell in squalls. A horseman advanced hiding a precious burden under his bourka.... But before he had shown his spoil Boudrys had invited his friends to a third wedding."

"Bravo! Professor," cried the Count; "you pronounce Jmoude to perfection. But who told you this pretty *daïna*?"

---

3 **Siatelstvo**, "Your **shining light**"; the title used in addressing a count.

4 The knights of the Teutonic order.

5 Felt cloak.

"A young lady whose acquaintance I had the honour to make at Wilno, at the house of Princess Katazyna Paç."

"What is her name?"

"The *panna* Iwinska."

"Mlle. Ioulka!"[6] exclaimed the Count. "The little madcap! I might have guessed it. My dear Professor, you know Jmoude and all the learned tongues; you have read every old book, but you have let yourself be taken in by a young girl who has only read novels. She has translated to you, more or less correctly, in Jmoudic, one of Miçkiewicz's dainty ballads, which you have not read because it is no older than I am. If you wish it I will show it to you in Polish, or, if you prefer, in an excellent Russian translation by Pouchkine."

I confess I was quite dumbfounded. How the Dorpat professor would have chuckled if I had published as original the *daïna* of the "Sons of Boudrys"!

Instead of being amused at my confusion, the Count, with exquisite politeness, hastened to turn the conversation.

"So you have met Mlle. Ioulka?" said he.

"I have had the honour of being presented to her."

"What do you think of her? Speak quite frankly."

"She is a most agreeable young lady."

"So you are pleased to say."

"She is exceedingly pretty."

"Oh!"

"Do you not think she has the loveliest eyes in the world?"

"Yes."

"A complexion of the most dazzling whiteness?... I was reminded of a Persian *ghazel*, wherein a lover extols the fineness of his mistress's skin. 'When she drinks red wine,' he said, 'you see it pass down her throat.' The *panna* Iwinska made me think of those Persian lines."

"Mlle. Ioulka may possibly embody that phenomenon; but I do not know if she has any blood in her veins.... She has no heart.... She is as white and as cold as snow!"

He rose and walked round the room some time without speaking, as though to hide his emotion; then, stopping suddenly—

"Pardon me," he said, "we were talking, I believe, of folk-poetry...."

"We were, Your Excellency."

"After all it must be admitted that she translated Miçkiewicz very prettily.... 'Frolicsome as a kitten,... white as cream,... eyes like stars,' ... that is her own portrait, do you not agree?"

"Absolutely, Your Excellency."

"With reference to this roguish trick ... a very ill-judged one, to be sure,... the poor child is bored to death by an old aunt. She leads the life of a nun."

"At Wilno she went into society. I saw her at the ball given by the officers of the—regiment."

"Ah, yes! the society of young officers suits her exactly. To laugh with one, to backbite with another, and to flirt with all of them.... Will you come and see my father's library, Professor?"

I followed him to a long gallery, lined with many handsomely bound books, which, to judge from the dust which covered their edges, were rarely opened. What was my delight to find that one of the first volumes I pulled out of a glass case was the *Catechismus Samogiticus*! I could not help uttering a cry of pleasure. It seemed as though some mysterious power were exerting its influence unknown to us.... The Count took the book, and, after he had turned over the leaves carelessly, wrote on the flyleaf: "*To Professor Wittembach, from Michael Szémioth.*" I did not know how to express my great gratitude, and I made a mental resolution that after my death this precious book should be the ornament of my own University library.

"If you like to consider this library your workroom," said the Count, "you shall never be disturbed here."

III

After breakfast the following day the Count proposed that I should take a walk with him. The object in view was to visit a *kapas* (the name given by the Lithuanians to tumuli, called by the Russians *kourgâne*), a very noted one in that country, because formerly poets and magicians (they are one and the same thing) gathered there on certain special occasions.

"I have a very quiet horse to offer you," he said. "I regret that I cannot take you by carriage, but, upon my word, the road we go by is not fit for carriages."

I would rather have stopped in the library taking my notes, but I could not express any wish contrary to that of my generous host, and I accepted. The horses were waiting for us at the foot of the steps in the courtyard, where a groom held a dog in leash.

"Do you know much about dogs, Professor?" said the Count, stopping for a minute and turning to me.

"Hardly anything, Your Excellency."

"The Staroste of Zorany, where I have property, sent me this spaniel, of which he thinks highly. Allow me to show him to you." He called to the groom, who came up with the dog. He was indeed a beautiful creature. The dog was quite used to the man, and leapt joyfully and seemed full of life; but when within a few yards of the Count he put his tail between his legs and hung back terrified. The Count patted him, and at this the dog set up a dismal howl.

"I think he will turn out a good dog with careful training," he said, after having examined him for some time with the eye of a connoisseur. Then he mounted his horse.

"Professor," he said, "when we were in the avenue leading from the château, you saw that dog's fear. Please give me your honest opinion. In your capacity of savant you must learn to solve enigmas.... Why should animals be afraid of me?"

"Really, Your Excellency does me the honour of taking me for an Oedipus, whilst I am only a simple professor of comparative philology. There might—"

"Observe," he interrupted me, "that I never beat either horses or dogs. I have a scruple against whipping a poor beast who commits a mistake through ignorance. But, nevertheless, you can hardly conceive the aversion that I inspire in dogs and horses. It takes me double the time and trouble to accustom them to me that it would other people. It took me a long time before I could subdue the horse you are riding, but now he is as quiet as a lamb."

"I believe, Your Excellency, that animals are physiognomists, and detect at once if people whom they see for the first time like them or not. I expect you only like animals for the services they render you; on the other hand, many people have an instinctive partiality for certain beasts, and they find it out at once. Now I, for instance, have always had an instinctive liking for cats. They very rarely run away from me when I try to stroke them, and I have never been scratched by one."

6 Julienne.

"That is very likely," said the Count; "I cannot say I have a real affection for animals.... Human beings are so much more to be preferred. We are now coming into a forest, Professor, where the kingdom of beasts still flourishes—the *matecznik*, the womb, the great nursery of beasts. Yes, according to our national traditions, no one has yet penetrated its depths, no one has been able to reach to the heart of these woods and thickets, unless, always excepted, the poets and magicians have, who go everywhere. Here the beasts all live as in a Republic ... or under a Constitutional Government, I cannot tell which of the two. Lions, bears, elks, the *joubrs,* our wild oxen or aurochs, all live very happily together. The mammoth, which is preserved there, is thought highly of; it is, I believe, the Marshal of the Diet. They have a very strict police force, and if they decide that any beast is vicious they sentence him to banishment. It falls thus out of the frying-pan into the fire; it is obliged to venture into the region of man, and few escape."[7]

"A very curious legend," I exclaimed, "but, Your Excellency, you speak of the aurochs, that noble animal which Cæsar has described in his *Commentaries*, and which the Merovingian kings hunted in the forest of Compiègne. I am told they still exist in Lithuania—is that so?"

"Certainly. My father himself killed a *joubr*, having obtained permission from the Government. You can see the head in the large dining-hall. I have never seen one. I believe they are very scarce. To make amends we have wolves and bears here in abundance. To guard against a possible encounter with one of these gentlemen I have brought this instrument" (and he produced a Circassian tchékhole[8] which he carried in his belt), "and my groom carries in his saddle-box a double-barrelled rifle."

We began to penetrate into the forest. Soon the narrow track that we were following disappeared altogether. Every few moments we were obliged to ride round enormous trees whose low branches barred our passage. Several of these, which were dead of old age and fallen over, looked like bulwarks crowned with a line of *chevaux-de-frise* (impossible to scale). Elsewhere we encountered deep pools covered with water lilies and duckweed. Further on we came to a clearing where the grass shone like emeralds; but woe to those who ventured on it, for this rich and deceptive vegetation usually hides abysses of mud in which both horse and rider would disappear for ever.... The arduousness of the route had interrupted our conversation. All my attention was taken up in following the Count, and I admired the imperturbable sagacity with which he guided his way without a compass, and always regained the right direction which had to be followed to reach the kapas. It was evident that he had frequently hunted in these wild forests.

At last we perceived the tumulus in the centre of a large clearing. It was very high and surrounded by a fosse still clearly recognisable in spite of the landslips. It looked as though it had recently been excavated. At the summit I noticed the remains of an erection built of stones, some of which bore traces of fire. A considerable quantity of ashes, mixed with pieces of charcoal, with here and there fragments of coarse crockery, attested that there had been a fire on the top of the tumulus for a considerable time. If one can put faith in popular tradition, human sacrifices had been offered several times in the kapas; but there is hardly any extinct religion to which these abominable rites have not been attributed, and I imagine one could justify a similar theory with regard to the ancient Lithuanians from historic evidence.

We came down from the tumulus to rejoin our horses, which we had left on the far side of the fosse, when we saw an old woman approaching us, leaning on a stick and holding a basket in her hand.

"Good day, gentlemen," she said to us as she came up, "I ask an alms for the love of God. Give me something for a glass of brandy to warm my poor body."

The Count threw her a coin, and asked what she was doing in the wood, so far from habitation. For sole answer she showed him her basket filled with mushrooms. Although my knowledge of botany was but limited, I thought several of the mushrooms looked like poisonous ones.

"My good woman," I said, "you are not going to eat those, I hope."

"Sir," the old woman replied, with a sad smile, "poor folk eat all the good God gives them."

"You are not acquainted with Lithuanian stomachs," the Count put in; "they are lined with sheet iron. Our peasants eat every kind of fungus they find, and are none the worse for them."

"At least prevent her from tasting the *agaricus necator* she has in her basket," I cried, and I stretched out my hand to take one of the most poisonous of the mushrooms, but the old woman quickly withdrew the basket.

"Take care," she said in a frightened tone; "they are protected ... *Pirkuns! Pirkuns!*"

"*Pirkuns*," I may explain in passing, is the Samogitian name for the divinity called by the Russians *Péroune*; it is the Jupiter *tonans* of the Slavs. If I was surprised when I heard the old woman invoke a pagan god, I was much more astonished to see the mushrooms heave up. The black head of a snake raised itself at least a foot out of the basket. I jumped back, and the Count spat over his shoulder after the superstitious custom of the Slavs, who believe that in this way they turn away misfortune, as did the ancient Romans. The old woman put the basket on the ground, and crouched by its side; then she held out her hand towards the snake, pronouncing some unintelligible words like an incantation. The snake remained quiet a moment, then it curled itself round the shrivelled arm of the old woman and disappeared in the sleeve of her sheepskin cloak, which, with a dirty chemise, comprised, I believe, all the dress of this Lithuanian Circe. The old woman looked at us with a little laugh of triumph, like a conjurer who has just executed a difficult trick. Her face wore that mixture of cunning and stupidity which is often noticeable in would-be witches, who are mostly scoundrels and dupes.

"Here you have," said the Count in German, "a specimen of local colour; a witch who tames snakes, at the foot of a kapas, in the presence of a learned professor and of an ignorant Lithuanian gentleman. It would make a capital subject for a picture of natural life by your countryman Knauss.... If you wish to have your fortune told, this is a good opportunity."

I replied that I did not encourage such practices.

"I would much rather," I added, "ask her if she knows anything about that curious superstition of which you spoke. Good woman," I said to her, "have you heard tell of a part of this forest where the beasts live in a community, independent of man's rule?"

The witch nodded her head in the affirmative, and she gave a low laugh, half silly, half malicious.

"I come from it," she said. "The beasts have lost their king. Noble, the lion, is dead; the animals are about to elect another king. If you go there perhaps they will make you king."

"What are you saying, mother?" and the Count burst into shouts of laughter. "Do you know to whom you are talking? Do you not know that this gentleman is.... (what the deuce do they call a professor in Jmoudic?) a great savant, a sage, a *waïdelote*?"[9]

---

7   See **Messire Thaddée**, by Miçkiewicz, and **Captive Poland**, by M. Charles Edmond.

8   A Circassian gun-case.

9   A bad translation of the word "professor." The **waïdelotes** were the Lithuanian bards.

The witch stared at him fixedly.

"I was mistaken," she said. "It is thou who ought to go there. Thou wilt be their king, not he; thou art tall, and strong, and hast claws and teeth."

"What do you think of the epigrams she levels at us?" said the Count. "Can you show us the way, mother?" he asked.

She pointed with her hand to a part of the forest.

"Indeed?" said the Count. "And how can you get across the marsh? You must know, Professor, that she pointed to an impassable swamp, a lake of liquid mud covered over with green grass. Last year a stag that I wounded plunged into this infernal marsh, and I watched him sink slowly, slowly.... In five minutes I saw only his horns, and soon he disappeared completely, two of my dogs with him."

"But I am not heavy," said the old woman, chuckling.

"I think you could cross the marsh easily on a broomstick."

A flash of anger shone in the old woman's eyes.

"Sir," she said, returning to the drawling and nasal twang of the beggar, "haven't you a pipe of tobacco to give a poor woman? Thou hadst better search for a passage through the swamp than go to Dowghielly," she added in a lower tone.

"Dowghielly!" said the Count, reddening, "what do you mean?"

I could not help noticing that this word produced a singular effect upon him. He was visibly embarrassed; he lowered his head in order to hide his confusion, and busied himself over opening the tobacco pouch which hung at the hilt of his hunting knife.

"No, do not go to Dowghielly," repeated the old woman. "The little white dove is not for thee, is she, *Pirkuns*?"

At that moment the snake's head appeared out of the collar of the old woman's cloak and stretched up to its mistress's ear. The reptile, trained doubtless to the trick, moved its jaws as though it spoke.

"He says I am right," said the old woman.

The Count gave her a handful of tobacco.

"Do you know me?" he asked.

"No, sir."

"I am the master of Médintiltas. Come and see me one of these days; I will give you tobacco and brandy."

The old woman kissed his hand and moved away with rapid strides. We soon lost sight of her. The Count remained thoughtful, tying and untying the fastenings of his bag, hardly conscious of what he was doing.

"Professor," he said to me after a somewhat long silence, "you will laugh at me. That old crone knew both me and the road which she showed me better than she pretended.... After all, there is nothing so very surprising in that. I am as well known in this countryside as the white wolf. The jade has seen me several times on the road to Dowghielly Castle.... A marriageable young lady lives there, so she concluded that I was in love.... Then some handsome boy has bribed her to tell me bad luck.... It is obvious enough. Nevertheless, ... in spite of myself, her words have affected me. I am almost frightened by them.... You have cause to laugh.... The truth is that I intended to go and ask for dinner at the Castle of Dowghielly, and now I hesitate.... I am a great fool. Come, Professor, you decide it. Shall we go?"

"In questions of marriage I never give advice," I said laughingly. "I take good care not to have an opinion."

We had come back to our horses.

"The horse shall choose for me," cried the Count, as he vaulted into the saddle and let the bridle lie slack.

The horse did not hesitate; he immediately entered a little footpath, which, after several turnings, descended into a metalled road which led to Dowghielly. Half an hour after we reached the Castle steps.

At the sound of our horses a pretty, fair head appeared at a window, framed between two curtains. I recognised the translator of Miçkiewicz, who had taken me in.

"You are welcome," she said. "You could not have come more apropos, Count Szémioth. A dress from Paris has just arrived for me. I shall be lovely past recognition."

The curtains closed again.

"It is certainly not for me that she is putting on this dress for the first time," muttered the Count between his teeth whilst mounting the steps.

He introduced me to Madam Dowghiello, the aunt of the *panna* Iwinska, who received me courteously and spoke to me of my last articles in the Koenigsberg *Scientific and Literary Gazette*.

"The Professor has come to complain to you," said the Count, "of the malicious trick which Mademoiselle Julienne played on him."

"She is a child, Professor; you must forgive her. She often drives me to distraction with her follies. I had more sense at sixteen than she has at twenty, but she is a good girl at heart, and she has many good qualities. She is an admirable musician, she paints flowers exquisitely, and she speaks French, German and Italian equally well.... She embroiders."

"And she composes Jmoudic verses," added the Count, laughing.

"She is incapable of it," exclaimed Madam Dowghiello; and they had to explain her niece's mischievousness.

Madam Dowghiello was well educated, and knew the antiquities of her country. Her conversation was particularly agreeable to me. She read many of our German reviews, and held very sane views upon philology. I admit that I did not notice the time that Mademoiselle Iwinska took to dress, but it seemed long to Count Szémioth, who got up and sat down again, looked out of the window, and drummed on the pane with his fingers as a man who has lost patience.

At length, at the end of three-quarters of an hour, Mademoiselle Julienne appeared, wearing with exquisite grace a dress which would require more critical knowledge than mine to describe. She was followed by her French governess.

"Do I not look pretty?" she said to the Count, turning round slowly so that he could see her from all sides.

She did not look either at the Count or at me, but at her new dress.

"How is it, Ioulka," said Madam Dowghiello, "that you do not say good day to the Professor? He complains of you."

"Ah, Professor!" she cried, with a charming little pout. "What have I done? Have you come to make me do penance?"

"We shall punish ourselves, Mademoiselle, if we deprive ourselves of your presence," I answered. "I am far from complaining; on the contrary, I congratulate myself on having learnt, thanks to you, that the Lithuanian Muse has reappeared more brightly than ever."

She lowered her head, and, putting her hands before her face, taking care not to disarrange her hair, she said, in the tones of a child who has just stolen some sweetmeats—

"Forgive me; I will not do it again."

"I will only pardon you, my dear Pani," I said to her, "if you will fulfil a certain promise which you were good enough to make to me at Wilmo, at the house of the Princess Katazyna Paç."

"What promise?" she asked, raising her head and laughing.

"Have you forgotten so soon? You promised me that if we met in Samogitia you would let me see a certain country dance which you said was enchanting."

"Oh, the roussalka! I shall be charmed; and the very man I need is here."

She ran to a table loaded with music-books, and, turning over one hastily, put it on the piano stand.

"Mind, my dear, *allegro presto*," she said, addressing her governess. And she played the prelude herself, without sitting down, to show the time.

"Come here, Count Michel! you are too much of a Lithuanian not to be able to dance the roussalka; ... but dance like a peasant, you understand."

Madam Dowghiello in vain tried to object. The Count and I insisted. He had his motives, for his part in the dance was extremely agreeable, as we soon saw. The governess, after several attempts, said she thought she could play that kind of waltz, strange though it was; so Mademoiselle Iwinska, after moving some chairs and a table that were in the way, took hold of her partner by the collar of his coat and led him into the centre of the room.

"You must know, Professor, that I am a roussalka, at your service."

She made a low bow.

"A roussalka is a water nymph. There is one in each of the big pools of black water which adorn our forests. Do not go near! The roussalka comes out, lovelier even than I, if that be possible; she carries you to the bottom, where, very likely, she gobbles you up...."

"A real siren," I cried.

"He," continued Mademoiselle Iwinska, pointing to Count Szémioth, "is a very foolish young fisherman who exposes himself to my clutches, and, to make the pleasure last longer, I fascinate him by dancing round him for a time.... But, alas! to do it properly I want a sarafane.[10] What a pity! You must please excuse this dress, which has neither character nor local colour.... Oh! and I have slippers on. It is quite impossible to dance the roussalka with slippers on ... and heels on them too."

She picked up her dress, and, daintily shaking a pretty little foot at the risk of showing her leg, she sent the slipper flying to the end of the drawing-room. The other followed the first, and she stood upon the parquetry floor in her silken stockings.

"We are quite ready," she said to the governess.

And the dance began.

The roussalka revolves and revolves round her partner; he stretches out his arms to seize her, but she slips underneath him and escapes. It is very graceful, and the music has movement and originality. The figure ends when the partner, believing that he has seized the roussalka, tries to give her a kiss, and she makes a bound, strikes him on the shoulder, and he falls dead at her feet.... But the Count improvised a variation, strained the winsome creature in his arms, and kissed her again and again. Mademoiselle Iwinska uttered a little cry, blushed deeply, and threw herself, pouting, into a couch, complaining that he had hugged her like the bear that he was. I saw that the comparison did not please the Count, for it brought to his mind the family misfortune, and his brow darkened. I thanked Mademoiselle Iwinska most warmly, and praised her dance, which seemed to me to have an antique flavour, and recalled the sacred dances of the Greeks. I was interrupted by a servant announcing General and Princess Véliaminof. Mademoiselle Iwinska leaped to the sofa for her shoes, hastily thrust in her little feet, and ran to meet the Princess, making successively two profound bows. I noticed that at each bow she adroitly drew on part of her slipper. The General brought with him two aides-de-camp, and, like us, had come to ask for hospitality. In any other country I imagine the mistress of the house would have been a little embarrassed to receive all at once six hungry and unexpected guests; but Lithuanian hospitality is so lavish that the dinner was not more than half an hour late, I think; there were too many pies, however, both hot and cold.

IV

The dinner was very lively. The General gave us a most interesting account of the dialects spoken in the Caucasus, some of which are Aryan, and others Turanian, although between the different peoples there is a remarkable uniformity in manners and customs. I had to talk of my travels because Count Szémioth congratulated me on the way I sat a horse, and said he had never met a minister or a professor who could have managed so easily such a journey as the one we had taken. I explained to him that, commissioned by the Bible Society to write a work on the language of the *Charruas*, I had spent three and a half years in the Republic of Uruguay, nearly always on horse-back, and living in the pampas among the Indians. This led me to relate how, when lost for three days in those boundless plains, without food or water, I had been reduced, like the *gauchos* who accompanied me, to bleed my horse and drink his blood.

All the ladies uttered a cry of horror. The General observed that the Kalmouks did the same in similar extremities. The Count asked me what the drink tasted like.

"Morally, it was most repugnant," I replied, "but, physically, I found it rather good, and it is owing to it that I have the honour of dining here to-day. Many Europeans, I mean white men, who have lived for a long time with the Indians, accustom themselves to it, and even get to like the taste. My good friend Don Fructuoso Rivero, President of the Republic, hardly ever missed a chance of gratifying it. I recollect one day, when he was going to Congress in full uniform, he passed a *rancho* where a young foal was being bled. He got off his horse to ask for a *chupon*, a suck; after which he delivered one of his most eloquent speeches."

"Your President is a hideous monster," cried Mademoiselle Iwinska.

"Pardon me, my dear Pani," I said to her, "he is a very distinguished person, with a most enlightened mind. He speaks several very difficult Indian dialects to perfection, specially the *Charrua*, the verbs of which take innumerable forms, according to whether its objective is direct or indirect, and even according to the social relations of the persons who speak."

I was about to give some very curious instances of the construction of the *Charrua* verb, but the Count interrupted me to ask what part of the horse they bled when they wanted to drink its blood.

"For goodness' sake, my dear Professor," cried Mademoiselle Iwinska, with a comic expression of terror, "do not tell him. He is just the man to slay his whole stable, and to eat us up ourselves when he has no more horses left!"

Upon this sally the ladies laughingly left the table to prepare tea and coffee whilst we smoked. In a quarter of an hour they sent from the drawing-room for the General. We all prepared to go with him; but we were told that the ladies only wished one man at a time. Very soon we heard from the drawing-room loud bursts of laughter and clapping of hands.

"Mademoiselle Ioulka is up to her pranks," said the Count.

He was sent for next; and again there followed laughter and applause. It was my turn after his. By the time I had reached the room every face had taken on a pretended gravity which did not bode well. I expected some trick.

---

10 A peasant's skirt, without a bodice.

"Professor," said the General to me in his most official manner, "these ladies maintain that we have given too kind a reception to their champagne, and they will not admit us among them until after a test. You must walk from the middle of the room to that wall with your eyes bandaged, and touch it with your finger. You see how easy it is; you have only to walk straight. Are you able to keep a straight line?"

"I think so, General."

Mademoiselle Iwinska then threw a handkerchief over my eyes and tied it tightly behind.

"You are in the middle of the room," she said; "stretch out your hand.... That is right! I wager that you will not touch the wall."

"Forward, march!" called out the General.

There were only five or six steps to take. I advanced very cautiously, sure that I should encounter some cord or footstool treacherously placed in my path to trip me up, and I could hear stifled laughter, which increased my confusion. At length I believed I was quite close to the wall, when my outstretched finger suddenly went into something cold and sticky. I made a grimace and started back, which set all the onlookers laughing. I tore off my bandage, and saw Mademoiselle Iwinska standing near me holding a pot of honey, into which I had thrust my finger, thinking that I touched the wall. My only consolation was to watch the two aides-de-camp pass through the same ordeal, with no better result than I.

Throughout the evening Mademoiselle Iwinska never ceased to give vent to her frolicsome humour. Ever teasing, ever mischievous, she made first one, then another, the butt of her fun. I observed, however, that she more frequently addressed herself to the Count, who, I must say, never took offence, and even seemed to enjoy her allurements. But when, on the other hand, she began an attack upon one of the aides-de-camp, he frowned, and I saw his eyes kindle with that dull fire which was almost terrifying. "Frolicsome as a kitten and as white as cream." I thought in writing that verse Miçkiewicz must surely have wished to draw the portrait of the *panna* Iwinska.

V

It was very late before we retired to bed. In many of the great houses in Lithuania there is plenty of splendid silver plate, fine furniture, and valuable Persian carpets; but they have not, as in our dear Germany, comfortable feather beds to offer the tired guest. Rich or poor, nobleman or peasant, a Slav can sleep quite soundly on a board. The Castle of Dowghielly was no exception to this general rule. In the room to which the Count and I were conducted there were but two couches newly covered with morocco leather. This did not distress me much, as I had often slept on the bare earth in my travels, and I laughed a little at the Count's exclamations upon the barbarous customs of his compatriots. A servant came to take off our boots and to bring us dressing-gowns and slippers. When the Count had taken off his coat, he walked up and down awhile in silence; then he stopped in front of the couch, upon which I had already stretched myself.

"What do you think of Ioulka?" he said.

"I think she is bewitching."

"Yes, but such a flirt!... Do you believe she has any liking for that fair-haired little captain?"

"The aide-de-camp?... How should I tell?"

"He is a fop!... So he ought to please women."

"I deny your conclusion, Count. Do you wish me to tell you the truth? Mademoiselle Iwinska thinks far more how to please Count Szémioth than to please all the aides-de-camp in the army."

He blushed without replying; but I saw that my words had given him great pleasure. He walked about again for some time without speaking; then, after looking at his watch, he said—

"Good gracious! we must really go to sleep; it is very late."

He took his rifle and his hunting knife, which had been placed in our room, put them in a cupboard, and took out the key.

"Will you keep it?" he said; and to my great surprise he gave it to me. "I might forget it. You certainly have a better memory than I have."

"The best way not to forget your weapons would be to place them on that table near your sofa," I said.

"No.... Look here, to tell you the truth, I do not like to have arms by me when I am asleep.... This is the reason. When I was in the Grodno Hussars, I slept one night in a room with a companion, and my pistols were on the chair near me. In the night I was awakened by a report. I had a pistol in my hand; I had fired, and the bullet had passed within two inches of my comrade's head.... I have never been able to remember the dream I had."

I was a little disturbed by his anecdote. I was guarded against having a bullet through my head; but, when I looked at the tall figure of my companion, with his herculean shoulders and his muscular arms covered with black down, I could not help recognising that he was perfectly able to strangle me with his hands if he had a bad dream. I took care, however, not to let him see that I felt the slightest uneasiness. I merely put a light on a chair close to my couch, and began to read the *Catechism* of Lawiçki, which I had brought with me. The Count wished me good night, and lay down on his sofa, upon which he turned over five or six times; at last he seemed asleep, although he was doubled up like Horace's lover, who, shut up in a chest, touched his head with his bent knees.

...Turpi clausus in arca,
Contractum genibus tangas caput...."

From time to time he sighed heavily, or made a kind of nervous rattle, which I attributed to the peculiar position in which he had chosen to sleep. An hour perhaps passed in this way, and I myself became drowsy. I shut my book, and settled myself as comfortably as was possible on my bed, when an odd giggling sound from my neighbour set me trembling. I looked at the Count. His eyes were shut; his whole body shuddered; from his half-opened lips escaped some hardly articulate words.

"So fresh!... so white!... The Professor did not know what he said.... Horse is not worth a straw.... What a delicious morsel!"

Then he began to bite the cushion, on which his head rested, with all his might, growling at the same time so loudly that he woke himself.

I remained quite still on my couch, and pretended to be asleep. Nevertheless, I watched him. He sat up, rubbed his eyes, sighed sadly, and remained for nearly an hour without changing his position, absorbed apparently in his reflections. I was, however, very ill at ease, and I inwardly vowed never again to sleep by the side of the Count. But in the long run weariness overcame disquiet, and when the servant came to our room in the morning, we were both in a profound sleep.

VI

We returned to Médintiltas after breakfast. When I found Dr. Froeber alone, I told him that I believed the Count was unwell, that he had had frightful dreams, was possibly a somnambulist and would be dangerous in that condition.

"I am aware of all that," said the doctor. "With an athletic organisation he is at the same time as nervous as a highly strung woman. Perhaps he gets it from his mother.... She has been devilishly bad to-day.... I do not believe much in stories of fright and longings of pregnant women; but one thing is certain, the Countess is mad, and madness can be inherited...."

"But the Count," I returned, "is perfectly sane: his mind is sound, he has much higher intelligence than, I admit, I should have expected; he loves reading...."

"I grant it, my dear sir, I grant it; but he is often eccentric. Sometimes he shuts himself up for several days; often he roams about at night. He reads unheard-of books.... German metaphysics ... physiology, and I know not what! Even yesterday a package of them came from Leipzig. Must I speak plainly? A Hercules needs a Hebe. There are some very pretty peasant girls here.... On Saturday evenings, when they have washed, you might mistake them for princesses.... There is not one of them but would be only too proud to distract my lord. I, at his age, devil take me!... No, he has no mistress; he will not marry, it is wrong. He ought to have something to occupy his mind."

The doctor's coarse materialism shocked me extremely, and I abruptly terminated the conversation by saying that I sincerely wished that Count Szémioth should find a wife worthy of him. I was surprised, I must admit, when I learnt from the doctor of the Count's taste for philosophical studies. It went against all my preconceived ideas that this officer of the Hussars, this ardent sportsman, should read German metaphysics and engage himself in physiology. The doctor spoke the truth, however, as I had proof thereof even that very day.

"How do you explain, Professor," he said to me suddenly towards the close of dinner—"how do you explain the *duality* or the *twofold nature* of our being?"

And when he observed that I did not quite follow him, he went on—

"Have you never found yourself at the top of a tower, or even at the edge of a precipice, having at the same time a desire to throw yourself down into space, and a feeling of terror absolutely the reverse?"

"That can be explained on purely physical grounds," said the doctor; "first, the fatigue of walking up hill sends a rush of blood to the brain, which—"

"Let us leave aside the question of the blood, doctor," broke in the Count impatiently, "and take another instance. You hold a loaded fire-arm. Your best friend stands by. The idea occurs to you to put a ball through his head. You hold assassination in the greatest horror, but all the same, you have thought of it. I believe, gentlemen, that if all the thoughts which come into our heads in the course of an hour ... I believe that if all *your* thoughts, Professor, whom I hold to be so wise, were written down, they would form a folio volume probably, after the perusal of which there would not be a single lawyer who could successfully defend you, nor a judge who would not either put you in prison or even in a lunatic asylum."

"That judge, Count, would certainly not condemn me for having hunted, for more than an hour this morning, for the mysterious law that decides which Slavonic verbs take a future tense when joined to a preposition; but if by chance I had some other thought, what proof of it could you bring against me? I am no more master of my thoughts than of the external accidents which suggest them to me. Because a thought springs up in my mind, it cannot be implied that I have put it into execution, or even resolved to do so. I have never thought of killing anybody; but, if the thought of a murder comes into my mind, is not my reason there to drive it away?"

"You talk with great certainty of your reason; but is it always with us, as you say, to guide us? Reflection, that is to say, time and coolness are necessary to make the reason speak and be obeyed. Has one always both of these? In battle I see a bullet coming towards me; it rebounds, and I get out of the way; by so doing I expose my friend, for whose life I would have given my own if I had had time for reflection...."

I tried to point out to him our duty as men and Christians, the obligation we are under to imitate the warrior of the Scriptures, always ready for battle; at length I made him see that in constantly struggling against our passions we gain fresh strength to weaken and to overcome them. I only succeeded, I fear, in reducing him to silence, and he did not seem convinced.

I stayed but ten days longer at the Castle. I paid one more visit to Dowghielly, but we did not sleep there. As on the first occasion, Mlle. Iwinska acted like a frolicsome and spoilt child. She exercised a kind of fascination over the Count, and I did not doubt that he was very much in love with her. At the same time he knew her faults thoroughly, and was under no illusions. He knew she was a frivolous coquette, and indifferent to all that did not afford her amusement. I could see that he often suffered internally at seeing her so unreasonable; but as soon as she paid him some little attention his face shone, and he beamed with joy, forgetful of all else. He wished to take me to Dowghielly for the last time the day before my departure, possibly because whilst I could stay talking with the aunt, he could walk in the garden with the niece; but I had so much work to do I was obliged to excuse myself, however much he urged. He returned to dinner, although he had told us not to wait. He came to table, but could not eat. He was gloomy and ill-tempered all through the meal. From time to time his eyebrows contracted and his eyes assumed a sinister expression. When the doctor returned to the Countess, the Count followed me to my room, and told me all that was on his mind.

"I heartily repent," he exclaimed, "having left you to go and see that little fool who makes game of me, and only cares for fresh faces; but, fortunately, all is over between us; I am utterly disgusted, and I will never see her again...."

For some time he paced up and down according to his usual habit.

"You thought, perhaps, I was in love with her?" he went on. "That is what the silly doctor thinks. No, I have never loved her. Her merry look amused me. Her white skin gave me pleasure to look at.... That is all there is pleasing about her,... her complexion especially. She has no brains. I have never seen anything in her but just a pretty doll, agreeable to look at when one is tired and lacks a new book.... There is no doubt she is beautiful.... Her skin is marvellous!... The blood under that skin ought to be better than a horse's.... Do you not think so, Professor?"

And he laughed aloud, but his laugh was not pleasant to hear.

I said good-bye to him the next day, to continue my explorations in the north of the Palatinate.

VII

They lasted nearly two months, and I can say that there is hardly a village in Samogitia where I did not stop and where I did not collect some documents. I may here be allowed, perhaps, to take this opportunity of thanking the inhabitants of that province, and especially the Church dignitaries, for the truly warm co-operation they accorded me in my researches, and the excellent contributions with which they have enriched my dictionary.

After staying a week at Szawlé, I intended to embark at Klaypeda (the seaport which we call Memel) to return to my home, when I received the following letter from Count Szémioth, which was brought by one of his huntsmen:—

MY DEAR PROFESSOR,—

Allow me to write to you in German, for I should commit too many errors in grammar if I wrote in Jmoudic, and you would lose all respect for me. I am not sure you have much of that as it is, and the news that I am about to communicate to you will probably not increase it. Without more ado, I am going to be married, and you will guess to whom. *Jove laughs at lovers' vows.* So said Pirkuns, our Samogitian Jupiter. It is, then, Mlle. Julienne Iwinska that I am to marry on the 8th of next month. You will be the kindest of men if you will come and assist at the ceremony. All the peasantry of Médintiltas and the neighbouring districts will come to devour several oxen and countless swine, and, when they are drunk, they will dance in the meadow, which, you will remember, lies on the right of the avenue. You will see costumes and customs worthy of your consideration. It will give me and also Julienne the greatest pleasure if you come, and I must add that your refusal would place us in a most awkward situation. You know that I belong to the Evangelical Communion, as does my betrothed; now, our minister, who lives about thirty leagues away, is crippled with gout, and I ventured to hope you would be so good as to act in his stead.

Believe me, my dear Professor,
Yours very devotedly,
MICHEL SZÉMIOTH.

At the end of the letter, in the form of a postscript, had been added in Jmoudic, in a pretty feminine handwriting:

I, the muse of Lithuania, write in Jmoudic. Michel is very impertinent to question your approval. There is no one but I, indeed, who would be so silly as to marry such a fellow as he. You will see, Professor, on the 8th of next month, a bride who may be called *chic*. That is not a Jmoudic word, it is French. But please do not be distracted during the ceremony.

Neither the letter nor the postscript pleased me. I thought the engaged couple showed an inexcusable levity concerning such a solemn occasion. However, how was I to decline? And yet I will admit that the promised pageant had its attractions for me. According to all appearance, I should not fail to find among the great number of gentlefolk, who would be gathered together at the Castle of Médintiltas, some learned people who would furnish me with useful information. My Jmoudic glossary was very good; but the sense of a certain number of words which I had learnt from the lips of the lowest of the peasants was still, relatively speaking, somewhat obscure to me. All these considerations combined were sufficiently strong to make me consent to the Count's request, and I replied that I would be at Médintiltas by the morning of the 8th.

How greatly had I occasion to repent of my decision!

VIII

On entering the avenue which led to the Castle I saw a great number of ladies and gentlemen in morning dress standing in groups on the steps of the entrance or walking about the paths of the park. The court was filled with peasants in their Sunday attire. The Castle bore a festive air; everywhere were flowers and wreaths, flags and festoons. The head servant led me to the room on the ground floor which had been assigned to me, apologising for not being able to offer me a better one; but there were so many visitors in the Castle that it had been impossible to reserve me the room I had occupied during my first visit, which had been given to the wife of the premier Marshal. My new chamber was, however, very comfortable; it looked on the park, and was below the Count's apartment. I dressed myself hastily for the ceremony, and put on my surplice,
but neither the Count nor his betrothed made their appearance. The Count had gone to fetch her from Dowghielly. They should have come back a long time before this; but a bride's toilette is not a light business, and the doctor had warned the guests that as the breakfast would not take place till after the religious ceremony, those whose appetites were impatient would do well to fortify themselves at a sideboard, which was spread with cakes and all kinds of drinks. I remarked at the time that the delay excited ill-natured remarks; two mothers of pretty girls invited to the fête did not refrain from epigrams launched at the bride.

It was past noon when a salvo of cannon and muskets heralded her arrival, and soon after a state carriage entered the avenue drawn by four magnificent horses. It was easily seen by the foam which covered their chests that the delay had not been on their part. There was no one in the carriage besides the bride, Madam Dowghiello and the Count. He got out and gave his hand to Madam Dowghiello. Mademoiselle Iwinska, with a gracefully coquettish gesture, pretended to hide under a shawl to avoid the curious looks which surrounded her on all sides. But she stood up in the carriage, and was just about to take the Count's hand when the wheelers, terrified maybe by the showers of flowers that the peasants threw at the bride, perhaps also seized with that strange terror which animals seemed to experience at the sight of Count Szémioth, pranced and snorted; a wheel struck the column at the foot of the flight of steps, and for a moment an accident was feared. Mademoiselle Iwinska uttered a little cry,... but all minds were soon relieved, for the Count snatched her in his arms and carried her to the top of the steps as easily as though she had been a dove. We all applauded his presence of mind and his chivalrously gallant conduct. The peasants yelled terrific hurrahs, and the blushing bride laughed and trembled simultaneously. The Count, who was not at all in a hurry to rid himself of his charming burden, evidently exulted in showing her picture to the surrounding crowd....

Suddenly a tall, pale, thin woman, with disordered dress and dishevelled hair, and every feature in her face drawn with terror, appeared at the top of the flight of stairs before anyone could tell from whence she sprang.

"Look at the bear!" she shrieked in a piercing voice, "look at the bear!... Get your guns!... He has carried off a woman! Kill him! Fire! fire!"

It was the Countess. The bride's arrival had attracted everybody to the entrance and to the courtyard or to the windows of the Castle. Even the women who kept guard over the poor maniac had forgotten their charge; she had escaped, and, without being observed by anyone, had come upon us all. It was a most painful scene. She had to be removed, in spite of her cries and resistance. Many of the guests knew nothing about the nature of her illness, and matters had to be explained to them. People whispered in a low tone for a long time after. All faces looked shocked. "It is an ill omen," said the superstitious, and their number is great in Lithuania.

However, Mlle. Iwinska begged for five minutes to settle her toilette and put on her bridal veil, an operation which lasted a full hour. It was more than was required to inform the people who did not know of the Countess's illness of the cause and of its details.

At last the bride reappeared, magnificently attired and covered with diamonds. Her aunt introduced her to all the guests, and, when the moment came to go into the chapel, Madam Dowghiello, to my great astonishment, slapped her niece on the cheek, in the presence of the whole company, hard enough to make those whose attention was not otherwise engaged to turn round. The blow was received with perfect equanimity, and no one seemed surprised; but a man in black wrote something on a paper which he carried, and several of the persons present signed their names with the most nonchalant air. Not until after the ceremony did I find the clue to the riddle. Had I guessed it I should not have failed to oppose the abominable custom with the whole weight of my sacred office as a minister of religion. It was to set up a case for divorce by pretending that the marriage only took place by reason of the physical force exercised against one of the contracting parties.

After the religious service I felt it my duty to address a few words to the young couple, confining myself to putting before them the gravity and sacredness of the bond by which they had just united themselves; and, as I still had Mlle. Iwinska's postscript on my mind, I reminded her that she was now entering a new life, no longer accompanied by childish pleasures and amusements, but filled with serious duties and grave trials. I thought that this portion of my sermon produced much effect upon the bride, as well as on everyone present who understood German.

Volleys of firing and shouts of joy greeted the procession as it came out of the chapel on its way to the dining-hall. The repast was splendid and the appetites very keen; at first no other sounds were audible but the clatter of knives and forks. Soon, however, warmed by champagne and Hungarian wines, the people began to talk and laugh, and even to shout. The health of the bride was drunk with enthusiastic cheers. They had scarcely resumed their seats when an old *pane* with white moustaches rose up.

"I am grieved to see," he said in a loud voice, "that our ancient customs are disappearing. Our forefathers would never have drunk this toast from glasses of crystal. We drank out of the bride's slipper, and even out of her boot; for in my time ladies wore red morocco boots. Let us show, my friends, that we are still true Lithuanians. And you, Madam, condescend to give me your slipper."

"Come, take it, Monsieur," replied the bride, blushing and stifling a laugh;... "but I cannot satisfy you with a boot."

The *pane* did not wait a second bidding; he threw himself gracefully on his knees, took off a little white satin slipper with a red heel, filled it with champagne, and drank so quickly and so cleverly that not more than half fell on his clothes. The slipper was passed round, and all the men drank out of it, but not without difficulty. The old gentleman claimed the shoe as a precious relic, and Madam Dowghiello sent for a maid to repair her niece's disordered toilette.

This toast was followed by many others, and soon the guests became so noisy that it did not become me to remain with them longer. I escaped from the table without being noticed and went outside the Castle to get some fresh air, but there, too, I found a none too edifying spectacle. The servants and peasants who had had beer and spirits to their hearts' content were nearly all of them already tipsy. There had been quarrelling and some heads broken. Here and there drunken men lay rolling on the grass in a state of stupidity, and the general aspect of the fete looked much like a field of battle. I should have been interested to watch the popular dances quite close, but most of them were led by impudent gipsies, and I did not think it becoming to venture into such a hubbub. I went back, therefore, to my room and read for some time; then I undressed and soon fell asleep.

When I awoke the Castle clock was striking three o'clock. It was a fine night, although the moon was half shrouded by a light mist. I tried to go to sleep again, but I could not manage it. According to my usual habit when I could not sleep I thought to take up a book and read, but I could not find matches within reach. I got up and was going to grope about the room when a dark body of great bulk passed before my window and fell with a dull thud into the garden. My first impression was that it was a man, and I thought possibly it was one of the drunken men, who had fallen out of the window. I opened mine and looked out, but I could not see anything. I lighted a candle at last, and, getting back into bed, I had gone through my glossary again just as they brought me a cup of tea. Towards eleven o'clock I went to the salon, where I found many scowling eyes and disconcerted looks. I learnt, in short, that the table had not been left until a very late hour. Neither the Count nor the young Countess had yet appeared. At half-past eleven, after many ill-timed jokes, people began to grumble—at first below their breath, but soon aloud. Dr. Froeber took upon himself to send the Count's valet to knock at his master's door. In a quarter of an hour the man came back looking anxious, and reported to Dr. Froeber that he had knocked more than a dozen times without getting any answer. Madam Dowghiello, the doctor and I consulted together. The valet's uneasiness influenced me. We all three went upstairs with him and found the young Countess's maid outside the door very scared, declaring that something dreadful had happened, for Madam's window was wide open. I recollected with horror that heavy body falling past my window. We knocked loudly; still no answer. At length the valet brought an iron bar, and we forced the door.... No! courage fails me to describe the scene which presented itself to our eyes. The young Countess was stretched dead on her bed, her face horribly torn, her throat cut open and covered with blood. The Count had disappeared, and no one has ever heard news of him since.

The doctor examined the young girl's ghastly wound.

"It was not a steel blade," he exclaimed, "which did this wound.... It was a bite...."

* * * * *

The doctor closed his book, and looked thoughtfully into the fire.

"And is that the end of the story?" asked Adelaide.

"The end," replied the Professor in a melancholy voice.

"But," she continued, "why have you called it '*Lokis*'? Not a single person in it is so called."

"It is not the name of a man," said the Professor. "Come, Théodore, do you understand what '*Lokis*' means?"

"Not in the very least."

"If you were thoroughly steeped in the law of transformation from the Sanskrit into Lithuanian, you would have recognised in *lokis* the Sanskrit *arkcha*, or *rikscha*. The Lithuanians call *lokis* that animal which the Greeks called [Greek: arktos], the Latins *ursus*, and the Germans *bär*.

"Now you will understand my motto:

Miszka su Lokiu,
Abu du tokiu.

"You remember that in the romance of *Renard* the bear is called *damp Brun*. The Slavs called it Michel, which becomes Miszka in Lithuanian, and the surname nearly always replaces the generic name *lokis*. In the same way the French have forgotten their new Latin word *goupil*, or *gorpil*, and have substituted *renard*. I could quote you endless other instances...."

But Adelaide observed that it was late, and we ought to go to bed.

THE END

STUDIO 5-6-7

And it never bothered me that much at first.
Back in those days I was so much more concerned
    with my hi-score, whatever that meant.
All those ten pence pieces that I spent.
My hand-eye co-ordination was second to none
    but as time went by, my wrist got numb...

Still I started to go there more and more
    and I started to notice the posters
    this guy came and he put up next door
There were actresses in varying states of
    deshabille,
for an audience in varying states of dishevelled.

Then this one time some pissed up bloke
came out of the fire door to throw up
and he just fucked off and he left open
so I wandered in and it was like I'd stumbled into a
    pornutopia
...in the Studio 5-6-7

Well, they say that it's darkest just before the dawn
    but before, during, and after a good dose of
    yon hardcore porn,
It's always dark in a XXX theatre.
Well, you can work it out while you're sitting there.
I'd never dreamed there was so much filth
and the lengths that some people will go to just to
    sneak into a film.

From then on my interest increased,
culminating during a showing of Walerian
    Borowczyk's opus entitled The Beast.
Now corruption and depravity are my middle
    names,
although to the uninititiated eye they probably
    both look the same.
From the silken sheets of a French chateau
    to a handkerchief in a steelworker's moleskins.
It's easy to look at, but it's hard to turn away
    and if even if you only went once,
there's a part of you
    that will always and forever stay
...in the Studio 5-6-7

A tune by Pink Stainless Tail, c. 2001.

INDEX

Entries are sorted with leading articles omitted, regardless of language. Foreign films are listed under their original language title (transliterated into Roman where appropriate) with cross-references to and from the English language variant title. Please note that cross-references retain their leading articles. Surnames with prefixes are sorted under their particle, e.g. "de Sade" under "D".

#

****
▶ *Four Stars*
17e Parallèle [*17th Parallel*] (1968) 29
17th Parallel
▶ *17e Parallèle*
2 ou 3 Choses Que je Sais d'Elle [*Two or Three Things I Know About Her*] (1967) **26**, 29
20,000 Leagues Under the Sea (1954) 86
20.000 Ans à la Française [*20,000 years of the French*] AKA *The French Way of Looking at It* (1967) .11, 15
491 (1964) 86
7 Murders for Scotland Yard (1971) 67
7/64: Leda mit dem Schwan [*Leda and the swan*] (1964) .90

A

"*A*" (1965) 29, 69
Abbott and Costello Meet Dr. Jekyll and Mr. Hyde (1953) 70, **71**
Abduction of Europa, The (painting) **90**
Accattone (cinema) 28
Act, The (12" single) 9
Adda, Valérie 78
Adler, Lou 8
Adult Version of Dr. Jekyll and Mr. Hyde, The (1972) 70, **71**
Affaire Manet, L' [the Manet affair] (1951) 29
Age D'Or, L' [the golden age] (1930) 42n
Ai no Borei
▶ *L'Empire de la Passion* [*Empire of Passion*]
Ai no Corrida
▶ *L'Empire des Sens* [*Empire of the Senses*]
Al Pereira vs. the Alligator Ladies (2012) . . .79
Alain Decaux Raconte [Alain Deccaux recounts] (TV) 98
Alazraki, Benito 10, 11
Albertini, Bitto 77
Albertini, Marcel .72
Albicocco, Jean-Gabriel 37
Albin, Karin 52
Albino, Coco 60
Alexander VI (pope) 30, 31, 59
Alexandra, Charlotte 30
Alexandrova, Inga 47
Alexeieff, Alexandre 13
Alice in Wonderland (book) 35, 67
Allegory of Earth, The (painting) 45
Alleton, Martine .69
Almanach des Adresses des Demoiselles de Paris [almanac of addresses of ladies of Paris] (TV) **17**
Alpha France (production company) 93
Alphaville (1965) 69
Alucarda AKA *Sisters of Satan* (1975) 56
Amati, Sandro 47
Amatucci, Bruno 47
Ambiguous Image, The (book) **92**
Ambrosini, Andreina 55
American Pie: The Wedding (2003) 88
Ammanati, Bartolomeo 90
Amore e Rabbia [*Love and Anger*] (1967) 37, 63
Amore, L' (1969) 37
Amour c'est Gai, l'Amour c'est Triste, L' [*Love Is Gay, Love Is Sad*] (1971) 29
Amour chez les Poids Lourds, L' [*Love in the Heavy Goods Vehicles*] (1978) 49
Amour Monstre de Tous les Temps, L' [the greatest love of all time] (1978) . . . **16**, 29
Anastasi, Domenico 49
Anatole Dauman: Pictures of a Producer (book) **92**
Anatomie du Diable [anatomy of the devil] (book) **92**
And God Ceated Woman
▶ *Et Dieu… Créa la Femme*
Andersen, Dominique 68
André, Carole 80, **81**
Andréani, Jean-Pierre 20
Angeloni, Carla .64
Angel's Games
▶ *Les Jeux des Anges* [*The Games of Angels*]
Anglais Décrit dans le Château Fermé, L' [*Portrait of an Englishman in his Castle*] (book) 80, 81
Animal Farm (n.d.) 85, 87
Animales Racionales [*Human Animals*] (1983) **87**
Année Dernière à Marienbad, L' [*Last Year in Marienbad*] (1961) **26**, 29
Aphrodite (1982) 37
Aquila [*The Eagle*] (constellation) 90
Araignée de Satin, L' [*The Satin Spider*] (1986) 37
Arcadi, Ari 20, 62
Arcimboldo, Giuseppe 45
Arduini, Paola 54
Arenkens, Paul 50
Argento, Dario 60, 61
Argos Films (production co.) 8, 13, 14, 16, 16, **27**, 28, 31, 80, 92
Armes, Roy 92
Armoire, L' [the wardrobe] (1979) . . . **16**, **62**
Armontel, Roland 38
Arno, Alice 49
Arno, Lisbeth 58
Arrow Films (company) 9
Ars Amandi [*The Art of Love*] AKA *L'Art d'Aimer* (1983) 16, 61, **72–73**, 73, 90, 90
Ars Amatoria (book) 73
Arsan, Emmanuelle 63, 74, 77
Art d'Aimer, L'
▶ *Ars Amandi* [*The Art of Love*]
Art of Love, The
▶ *Ars Amandi*
Art Theatre Guild (production co.) 63
Arthur (TV) 70
Assault! Jack the Ripper (1976) 67
Assonitis, Ovidio G. 87
Asteroids (video game) 7
Astronautes, Les [*The Astronauts*] (1963) 13, 23, 27, **28**, 29, 45
Astronauts, The
▶ *Les Astronautes*
Astruc, Alexandre 29
Astruc, Renata 18
Atelier de Fernand Léger [Fernand Léger's studio] (1954) .12
Atellian, Robert .38
Au Hasard Balthazar (1966) **26**, 29
Audibert, Mireille 52
August
▶ *Sierpień*
Augustyniak, Piotr 50
Aurel, Jean 29
Autumn
▶ *Jesień*
Awful Dr. Orloff, The
▶ *Gritos en la noche* [night visions]

B

Baba Yaga (1973) 66
Baba Yaga (comic) 66
Babies (tune) 41n
Bachelet, Pierre .74
Bachelor Party (1983) 77
Bagella, Bruno 55
Baker, Robert S. .67
Balch, Antony 9, 93
Baldaccini, Anna 38
Ballet Mecanique (1924) 12
Balletta, Francesca 54
Banner of Youth (newspaper) 12
Baratier, Jacques 29, 37, 69
Bardot, Brigitte .46
Bargielowski, Marek 50
Bariha, Khadicha 62, 64, 68

Barnett, Steve 74, 76
Barra, Gérard 69
Barrère, Igor 19
Barry, Maurice 29
Barry, Stanley 24
Barrymore, John .70
Barska, Teresa 51
Bartanowski, Anny 69
Bataille, George 39, 41n, 76
Bathory, Erzsébet 30–33
Batzella, Luigi 47
Baudet, Jacky 58
Baum, Ralph 68
Beano (comic) 7
Beast from 20,000 Fathoms, The (1953) . . .86
Beast in Heat, The
  ▸ *La Bestia in Calore*
Beast in Space, The
  ▸ *La Bestia nello Spazio*
Beast of Gévaudan, The
  ▸ *La Bête du Gévaudan*
Beast, The
  ▸ *La Bête*
Beatles, The (group) 7, 87
Beau Samedi, Le [the beautiful Saturday]
  (1974) 29
Beaumont, Georges 25
Beautiful Dead Body
  ▸ *Spooky Kama Sutra*
Beautiful Prisoner, The
  ▸ *La Belle Captive*
Beauty and the Beast (1991) 83, 84
Beauty and the Beast (story) . . . .
  35, 39, 95, 101–105
Beauty and the Beast (1946)
  ▸ *La Belle et la Bête* (1946)
Becker, Vernon P. 8, 67
Bednarczyk, Antoni 51
Behind Convent Walls
  ▸ *Interno di un Convento* [inside a convent]
Beldent, Joël .62, 78
Beldent, Marc-Antoine 79
Bella e la Bestia, La [beauty and the beast]
  (1977) **82**, **86**
Bellamy, Florence 30, 33
Belle Captive, La [*The Beautiful Prisoner*]
  (1983) **26**, 28, 29
Belle et la Bête, La [*Beauty and the Beast*]
  (1946) 84, **100**
Belle et la Bête, La [*Beauty and the Beast*]
  (2014) 99
Belleval, Sabrina .78
Bellmer, Hans 16, 41n
Ben Hur (1959) 73
Benayoun, Robert 92
Bénazéraf, José 92
Bene, Carmelo 31
Benedetti, Pierre 38, 58
Bennent, Anne 64, 65

Bennent, Heinz 35, 64
Benussi, Femi 47
Bercher, Fernand 20
Berg, Claudine 78
Bergman, Ingmar 10, 11, 60, 92
Bergonzelli, Sergio 60, 61
Berinizi, Jacopo .30
Berinizi, Lorenzo 30
Berman, Monty .67
Bernabei, Silvano 54
Bernard, Josy 78
Berroyer, Odette .38
Berruti, Giulio 53, 56
Bestia in Calore, La [*The Beast in Heat*]
  (1977) 47
Bestia nello Spazio, La [*The Beast in Space*]
  (1978) **48**
Bestialità [*Bestiality*] AKA *Dog Lay Afternoon*
  (1976) **86**
Bestiality
  ▸ *Bestialità*
Bête, La [*The Beast*] AKA *Death's Ecstasy*
  (1974) 8,
  9, 15, 16, **26**, **27**, 29, **38–44**, 46, 47, 48,
  60, 63, 76, 84, 86, 87, 89, 92, **94**, 98, 119
Bête du Gévaudan, La [the Beast of Gévaudan]
  (2001) 98
Bête du Gévaudan, La [the Beast of Gévaudan]
  (2003) 99
Bête du Gévaudan, Véritable Fléau de Dieu, La
  [the Beast of Gévaudan, God's true plague]
  (book) 99
Betti, Laura 72
Bianchi Montero, Roberto 48
Bianchi, Andrea 47, 49
Bianchini, Cesare 48
Bianco, Carmelo .55
Bibliotheques, Les [libraries] (1963) 14
Big Tit Monastery
  ▸ *Kyonyû shûdōin* / 巨乳修道院
Bird, Daniel 5
Biribicchi, Enrico 49
Bizarre (mag) 63
Bizet, Georges 15
Black Emanuelle (1975) 77
Black Moon (1975) 53
Black, Cilla 7
Blacula (1972) 70
Blanc, Nathalie 78
Blanchard, Marc .62
Blanchard, Sophie 62
Blanche (1972) 15, 23, **24–25**, 75, 92
Blanche, Roland **63**
Blaszynska, Felicja 51
Blaze of Embers (book) 81
Blechtrommel, Die [*The Tin Drum*]
  (1979) **26**, 28, 29
Blondel, Claude .18

Blondy
  ▸ *Vortex*
Blood for Dracula (1974) 53, 69
Blood of Doctor Jekyll, The
  ▸ *Docteur Jekyll et les Femmes*
Bloodbath of Doctor Jekyll, The
  ▸ *Docteur Jekyll et les Femmes*
Bloodlust
  ▸ *Docteur Jekyll et les Femmes*
Bloody Hands of the Law, The
  ▸ *La Mano Spietata della Legge*
Blue Angel, The (1930) 83
Blues Brothers, The (1980) 8
Bo Peep (nursery rhyme) 84
Boccaccio, Giovanni 17
Boiron, Serge 38
Boisrond, Michel 17
Boissonnade, Christian 24
Boite a Musique, La [the music box]
  (1961) 13
Boivin, Jacqueline 18
Bokusā / ボクサー [*The Boxer*] (1977) . . .63
Bolscher, Piet 24, 30, 38, 62, 68
Bonan, Jean-Denis 29
Bonnafoux, Guy 20, 24, 78
Bordier, Philippe 98
Borgia, Cesare 30
Borgia, Lucrezia 30, 31, **33**, 48
Borgia, Rodrigo .33
Borgias, The (TV) 33
"Boro"
  ▸ Walerian Borowczyk
Borowczyk, Ligia AKA Ligia Branice . . . . .
  11, 13, 14, 20, **22**, **23**, 24, 27, 33, 54, 55
Borowczyk, Walerian AKA "Boro" 1, 4–97
Bory, Florence 38
Bosé, Lucia **32**
Boucher, Bruno .75
Bougie, Robin 5
Bouillon, Brahim 62
Boullu, Jean 58
Bourdon, Thierry 38
Bouyxou, Jean-Pierre 93
Boxer, The
  ▸ *Bokusā* / ボクサー
Boy and his Dog, A (1975) 87
Bradley, Al 48
Brahm, John 67
Brandon, David .73
Branice, Ligia
  ▸ Ligia Borowczyk
Brass, Tinto 47, 73
Brasseur, Pierre .20
Braun Munk, Eugene 68
Braunberger, Gisèle 58, 62
Braunberger, Pierre 58, 62, 68, 79
Brescia, Alfonso .48
Bresson, Robert 29, 92
Bretoneiche, Charles 20, 24

Bride of the Monster (1955) 86
Brief von Paris [letter from Paris] (1977) . **16**
Brisseau, Daniel 25
Broadway by Light (1958) 29
Broglio, Carlo 48
Brooks, Louise 66, 67
Brotherhood of the Wolf, The
   ▸ Le Pacte de Loups
Brouillard, Pascale 20
Browning, Tod 84
Brûlure de Mille Soleils, La [The Heat of a
   Thousand Suns] (1965) 29
Bruna, Claude 74
Brunelin, André G. 18
Buchheim, Wilhelm 72
Büchse der Pandora, Die [Pandora's Box]
   (1929) **66**, 67
Büchse der Pandora, Die [Pandora's Box]
   (play) 64
Buczkowski, Leonard 10, 11
Bufo, Filippo 55
Bull, The
   ▸ Taurus
Buniejew, Borys 10, 11
Buñuel, Luis 42n, 45, 60
Burawska, Irena .50
Burger, Michele .74
Burns Westburg, Dana 74
Burroughs, Edgar Rice 83
Burroughs, William 9, 41n
Byl Sobie Raz [once upon a time] (1957) . **12**

C

Cadet, Véronique 62
Café Flesh (1983) 87
Cagnat, Isabelle .68
Caiano, Mario 47
Caligola: La storia mai raccontata [Caligula:
   The Untold Story] AKA Caligula 2 (1982) 73
Caligula (1979) 73
Caligula (bastard) 73
Caligula 2
   ▸ Caligola: La storia mai raccontata
   [Caligula: The Untold Story]
Caligula and Messalina (1981) 73
Caligula: The Untold Story
   ▸ Caligola: La storia mai raccontata
Calindri, Dora 54
Camera Obscura (1965) 14
Camus, Marcel 37
Canari (actor) 20
Cannibal Holocaust (1980) 47
Cap, Jean-Louis .81
Capellani, Albert .33
Capia, Robert 20, 30, 38, 58
Capra, Claude 46
Cardiff, Jack 28, 35, 37, 80
Caribbean Papaya
   ▸ Papaya dei Caraibi

Carol, Martine 33
Carole Fouanon, Raymonde 54
Carrière, Mathieu 46, 78
Carroll, Lewis 67
Carrot cake (cake) 9
Carry On Emmanuelle (1978) 77
Casa Sperduta nel Parco, La [The House on the
   Edge of the Park] (1980) 47
Caserini, Mario 33
Cassan, André 20
Castor and Pollux (constellation) 63
Cat People (1942) **84**
Cat People (1982) 84
Catau, Muriel 74
Catry, Edith 18
Caubet, Laurence 62
Cayrade, Alain 30, 38
Cayrol, Jean 29
Ceremonia Sangrienta [blood ceremony]
   (1973) **32**
Cérémonie d'amour [Love Rites] AKA Queen of
   the Night (1987) . . 61, 75, **78–79**, 80, 81
Ceriani, Umberto 48
Cerrato, Renzo 80, 81
Cesar, Robert 25
Cetra Records (label) 64
Challan, Annie 24
Chandrasekhar, Jay 88
Chantons sous l'Occupation [Singing During the
   Occupation] (1976) 29
Chantrell, Tom 8
Charlet, Sylvaine .52
Charlotte: The Diary of a Nymphomaniac
   ▸ La Jeune Fille Assassinée [a
   young girl murdered]
Charrel, Michel 20
Chastel, Jean 99
Chaval (actor) 29
Chavalanthrope, La [the horse-man]
   (1972) 29
Chazel, Robert 94
Cheutin, Claude .21
Chevalier, Louise 52
Chianese, Francesco 55
Chiaramello, Giancarlo 64
Chien, Le [the dog] (tune) 59
Chimenti, Melissa 47
Chocolat, Marie .74
Choderlos de Laclos, Pierre 53
Chojnacka, Jadwiga 50
Christensen, Benjamin 56
Christian-Jaque (actor) 33
Christie, Tony 7
Christophe, Pascale 30, 58
Chronicle of a Summer
   ▸ Chronique d'un été
Chronique d'un été [Chronicle of a Summer]
   (1961) **26**, 29
Ciao Manhattan (1972) 46

Ciganer, André 40n, 44
Cikan, Miroslav **10**, 11
Cinéaste Onirique: le cas étrange du Dr Jekyll et
   Miss Osbourne (book) **92**
CineCenta Twin (cinema) 7, 8
Cinema Sewer (mag) 5
Cipriani, Stelvio .47
Circle of Deceit
   ▸ Die Fälschung [the forgery]
Cités de la Plaine [cities of the plain]
   (2001) 36
Citizen Kane (1941) 76
Clark, Bob 67
Clavel, Maurice 29
Clavier, François .74
Claxton, William F. 59
Clément, René 11, 14, 46
Cleopatra (empress) 89
Clerc, Adrien 9
Clerici, Gianfranco 47
Clock DVA (group) 9
Cloistered Nun: Runa's Confession
   ▸ Shudojo Runa no Kokuhaku
   ／修道女ルナの告白
Clos, Luis 75
Cocker, Jarvis 9, 41n
Cocker, Joe 7
Cocteau, Jean 46, 84
Cohen, Howard R. 74
Cohn, Bernard 25
Colla, Louis-Michel 62, 68
Collections Privée [Private Collections]
   (1979) 16, 17, 41n, **63**
Collet, Pierre 18
Collet, Pierre 20
Colpi, Henri 29
Combes, Georges 21
Comolli, Jean-Louis 29
Concert de M. et Mme Kabal, Le [the concert
   of Mr. and Mrs. Kabal] (1962) 13
Contacts (TV) (1989) 36
Contes Immoraux [Immoral Tales] (1974) . . . .
   8, **9**, 15, 15, 16, **26**, 28, 29, **30–31**, 33,
   36, 41n, 59, 60, 63, 73, 75, 76, 80, 81, 86
Conti, Marie-Catherine 62
Continental Film Review (mag) 8, 9, **9**, 92, 93
Convent of Sinners
   ▸ La Monaca del Peccato
Cooper, Merian .83
Copin, Claude 18
Corbucci, Sergio 8
Corman, Roger .75
Corps Profond [deep body] (1960) 19
Coste, Catherine 68
Cotte, Roger 24
Couderc, Jacques 78
Coudeville, Martine 74
Coulant, Claudette 18
Coulant, Renée 20

Countess Dracula (1970) **32**
Coup de Grâce (1976) 29
Courbet, Gustave 43n
Cowie, Peter .93
Cox, Gérard .18
Crain, William 70
Cranitch, Brid 54
Crepax, Guido 66, 77
Crimes de l'Amour, Les [crimes of love] AKA *Two Love Crimes* (1953) 29
Crudo, Aldo .48
Cueille, Colette 21
Cumari Quasimodo, Maria 54
Cunningham, Alex 74
Cut! The Unseen Cinema (book) 92, **93**
Cygnus [*The Swan*] (constellation) 90
Czerwinski, Jan 51

D

D'Agostino, Antonio 87
D'Amario, Stefania 54
D'Amato, Joe 47, 56, 73
d'Aram, Philippe 58, 59
d'Argila, Philippe 24
D'Ovidio, Jacques 24, 38
da Vinci, Leonardo 59, 90
Daems, Agnès 68
Dagbert, Alain 21
Daillencourt, Bernard 30, 38, 58
Dal Pra, Rodolfo 54
Dali, Salvador 45
Dalio, Marcel 38
Dallesandro, Joe 52, 53, 56, 69
Dalmasso, Dominique 78
Dalmet, Michel 79
Damiano, Gerard 85
Dandy (comic) 7
Dangerous Liaisons
▸ *Les Liaisons Dangereuses*
Danglade, Robert 25
Danvers, Lise 30
Darblay, Raoul 20
Darnton, Robert 33
Dary, René 20
Das Wachsfigurenkabinett [waxworks] (1924) 67
Dassault, Olivier 58, 59
Daughters of Darkness (1971) 32
Dauman, Anatole
    8, 13, 15, 27, **28**, 30, 35, 38, 63, 79, 92
Dauman, Florence 28, 38
Dauphy, Robert 25
Day the Clown Cried, The (1972) 15
de Beaumont, Marie Leprince . . .39, 95, 101
de Beauterne, Antoine 98, 99
de Bos, Cornelis 90
de Boyer, Jean-Baptiste 33
de Chirico, Giorgio 14

de Funès, Isabelle 66
de Gourmont, Remy 16
de la Chaumette, M. 97
de Lagarde, Gérard 21
de Masi, Francesco 47
de Maupassant, Guy 14, 17, 62, 63
de Mirabeau, Comte 17
de Monfred, Avenir 13
de Monfred, Avenir 18
de Pisis, Filippo 16, 80
de Rais, Gilles 32
de Rola, Stash 46
de Sade, Marquis 17, 33, 76
de Vidas, Jean-Paul 58, 62
de Vidas, Michel 58
Death's Ecstasy
▸ *La Bête* [*The Beast*]
Debord, Guy 28
Decameron (book) 17
Deep Throat (1972) 85
Dehors-dedans (1975) 36, 37
Delahaye, Michel 24
Delbo, Jean-Jacques 64
Delon, Alain 14, 80
Delon, Claude 38
Delume, Daniel 78
Demain la Chine [tomorrow China] (1966) **26**, 29
Dembinska, Barbara 50
Démons, Les [*The Demons*] (1973) . . . **56**, 57
Demons, The
▸ *Les Démons*
Deneige, Alice 62
Den-en Ni Shisu / 田園に死す [*Pastoral: To Die in the Country*] (1974) 63
Deneuve, Catherine 14
Denis, Jacques 97, 98
Denis, Jeanne 97
Denis, Julienne 97
Denneval, M. 97
Deodato, Ruggero 47
Derek, Bo 88
Derek, John .88
Dernier Voyage de Gulliver, Le [the last voyage of Gulliver] (uncompleted) 11
des Mandiargues, André Pieyre . . . .
    15, 16, 16, 27, 28, 30, 31, 35, 41n, 52, 58, 59, 73, 76, 78, 80, **81**, 92, 92
des Mandiargues, Bona 27, 86
des Mandiargues, Sibylle Pieyre 80
Des Morts [*Of the Dead*] (1972) 85
Desboeuf, Philippe 30, 58
Désordre a 20 ans, Le [disorder is 20 years old] (1967) **26**
Deuil des Roses, Le [funeral roses] (book) . .81
Deux Marseillaises, Les [the two Marseillaises] (1968) 29
Devil and the Lady, The
▸ *El diablo y la Dama*

Devil in Miss Jones, The (1973) **85**
Devils, The (1971) 56, **57**
di Carlo, Carlo 61
Diaboliche, Le [diabolical] (1989) 86
Diary of a Chambermaid, The (1964) 45
Dictionnaire de Joachim, Le [Joachim's dictionary] (1965) **14**, 69
Dictionnaire Philosophique [*Philosophical Dictionary*] (book) 40n
Dietrich, Marlene 83
Diptyque [diptych] (1967) **15**
Dirty Dr. Jekyll (1973) 70
Disc Az (label) 59
Dlugolecka, Grazyna 50
Dni Oswiaty [school days] (1957) 12
Dobracki, Zbigniew 51
Docteur Jekyll et les Femmes [Dr. Jekyll and the Women] (1981) 16, 61, **68–69**, 92
Dog Lay Afternoon
▸ *Bestialità* [*Bestiality*]
Dogarama (n.d.) 85
Doll, The
▸ *La Poupée*
Dolly il sesso biondo [Dolly the blonde sex] (1979) 86
Dom [*House*] (1958) **13**, 23
Dom na Przedmiesciu [house in the suburbs] (1955) **10**, 11
Don't Torture a Duckling
▸ *Non si sevizia un paperino*
Don't Touch the White Woman
▸ *Touche pas la Femme Blanc*
Doniol-Valcroze, Jacques 29
Donna Velata, La [the veiled woman] (painting) .59
Douglas, Kirk 86
Dr. Black, Mr. Hyde (1976) 70
Dr. Dolittle (1967) 45
Dr. Jekyll and Mr. Black (1973) 70
Dr. Jekyll and Mr. Hyde (1920) 70, **71**
Dr. Jekyll and Mr. Hyde (1931) 70, **71**
Dr. Jekyll and Mr. Hyde (1941) 70
Dr. Jekyll and Mr. Hyde (play) **70**, 71
Dr. Jekyll and Sister Hyde (1971) . .67, 70, **71**
Dr. Jekyll and the Women
▸ *Docteur Jekyll et les Femmes*
Dr. Jekyll Likes Them Hot (1979) **71**
Dr. Jekyll's Dungeon of Death (1979) **71**
Dracula (1931) 84
Dream of the Fisherman's Wife, The (shunga) 86
Dream, Rinse 87
Dreyer, Carl .60
Dreyfus, Jean-Claude 58
Du Côté de la Côte [from coast to coast] (1958) 29
Dubreuil, André 24
Duchaussoy, Michel 46
Duchesne, Louis 20, 21

Duck You Sucker!
  ▸ *Il Était Une Fois la Révolution* [once upon a time the revolution]
Dufour, Pierre 75
Duguet, Jean 38
Duhamel, Captain 97
Duke of Yorks (cinema) 8
Dunning, George 13, 87
Duran Duran (group) 99
Durand, Claude .29
Duras, Marguerite 27
Durban, Guy 11, 15, 18, 20, 24, 30
Dürer, Albrecht .89
Duval, Jacques-Clément 21
Duval, Jean-Clément 25
Duvergé, Brigitte 18
Duvergé, Dominique 20, 24, 30, 38, 62
Dylan, Jesse 88
Dzieje Grzechu [Story of a Sin] (1911) 51
Dzieje Grzechu [Story of a Sin] (1933) 51
Dzieje Grzechu [Story of a Sin] (1975) **9**, 16, **50–51**, 90
Dzieje Grzechu [Story of a Sin] (novel) . .50, 51

E

Early Morning (1971) 37
Earth Spirit
  ▸ *Erdgeist*
Easy Rider (1969) 8
Ecaré, Désiré 29
Écoles, Les [schools] (1963) 14
Écriture, L' [handwriting] (1963) 14
Eden and After
  ▸ *Eden et Apres*
Eden et Apres [Eden and After] (1970) .35, **36**, 37
Eden Miseria [Eden misery] (1967) 29
Eden misery
  ▸ *Eden Miseria*
Edge of Sanity (1989) 67
Edo Porn
  ▸ *Hokusai Manga*
El diablo y la Dama [The Devil and the Lady] (1984) 37
Elvey, Maurice 67
Emmanuelle (1974) 8, 53, 63, **77**
Emmanuelle (comic) 77
Emmanuelle (computer game) 77
Emmanuelle (novel) 63
Emmanuelle (TV) 77
Emmanuelle 2 (1975) **77**
Emmanuelle 2 (book) 77
Emmanuelle 2000 (TV) 77
Emmanuelle 3
  ▸ *Emmanuelle à Cannes* [Emmanuelle Goes to Cannes]
Emmanuelle 4 (1984) **77**
Emmanuelle 5 AKA *Emmanuelle V* (1986) 60, **74–76**, 77

Emmanuelle 6 (1988) **77**
Emmanuelle 7 (1992) 77
Emmanuelle 77
  ▸ *La Marge* [the margin]
Emmanuelle à Cannes [Emmanuelle Goes to Cannes] AKA *Emmanuelle 3* (1978) 49, 76, 77
Emmanuelle Goes to Cannes
  ▸ *Emmanuelle à Cannes*
Emmanuelle II (1975) 53
Emmanuelle in Rio (2003) 77
Emmanuelle in Space (1994) 77
Emmanuelle in Wonderland (2011) 77
Emmanuelle l'antivierge [Emmanuelle the anti-virgin] (1975) 77
Emmanuelle Pie (2000) 77
Emmanuelle Private Collection (TV) 77
Emmanuelle Tango (2004) 77
Emmanuelle Through Time (TV) 77
Emmanuelle V
  ▸ *Emmanuelle 5*
Emmanuelle: A Hard Look (2000) 77
Emmanuelle: The Joys of a Woman
  ▸ *Emmanuelle II*
Emmanuelle: The Joys of a Woman (book) . .77
Emmanuelle's Seventh Heaven (1992) 77
Emperor Tomato Ketchup
  ▸ *Tomato Kecchappu Kotei* / トマトケッチャップ皇帝
Empire de la Passion, L' [Empire of Passion] AKA *Ai no borei* (1978) **26**, 28, 29
Empire des sens, L' [Empire of the Senses] AKA *Ai No Corrida* / *In the Realm of the Senses* (1976) **26**, 28, 29, 88
Empire of Passion
  ▸ *L'Empire de la Passion*
Empire of the Senses
  ▸ *L'Empire des sens*
Enard, Patrice 37
Encyclopedie de Grand'maman en 13 Volumes, L' [Grandmama's encyclopedia in 13 volumes] (1963) 13
Enrici, Carlo 64
Erdgeist [Earth Spirit] (play) 64
Erlanger, Dominique 52
Ernst, Max 13
Erotic Diary of a Lumberjack
  ▸ *Le Journal érotique d'un Bûcheron*
Erotic Diary of Woman of Thailand
  ▸ *Le Journal Érotique d'une Thailandaise*
Erotic Dr. Jekyll, The (1976) 70
Errigo, Raffaele .55
Erzebet Báthory (1974) 31, 76
Escargot de Venus [snail of Venus] AKA *Venus on the Half-Shell* **16**, 29
Escargots, Les [The Snails] (1965) 27, 45
Et Dieu... Créa la Femme [And God Ceated Woman] (1956) 46
Eurociné (production company) 93
"Even the Old Dude is Cool!" (book) 4

Exciting Love Girls
  ▸ *Giochi Carnali* [carnal games]
Experiment, The
  ▸ *Docteur Jekyll et les Femmes*
Expert Halima, L' [Halima the expert] (TV) **17**
Eye for the Girls, An (1966) 13

F

Fabiani, Noelle .74
Faceless (1987) .69
Faithfull, Marianne **36**, 80, **81**
Falcon, André 52
Falconetti, Gérard 58
Fall, Hassane 38, 58
Fälschung, Die [the forgery] AKA *Circle of Deceit* (1981) **26**, 29
Fanetti, Pasquale 47
Fano, Michel 35
Fantastic Planet
  ▸ *La Planète Sauvage* [wild planet]
Fanu, Sheridan, Le 32
Far from Vietnam
  ▸ *Loin du Vietnam*
Farfan, Esther 52
Farina, Corrado .66
Farouk, King 83
Fascination (1979) 40n
Fassbinder, Rainer Werner 60
Father and Master
  ▸ *Padre Padrone*
Faucheux, Agnès 24
Félines, Les [felines] AKA *Joy House* / *The Love Cage* (1964) 11, 14, **14**
Female Vampire, The (1973) **32**
Femme Fleur, La [the woman flower] (1965) 29, 80, 81
Femme-Bourreau, La [the woman executioner] (1968) 29
Ferbus, Jean-Pol .85
Fernand Léger's studio
  ▸ *Atelier de Fernand Léger*
Ferreri, Marco 79
Ferry, Jean 83
Fête Prisonnière, La [the prisoners' party] (1962) 29
Fêtes du Corps, Les [feasts of the body] (TV) 81
Feu de Braise [charcoal fire] (book) 81
Feuillère, Edwige 33
Fiches de Monsieur Cinema, Les (trading cards) 4
Fille Sage, La [the wise girl] (1963) 14
Film as a Subversive Art (book) **93**
Fine, Itza 83
Fisher, Terence .70
Flammarion engraving (artwork) **91**
Flashdance (1983) 77
Flavia the Heretic
  ▸ *Flavia, la Monaca musulmana*

Flavia, la Monaca Musulmana [*Flavia the Heretic*] (1974) **56**, 57
Fleischer, Alain 15, 28, 29, 35, **36**, 37
Fleischer, Richard 45, 86
Flesh (1968) 27, 53
Flesh for Frankenstein (1973) 53, 69
Floaters (2006) 60, 61
Fonda, Henry .87
Fonda, Jane 14
Forbidden Games
  ▸ *Jeux Interdits*
Ford, Jennifer .78
Forever Emmanuelle (1976) 77
Forgeot, Jacques 11, 15, 18
Fornarina, La [the baker] (painting) 59
Fornelli, Christine 24, 68
Fossey, Brigitte 46
Foule, La [the crowd] (1961) 13
Four Charlots Musketeers 2, The (1974) . . .37
Four Charlots Musketeers, The (1974) . 36, **37**
Four Stars AKA **** (1967) 53
Fragments of Conversations with Jean-Luc Godard (2007) 36
Francesco Aiello, Pier 72
Franco, Jesús . . . .
  9, 32, 56, 67, 69, 70, 73, 79, 87, 92, 93
Franval, Emmanuel 52
Fraschetti, Silvio 48
Fraticelli, Maria-Luisa 55
Freddy Got Fingered (2001) 88
Fregonese, Hugo 67
French Way of Looking at It, The
  ▸ *20.000 Ans à la Française*
    [20,000 years of the French]
Frenzy of Exultations
  ▸ *Szał Uniesień*
Freud, Sigmund 84, 99
Fried, Jakow .11
Fried., Jakow .10
Friedman, David 47
Fruits de la Passion, Les [*Fruits of Passion*] (1981) **26**, 28, 29, 63
Fruits of Passion
  ▸ *Les Fruits de la Passion*
Fruytier, Roland 69
Fuest, Robert .37
Fulci, Lucio 8, 47
Futz! (1969) .84

G

Gabrielle, Monique 74, 75, 76, 77
Gainsbourg, Serge 53
Galaxians (video game) 7
Gallotti, Dada .48
Games of Angels, The
  ▸ *Les Jeux des Anges*
Gance, Abel 33
Gancia (1963) 11, 14
Gandus, Roberto 47

Gans, Christopher 98
Garbo, Greta .83
Gardès, Renée 35
Gariazzo, Mario 46
Garner, James .73
Gasior, Halina .51
Gavotte (1967) **15**
Gawrysiak, Eugeniusz 51
Geek, the (1971) 86
Gemser, Laura **63**, 73, 77
George III (king) 7
Gerber, Jacques 28, 92
Gernolle, Norbert 21
Gesbert, Jérome 25
Giacobbe, Gabriella 54
Giacobetti, Francis 77
Gienieczko, Zofia 50
Gilberti, Nina .74
Gill, Lucette 78
Gilliam, Terry .14
Giochi Carnali [carnal games] AKA *Exciting Love Girls* (1983) 49
Gioconda AKA *Mona Lisa* (painting) 43n
Giombini, Marcello 48
Girl Beneath the Lion, The
  ▸ *Le Lis de Mer* (book)
Girl on the Motorcycle, The AKA *Naked under Leather* (1968) 28, 35, **36**, 37, 80, 81
Girl on the Motorcycle, The (book)
  ▸ *La Motocyclette* [the motorcycle girl]
Girotti, Massimo 72
Giulio Majano, Anton 64
Glenn, Pierre-William 46
Glowa [the head] (1949) 12
Gobbi, Sergio .37
Godard, Jean-Luc .27, 29, 37, 63, 69, 79, 92
Godard, Thierry 78
Golden Lotus, The
  ▸ *Le Lotus d'Or*
Gonzáles, Francisco Rojas 11
Goodbye Emmanuelle (1977) **77**
Gordon, Konstanty 12
Gordon, Robert 86
Goto, Island of Love
  ▸ *Goto, L'Ile d'Amour*
Goto, L'Ile d'Amour [*Goto, Island of Love*] (1968) 15, **20–21**, 23, 25, 27, 75, 92
Goulet, Pierre-Marie 29
Gourrier, Maurice-Pierre 24
Gourvil, Yves .58
Gradiva (2006) 79
Grandmama's encyclopedia in 13 volumes
  ▸ *L'Encyclopedie de Grand'maman en 13 Volumes*
Grant, David .46
Gras, Jean 24
Grass Labyrinth, The
  ▸ *Kusa-Meikyû* / 草迷宮
Grau, Jorge 32

Graves, Genevieve 24
Grayson, Godfrey 67
Greatest Love of all Time, The
  ▸ *L'Amour Monstre de Tous les Temps*
Green, Tom 88
Greenaway, Peter 90
Greenberg, Steve 74
Grégory, Gérard 78
Grieco, Sergio .56
Grignon, Bernard 30
Grignon, Marcel 35, 38
Gritos en la noche [night visions] AKA *The Awful Dr. Orloff* (1961) 70
Groffe, Serge 18, 20
Groffsky, Maxine 30
Groom, Jim 88
Gruel, Henri 29
Guccione, Bob 73
Guerbette, Jean 18
Guerre est Finie, La [*The War is Over*] (1966) 29
Guétary, François 58
Guez, Philippe 78
Guillé, Alain 38
Guillou, Patrice 79
Gustavsson, Kjell 30
Gwendoline (1984) 63

H

Hadley-Chase, James 66
Hakim, Raymond 52
Hakim, Robert 52
Halimi, André 29
Halperin, Victor 84
Hamano, Sachi 56
Hamilton, David 46
Hanany, Julien 38
Hancza, Wladyslaw 50
Hands of the Ripper (1971) 67
Harari, Clément 68
Hardester, Crofton 74
Hardiman, Olinka 49, 76
Harrington, Curtis 53
Harvey (1950) 59
Hasebe, Yasuharu **67**
Häxan [the witch] (1922) 56, **57**
Hayashi, Yoshifumi 16
Hearst, William Randolph 76
Heat (1972) 53
Heat of a Thousand Suns, The
  ▸ *La Brûlure de Mille Soleils*
Heroines du Mal, Les [*Heroines of Evil*] AKA *Three Immoral Women* (1979) . . . .
  16, **58–59**, 61, 63, 73, 80, 81
Heroines of Evil
  ▸ *Les Heroines du Mal*
Héron, Marcelle 62
Herpe, Alain .30

125

Herrero, Eligio 87
Hiard, Bernard 58
Hill, James 67
Hill, Terence 48
Hilton, George 48
Himmel über Berlin, Der [Heaven over Berlin]
  AKA *Wings of Desire* (1987) . . . **26**, 28, 29
Himorogi (2012) 60, 61
Hiroshima Mon Amour [Hiroshima my love]
  (1959) **26**, 29
Hirsh, Hy 13
Histoire d'O [*The Story of O*] (1975) . . .63, 69
Histoire d'O [*The Story of O*] (book) . . .28, 63
Histoire, Geographie [history, geography]
  (1982) 36
Hitchcock, Alfred 44n, 60, 67, 70, 87
Hnevsa, Thomas 30
Hochstätter, Zoran 74
Hokusai Manga AKA *Edo Porn* (1981) . 86, **87**
Hokusai, Katsushika 86
Holbrook, John 83
Holoubek, Gutaw 25
Holy Smoke (1963) 11, 14
Hopper, Dennis 8
Horse (1965) **84**
Horulu, Kemal 83
Hourglass Sanatorium, The
  ▸ *Sanatorium pod klepsydra*
House of Dolls (book) 47
House
  ▸ *Dom*
Hubert, Yves-André 98
Hübner, Bruno 64
Hughes, Howard 76
Huhardeux, Odile 78
Human Animals
  ▸ *Animales Racionales*
Human League, The (group) 9
Hummel, Lisbeth 38, 86
Hundar, Robert 48
Hunebelle, André 37
Hungry Like the Snake (non-existent tune) .99
Hunko, Henryk 50
Huston, John 87
Hvorfor gør de det? [*Why do They Do it?*]
  (1971) 85
Hyper Auto Erotic Art — Hayashi (1984) . .16

I

I am Curious (*George*) (non-existent film) .88
I Prosseneti [the pimps] (1976) 61
I, Monster (1971) 70
Il Était Une Fois la Révolution [once upon a
  time the revolution] AKA *Duck You Sucker!*
  (1971) 27
Ile aux Sirenes, L' [island of sirens] (1979) **63**
Ilsa, She Wolf of the SS (1975) 47
Images in a Convent
  ▸ *Immagini di un Convento*

Imbert, Jean-Paul 79
Immagini di un Convento [*Images in a
  Convent*] (1979) 56
Immoral Novices (non-existent film) 65
Immoral Tales
  ▸ *Contes Immoraux*
*Immoral Tales: Sex and Horror Cinema in
  Europe 1956-1984* (book) 9, **92**
In the Folds of the Flesh
  ▸ *Nelle Pieghe della Carne*
In the Realm of the Senses
  ▸ *L'Empire des sens* [Empire of the Senses]
In Versi (2008) 61
Inconnus de la Terre, Les [Strangers of the Earth]
  (1961) 29
Innocent, The
  ▸ *L'Innocente*
Innocente, L' [*The Innocent*] (1976) . . . 60, **61**
Interno di un Convento [inside a convent]
  AKA *Behind Convent Walls / Sex Life in a
  Convent* (1978) 16, 23, **54–55**, 60, 61, 76
Island of Death
  ▸ *Ta Paidiá tou Diavólou* /
    Τα παιδιά του Διαβόλου
Ismaël, Gérard 58
Israel, Neal 77
It Came from Beneath the Sea (1955) . . .86
It Came from the Deep (2000) **88**
Ivens, Joris 29
Iwaszkiewicz, Marek 51
Iwinski, Kazimierz 51
Izykowska, Anna 51

J

Jack the Ripper (1959) 67
Jack the Ripper (1976) 67
Jack the Ripper (bastard) . . . .
  64, 67, 69, 70, 84, 99
Jack the Ripper, Light-Hearted Friend
  (book) 67
Jacques Adiba, Alain 78
Jaeckin, Just 8, 53, 63, 69, 77
Jarry, Alfred .19
Jaws (1975) .87
Je t'Aime Moi Non Plus [i love you me neither]
  (1976) 53
Jeannette, Isabelle 62
Jedryka, Stanislaw 13, 23
Jekyll Jekyll Hyde Jekyll Hyde Hyde Jekyll
  (song) 70
Jendrusch, Angelika 64
Jesien [autumn] (1955) 12
Jess, Marilyn .49
Jetée, La [the jetty] (1962) 13, 21, **23**, 27, 29
Jeu avec Le Feur [*Playing with Fire*] (1975) .53
Jeune Fille Assassinée, La [a young girl
  murdered] AKA *Charlotte: The Diary of
  a Nymphomaniac / Ein Wildes Leben* [a
  wild life] **46**

Jeux des Anges, Les [*The Games of Angels*] AKA
  Angel's Games (1964) **14**, 69
Jeux Interdits [*Forbidden Games*] (1952) . .46
Jewison, Norman 73
Jez, Ewa 50
Joachim's dictionary
  ▸ *Le Dictionnaire de Joachim*
Joconde: Histoire d'une obsession, La [Mona
  Lisa: story of an obsession] (1958) 29
Joensen, Bodil 85
Johnson, Don 87
Jojot, Louis 18
Jones, L.Q. 87
Jouet Joyeux [happy toys] (1979) 16
Jourdan, Catherine **34**, **35**, **36**, **37**
Journal Érotique d'un Bûcheron, Le [Erotic
  Diary of a Lumberjack] (1974) 49
Journal Érotique d'une Thailandaise, Le [Erotic
  Diary of Woman of Thailand] (1980) . . .76
Joy House
  ▸ *Les Félines* [felines]
Julius II (pope) 59
Jupiter and Aquila
  ▸ *Jupiter und Asteria*
Jupiter und Asteria [Jupiter and Aquila]
  (painting) **90**

K

Kalfa, Steve 20
Kamizelka (TV) 23
Karamesinis, Vassili 48
Karen, Nicole 30
Karisn, Vassili 48
Kast, Pierre 29, 69
Ka-tzetnik 135633 (writer) 47
Kawalerowicz, Jerzy 10, 11, 56
Kay, André 74
Kaza, Elisabeth 38
Kennedy, John F. 31
Kennedy, Pluto 48
Kerdoncuff, Victor 21
Khan, Yaseen 74
Kharat, Michel 79
Kier, Udo 64, 68, 69
Kikoïne, Gérard 67
Killer Nun
  ▸ *Suor Omicida*
King Kong (1933) **83**
Kinski, Klaus 28, 36
Kirkham, Carole 87
Klein, Harold 13
Klein, William 29
Klossowski, Stash 46
Koczanowicz, Zbigniew 50
Kofman, Jacqueline 68
Konuma, Masaru 56
Kopp, Beate .64
Korzenie [roots] (1954) **10**, 11
Koskas, David 79

Koster, Henry 59
Kotoński, Włodzimierz 13
Kowalik, Maria 50
Kramer, Robert 36
Kren, Kurt 90
Kristel, Sylvia 46, 52, 53, 75, 77
Kronhausen, Eberhard 85
Kronhausen, Phyllis 85
Krvavá Paní [the bloody lady] (1980) . . . **32**
Krzyż Walecznych [cross of valour] (1958) **23**
Kubal, Viktor 32
Kubik, Andrzej 51
Kümel, Harry 17, 32
Kuperberg, Robert 64, 68
Kuroneko (1968) .86
Kusa-Meikyû / 草迷宮 [*The Grass Labyrinth*]
   (1979) **63**
Kutz, Kazimierz .23
Kyonyû shûdôin / 巨乳修道院 [*Big Tit
   Monastery*] (1995) 56

L

Labarthe, André S. 29
Labrande, Jean-Pierre 64, 68
Lacassin, Francis .98
Lacoste, Frédéric .79
Lady Chatterley's Lover (1981) 53, 63
Lahaie, Brigitte 49
Lalanne, Louis 62
Lalou, Etienne 19
Laloux, René 27, 28, 29, 45
Lambert, Anne-Louise 33
Landis, John 8
Landry, Yvonne .18
Lane, Sirpa AKA Sirpa Salo 33, 35, 38, **46–49**
Langiano, Bruno .79
Lannutti, Angelo 48
Lara, Jean 52
Larivière, Camille 52
Larraz, José 92
Lassailly, Florence 24
Lassiat, Hubert 20, 62
Last Voyage of Gulliver, The
  ▸ *Le Dernier Voyage de Gulliver*
Last Year in Marienbad
  ▸ *L'Année Dernière à Marienbad*
Lathuilliere, A.C. 75
Laure (1976) 77
Laurent, Luz 52
Laurent, Michel .38
Lawrence, D.H. .63
Lebovici, Gerard 28
Lebras, Jean-Louis 79
Leclerc, Ginette .20
Leconte, Patrice .25
Lecoq, Jacques 69
Leda and the Swan (painting) 90
Lee, Christopher 70

Lee, Julian 78
Leenhardt, Roger 29
Lefrere, Roger 58
Léger, Fernand 12, 14
Legrand, Gaëlle .58
Lemaire, Philippe 72
Lemoine, Michel .7
Lenartowicz, Stanislaw 23
Lengren, Tomasz 50
Leni, Paul 67
Lenica, Jan . . .11, 12, 13, 27, 29, 69, 80, 81
Lenoir, Rudy 20
Leo X (pope) 59
Léon XIII (pope) 99
Leoncini, Leonida 47
Leone, Sergio 27
Leroi, Francis 77
Lerouge, Marcellin 18
Leroux, Maurice .30
LeRoy, Mervyn .73
Leszczynski, Mariusz 51
Letans, Iris 77
Leterrier, François 77
Letter from Siberia
  ▸ *Lettre de Siberie*
Lettre de Siberie [*Letter from Siberia*]
   (1957) 27, 28, 29
Level Five (1997) **26**, 28, 29
Levitte, Bernard .74
Lévy, Michel 62
Lewis, Jerry 15, 70
Liaisons Dangereuses, Les [*Dangerous Liaisons*]
   (book) 53
Liberi, Marco 90
*Liebesbriefe einer Portugiesischen Nonne,
   Die* [*Love Letters of a Portuguese Nun*]
   (1976) 56, **57**
Lifchitz, Philippe 13, 14, 27, **28**
Lis de Mer, Le [the sea-lily] (book) 80, 81
Little Red Riding Hood (story) 84
Living Dead Girl, The
  ▸ *La Morte Vivante*
Ljuba
  ▸ *Ljubomir Popović*
Ljubomir Popović AKA Ljuba) 16
Llidó, Ramón 48
Lodger, The (1944) 67
Lodger, The (book) 67
Lodger: A Story of the London Fog, The
   (1926) **67**
Loin du Vietnam [*Far from Vietnam*]
   (1967) 27
Lokis — from the ms. of Professor Wittembach
   (story) 36, 39, 95, 106, 107–118
Lokis (1970) **106**, 107
Lonesome Cowboys (1968) 53, 84
Long, Elisabeth Jane 54
Longardi, Mario .55
Loro, Michel 78

Los Amantes de Lulú [Lulu's lovers]
  ▸ *Lulu* (1980)
Lotar, Marina 48
Lotus d'Or, Le [the golden lotus] (TV) . . . **17**
Loucif, Joëlle 25
Louis Stevenson, Robert 68, 70, 99
Louis XV (king) 97, 98
Lourié, Eugène 86
Louys, Pierre 76
Love and Anger
  ▸ *Amore e Rabbia*
Love Cage, The
  ▸ *Les Félines* [felines]
Love Express (non-existent film) 75, 76
Love in the Heavy Goods Vehicles
  ▸ *L'Amour chez les Poids Lourds*
Love in the Night
  ▸ *Vivre la nuit* [night life]
Love Is Gay, Love Is Sad
  ▸ *L'Amour c'est Gai, l'Amour c'est Triste*
Love Letters of a Portuguese Nun
  ▸ *Die Liebesbriefe einer
    Portugiesischen Nonne*
Love Rites
  ▸ *Cérémonie d'Amour*
Love, Kimberly .75
Lovelace, Linda .85
Lowell, Peter 74
Lowndes, Marie Belloc 67
Lubienska, Karolina 50
Luc, Kathy 18
Lucchini, Maurizio 55
Luchini, Fabrice .30
Lucrezia Borgia (1974) 31
Ludo (actor) 15
Lukaszewicz, Olgierd 50
Lulu AKA *Los Amantes de Lulú* [Lulu's lovers]
   (1980) 16, 60, **64–65**, 69
Lulu AKA *No Orchids for Lulu* (1962) . **66**, 67
Lulu (LP) 64
Lulu (plays) .66, 67
Lupi, Mario 72
Luti, Margherita .59
Lyne, Adrian 77

M

Mabe, Byron 70
Macinska, Zofia .51
Madame se Meurt [madame dies] (1961) . .29
Madrid, José Luis **67**
Maeda, Toshio 87
Magee, Patrick 68, 69
Magicienne, Le [the magician] (1961) 13
maid of Orleans, The
  ▸ *La Pucelle d'Orléans*
Maiden, Rita 68
Maietto, Carlo 47
Maietto, Renzo .47
Maillet, Guy 79

Maîtresses du Docteur Jekyll, Les [the mistresses of Dr. Jekyll] AKA *The Secret of Dr. Orloff* (1964) 70
Majewski, Janusz 107
Makavejev, Dusan 92
Malabestia [evil beast] (1978) **47**
Malabimba (1979) 49
Malémont, Philippe 18
Malle, Louis .53
Mallinson, Sarah 62
Mamet, Daniel 18
Man in the Attic (1953) 67
Mancuso, Ennio 49
Mano Spietata della Legge, La [The Bloody Hands of the Law] (1973) 46
Mansfield, Richard 70
Mansoura, Maïté 18
Manuel, Denis 52
Marani, Imelde 54
Maranzana, Mario 54
Marbre [marble] (book) 81
Marcas, Dominique 52
Marceline (1979) 80
Marceline (story) 58
Marceline (tune) 59
March, Frederic 70
Marco, Allain 20
Mardore, Michel 37
Marée, La [the tide] (1974) 31, 36
Marée, La [the tide] (story) 30, 31, 80
Maret, Sophie 75
Marge, La [the margin] AKA *The Streetwalker / Emmanuelle 77* (1976) **8**, 16, **52–53**, 56, 65, 81
Marge, La [*The Margin*] (book) **80**, 81
Maria Bifarini, Anna 55
Marie Claire (mag) 63
Maritin (actor) 20
Mark Robinson, Jeremy 92
Marker, Chris 13, 21, 23, 27, 29, 63
Marriage a la Mode (1973) 37
Marszalek, Barbara 50
Martin, Marguerite 98
Martinelli, Jean 38, 58
Martinelli, Sergio 47
Martínez Solares, Gilberto 56
Martínez, Loredana 54
Marty, Daniel 58
Mascarets [tidal bores] (book) . . .31, 80, 81
Masculin Féminin [masculine feminine] (1966) **26**, 29
Mask of Medusa
▸ *Le Masque de la Méduse*
Mason, James 86
Masque de la Méduse, Le [Mask of Medusa] (2010) 79
Massaccesi, Aristide
▸ Joe D'Amato

Mastorakis, Nico 85
Mata Hari (1985) 53
Matka Joanna od Aniołów [Mother Joan of the Angels] (1961) 11, 56, **57**
Mattei, Bruno 73
Matter of Resistance, A
▸ *La Vie de Château* [life in a castle]
Matthews, Denise K.
▸ Vanity (actor)
Maturin, Charles 40n
Maurice, Michel 24
Maurin, Yves-Marie 62
Mauritzson, Camilla 75
Mauro, Patrizia 54
Max Mon Amour [max my love] (1986) . . **88**
Mays, Fred 79
Maze, Michèle 68
Mazepa (1965) 25
Mazepa (1969) 25
Mazepa (1975) 25
Mazepa (1992) 25
Mazepa (play) 24, 25
Mazières, Catherine 78
McDowell, Curt 83
Medak, Peter 67
Meetings in the Forest
▸ *Les Rendez-Vous en Forêt*
Mei-Chen (actor) 18
Mekki, Hamida 62
Melmoth the Wanderer (book) 40n
Melville, Jean-Pierre 37
Memoria e Osaka, La [memory and Osaka] (play) 60
Mercanton, Isabelle 52
Mercanton, Victoria 46
Meriko, Maria 35
Mérimée, Prosper 36, 39, 95, 107
Merisi, Miana 54
Messeri, Gianmaria 47
Metamorphoses (book) 73
Meyer, Nicholas 67
Meyer, Russ 8
Michaels, Roxanna 74
Michel, Théo 21
Michelangelo (artist) 59, 90
Michisanti, Mario 55
Mickely, Noël 20
Miklas, Julie .74
Miller, Henry 76
Milt, Victor .70
Mingozzi, Gianfranco 56
Minotaur (mag) 83
Mirmant, Anne 21
Miró, Joan 12
Mishima, Yukio 80
Mitchell., Gordon 49
Mocati, Roger 25
Mocky, Jean-Pierre 53

Moctezuma, Juan López 56
Molinari, Giulio 55
Mona Lisa
▸ La Gioconda
Mona: l'Étoile sans Nom [Mona: nameless star] (1966) **26**, 29
Monaca del Peccato, La [Convent of Sinners] (1986) 56
Monache di Sant'Arcangelo, Le [the nuns of St Archangel] AKA *The Nun and the Devil* (1973) 56
Monceau, Gérard 78
Monge, Jacques 75
Monsieur Tête [Mr. Head] (1959) 29
Monster Munch (confectionary) 7
Montage IV (1968) 36
Monteillet, Max 49, 74
Montero, Roberto 33
Monti, Romana 54
Montori, Sergio 55
Moreau, Gustave 90
Morin, Edgar 29
Moroszkiewicz, Stanislaw 51
Morra, Paola 54
Morris, Marc .5
Morris, Mike 54
Morrissey, Paul 27, 53
Morte Vivante, La [The Living Dead Girl] (1982) **60**, 61
Mother Joan of the Angels
▸ *Matka Joanna od Aniołów*
Motocyclette, La [the motorcycle girl] (book) **80**, 81
Mouchette (1967) **26**, 29
Mrozewski, Zdzislaw 50
Muñoz Bachs, Eduardo 107
Murder by Decree (1979) 67
Muriel ou Le Temps d'un Retour [Muriel, or The Time of Return] (1963) **26**, 29
Muriel, or The Time of Return
▸ *Muriel ou Le Temps d'un Retour*
Murray, Scott 5, 59
Musée Noir, Le [the black museum] (book) 59, **80**, 81
Musée, Le [the museum] (1963) 14
Muslin, Alain 79
Mylonas, Jean 68

N

N. a Pris les Dés... [N. Takes the Dice] (1971) 37
N. Takes the Dice
▸ *N. a Pris les Dés...*
Na Konci Mesta [at the end of the city] (1955) 11
Nagrodzone Uczucie [love requited] (1957) **12**
Nahum, Jacques 72
Naked Under Leather (1968) 80
Naked under Leather
▸ The Girl on the Motorcycle

National Geographic (mag) 40n
Naudin, Julien .79
Nazi Love Camp 27
▸ *La Svastica nel Ventre*
[swastika on the belly]
Negrin, Alberto 61
Négroni, Jean .78
Nel Profondo del Delirio [deep in delirium]
▸ *Docteur Jekyll et les Femmes*
Nell, Carlo 52
Nelle Pieghe della Carne [In the Folds of the Flesh] (1970) .60
NeverEnding Story, The
▸ *Die Unendliche Geschichte*
New Realm Distribution (company) **27**
Newton, Adi 9
Newton, Helmut 46
Niay, Nelly 79
Night and Fog
▸ *Nuit et Brouillard*
Night of the Lepus (1972) 59
Nitsch, Hermann 47
No Orchids for Lulu
▸ *Lulu* (1962)
Noaro, Magali .68
Noël, Alain 20
Noi e l'Amore: comportamento sessuale deviante [us and love: deviant sexual behaviour] (1986) 87
Non si Sevizia un Paperino [Don't Torture a Duckling] (1972) 47
Norman, Barry .7
Notti Segrete di Lucrezia Borgia, Le [Secret Nights of Lucretia Borgia] (1982) 33, 48–**49**
Nous Deux France, À (1970) 29
Nouveaux Pictures (company) 9
Novelli, Armando 48
Novello, Ivor 67
Nowak, Zygmunt 51
Nowicka, Helena 51
Nubi Ardenti [burning clouds] (book) . . .60
Nude per l'Assassino [Strip Nude for Your Killer] (1975) 47, 49
Nuit de mil neuf cent quatorze, La [night of 1914] (book) 81
Nuit des Toiles, La [night of the canvasses] (1989) .36, 37
Nuit et Brouillard [Night and Fog] (1955) 27, 29
Nun and the Devil, The
▸ *Le Monache di Sant'Arcangelo*
[the nuns of St Archangel]
Nutty Professor II: The Klumps (2000) 88
Nutty Professor, The (1963) 70
Nyby, Christian 44n
Nympho-Teens of Roma Meet Son of the Wolfman (1979) 49

O

Ô Gaule (1974) 29
O'Horgan, Tom 84
Obidniak, Karol 51
Oeil Écoute, L' [the listening eye] (1970) . .69
Of the Dead
▸ *Des Morts*
Offret [The Sacrifice] (1986) **26**, 28, 29
Ohanessian, Suzanne 21, 25
Oiseaux sont des Cons, Les [birds are twats] (1965) 29
Oldfield, Mike 46
Olivieri, Roberto 55
Onassis, Aristotle 83
Onibaba (1964) 86
Orchestra of the Musicians' Union of Rome (group) 64
Origin of the World, The
▸ *L'Origine du Monde*
Origine du Monde, L' [The Origin of the World] (painting) 43n
Orkiestra Deta Gazowni Miejskiej (group) 12
Orlando, Antonio 72
Ôshima, Nagisa 28, 29, 88
Oswald, Lee Harvey 46
Otzenberger, Claude 29
Ould-Abderrahmane, Mazouz 58
Ovid (writer) 72, 73, 76

P

Pabst, G.W. **67**
Pacewicz, Lidia 51
Pacte de Loups, Le [The Brotherhood of the Wolf] (2001) .98
Padre Padrone [Father and Master] (1977) .86
Padre Padrone [Father and Master] (book) .86
Paget, Robert 46, 49
Paine, Heidi 74
Pallardi, Paul 20
Pallardy, Jean-Marie 49, 76, 77
Palmer, John 47
Palmieri, Carlo 55
Pame, Mireille .72
Pandora's Box
▸ *Die Büchse der Pandora*
Paolella, Domenico 56
Papaya dei Caraibi [Caribbean Papaya] aka *Papaya: Love Goddess of the Cannibals* (1978) **47**
Papaya: Love Goddess of the Cannibals
▸ *Papaya dei Caraibi* [Caribbean Papaya]
Parajanov, Sergei 60
Parete della Stanza Accanto, La [the walls of the next room] (1987) 61
Paris 1900 (1947) 63
Paris Seen by...
▸ *Paris vu Par...*
Paris Vogue (mag) 46
Paris vu Par... [Paris Seen by...] (1965) . . .63
Paris, Texas (1984) **26**, 28, 29
Pariscope: Un semaine de Paris (mag) 94
Parisi, Franco .49
Parmegiani, Bernard 68, 69
Parreton, Roger 25
Partexano, Alessandro 54
Pascal, Olivia .54
Pasolini, Pier Paolo 9, 46, 47, 92
Pastoral: To Die in the Country
▸ *Den-en Ni Shisu* / 田園に死す
Patriarca, Antonietta 54
Paul Rubens, Peter **90**
Paulsen, David .7
Pauquet, Daniel 18
Pawlak, Kazimierz 51
Paz, Octavio 80
Pearl Fishers, The (tune) 15
Pecker, Slim 70
Pedrazzi, Elisabetta 54
Pellegrini, Alessandrina 55
Penrose, Valentine 32
Penthouse (mag) 77
Péronne, Denise 24
Perrin, Jacques 24
Perrin, Louis .18
Perverted Stories (series) 88
Pescatore, Rossella 54
Pescatore, Valeria 54
Peter, Francis .98
Petersen, Wolfgang 45
Petit Poucet, Le [Tom Thumb] (1965) . 11, **14**
Phantom Fiend, The (1932) 67
Philips, Baxter 92
Philosophical Dictionary
▸ *Dictionnaire Philosophique*
Phonographe, Le [the phonograph] (1969) .15
Photo (mag) 60
Photographie et Cinema [photography and cinema] (1984) 36
Physique de l'Amour [natural history of love] (book) 16
Picadilly, Norma 52
Picasso, Paloma 30
Piechocinski, Jan 50
Pieczec, Siodma 11
Pieczynski, Boleslaw 51
Piégay, Henri .58
Pieri, Umbert .18
Pierro, Alessio 60, 61
Pierro, Marina . . . .
17, 54, 55, 58, **60**, 61, 68, 69, 72, 78
Pig Fucking Movie, The
▸ *Vase de Noces* [The Wedding Trough]
Pignard, Jean-François 62
Ping Mei, Jin .17
Pink Stainless Tail (group) 119
Pisano, Berto .49
Pitt, Ingrid **32**

Placido, Michele .64
Placido, Michele .72
Planète Sauvage, La [wild planet] AKA *Fantastic Planet* (1973) **26**, 28, 29
Plaskocinskiego, Jana 12
Platel, Jean-Pierre 21, 25, 30, 38, 62, 69
Playboy France (mag) 48
Playboy (mag) 73
Playgirls and the Vampire (1960) 8
Playing with Fire
▸ *Jeu avec Le Feur*
Plazewski, Jan 51
Pluet, Eric 35
Plus Belles Escroqueries du Monde, Les [*The World's Most Beautiful Swindlers*] (1963) 63
Podkowinski, Władysław 4, 40n
Poirier, Alain 21
Poisson, Isabelle .79
Polanski, Roman 79
Poli, Maurice 47
Pollet, Jean-Daniel 29
Popioły [the ashes] (1965) 51
Popović, Ljubomir 16, 27
Porte dévergondée [shameless door] (stories) 81
Porte, Régis 52
Portrait of an Englishman in his castle
▸ *L'Anglais Décrit dans le Château Fermé*
Positif (mag) **22**
Posse, Roberto 47
Pottiez, Alain 21
Poulain, Florence 78
Poupée, La [the doll] (1962) 69
Pour en Finir avec le Pouvoir d'Orphée [to have done with the power of Orpheus] (music) 69
Pourcher, L'abbé 99
Pouret, Robert 25
Pourvoir [provide] (1982) 37
Power, Romina .56
Powers, Jim 88
Prawdziwy Koniec Wielkiej Wojny [the real end of the great war] (1956) **10**, 11
Précaution Inutile, La [the useless precaution] (story) 17
Préville, Gisèle 68
Prim, Monique .38
Prima Donna, La (1963) 14
Private Collection, A
▸ *Une Collection Particulière*
Private Collections
▸ *Collections Privée*
Private Eye (mag) 88
Promenades dans Rome [walks in rome] (book) 55
Pronier, Francis .18
Pront, Alex 38, 69
Prosdogemi, Paola 54
Psycho (1960) 44n, 70, 85

Publius Ovidius Naso
▸ Ovid
Pucelle d'Orléans, La [the maid of Orleans] (book) 41
Pulp (group) 9, 41n
Puppo, Romano 54
Putin, Vladimir .46

Q

Queen of the Night
▸ *Cérémonie d'amour*
Queré, Françoise 58, 62
Question of Rape, A
▸ *Le Viol* [rape]
Quinta Donna, La [the fifth woman] (1982) 61
Quiquandon, Madeleine 18, 24
Quo Vadis (1951) 73

R

Rabelais (writer) 76
Rainy Taxi, The (installation) 45
Rambal, Jean-Pierre 62
Ramel, Bernard .62
Rampling, Charlotte 88
Ramsamy, Sylvain 58
Raped on the Beach
▸ *Violentata Sulla Sabbia*
Raphael (artist) .59
Rappeneau, Jean-Paul 11, 14
Reagé, Pauline 63
Red Light Zone (TV) 9
Redemption Video (company) 9
Redlich, Marian 51
Régis, Colette 20
Règlement, Le [regulations] (1969) 36
Règles, Rites (1982) 36
Regnault, Christiane 25
Regnoli, Piero 8, 48, 49
Reid, Gordon 93
Rekopis znaleziony w Saragossie [*The Saragossa Manuscript*] (1965) 25
Ren, Xin 85
Renaissance (1963) 13, **14**, 15
Rendez-vous de Minuit, Le [the appointment at midnight] (1961) **26**, 29
Rendez-Vous en Forêt, Les [meetings in the forest] (1971) 15, 28, 29, **34**–37
Repollero (animation technique) 12
Resnais, Alain 27, 29, 63, 92
Restif de La Bretonne, Nicolas-Edme 17
Return to the Chateau (book) 63
Revenge of Billy the Kid, The (1991) **88**
Reynolds, Willey 48
Ricci, André-Paul 79
Ricci, Paul 74
Riché, Daniel 24
Rios, Jean 62
Rivault, Pascale .38

Riviere, Georges-Henri 98
Rivollier, Mathieu 30, 38, 58
Rizzo, Alfredo 61
Robaszkiewicz, Maria 50
Robbe-Grillet, Alain 9, 27, 28, 29, 35, 36, 37, 53, 76, 79, 80, 92
Roberto (actor) 15, 24
Robertson, John S. 70
Robinson, W. Heath 105
Rogers, Michael 74
RoGoPaG (1963) 63
Rohellec, Régis, Le 62
Rolla, Micheline 24
Rollet-Andriane, Louis-Jacques 77
Rollet-Andriane, Marayat 77
Rollin, Jean . . 9, 40n, 60, 61, 77, 79, 92, 93
Rolling Stone (mag) 53
Rolling Stones, The (group) 53
Romay, Lina **32**
Rome Roméo (1992) 36
Rondi, Brunello 61
Room to Let (1950) 67
Rophé, Guy 78
Rosa, Jole 54
Rosalie (1966) 14, **15**, 23
Rosalie Prudent (story) 14
Rosen, Martin 59
Rosette (actor) 52
Ross, Howard 54
Rouch, Jean .29, 63
Rousseau, Louisette 18
Route est Belle, La [the road is fine] (1929) .63
Rovere, Gina 54
Rowney, William 45
Rufini, Franco 55
Ruh, Jean-Pierre 25, 38
Ruling Class, The (1972) 67
Rumilly, France .58
Ruspoli, Mario 27, 29
Russel, Percival .20
Russell, Ken 56
Russo, Luigi 86
Rustichelli, Carlo 62

S

Sacrifice, The
▸ *Offret*
Sadomania (1981) **87**
Saglio, Patrick 21
Saint-Aubin, Mr 98
Saint-Jean, Guy .20
Saintons, Pierre .64
Salama, Guila 78
Salò (1975) 9, 47
Salo, Sirpa
▸ Lane, Sirpa
Salon Kitty (1976) 47
Samosiuk, Zygmunt 51

Samouraï, Le [*The Samuraï*] (1967) 37
Samurai, The
▸ *Le Samouraï*
San Diego Surf (1968) 53
Sanatorium pod klepsydra [*The Hourglass Sanatorium*] (1973) 25
Sang de l'Agneau, Le [blood of the lamb] (story) 59, 80
Sans Soleil [sunless] (1983) **26**, 29
Santagada, Pietro 61
Santaniello, Oscar .49
Sanzio da Urbino, Raffaello 59
Saragossa Manuscript, The
▸ *Rekopis znaleziony w Saragossie*
Sarde, Alain 78, 79
Sarnelli, Trieste 24
Sasdy, Peter 32, 67
Satánico Pandemonium (1975) 56, **57**
Satin Spider, The
▸ *L'Araignée de Satin*
Savage Weekend (1979) 7
Savonarola, Hyeronimus 30
Scarlatti, Domenico 41n, 42n
Schaeffer, Pierre 69
Schamoni, Peter 35
Schatz, Hans-Jürgen 64
Scheherazade (writer) 17
Scherzo Infernal (1984) **16**, 28, 29, 69
Schlöndorff, Volker 28, 29
Schmidt-Keune, Thea 50
Schmitt, Tom 16
Schoedsack, Ernest 83
School of the Holy Beast
▸ *Seijū Gakuen* / 聖獣学園
School
▸ *Szkola*
Schrader, Paul 84
Scommessa, La [the bet] (1990) 61
Scomunicate di San Valentino, Le [*The Sinful Nuns of St Valentine*] (1974) 56
Scrabble (board game) 11
Screen International (mag) 46
Secret Nights of Lucretia Borgia
▸ *Le Notti Segrete di Lucrezia Borgia*
Secret of Dr. Orloff, The
▸ *Les Maîtresses du Docteur Jekyll* [the mistresses of Dr. Jekyll]
Sedgwick, Edie 84
Segal, Peter 88
Seguin, Elise 98
Seijū Gakuen / 聖獣学園 [*School of the Holy Beast*] (1974) 56, **57**
Sept Péchés Capitaux, Les [*The Seven Deadly Sins*] (1961) 63
Serfran, Michael 48
Sergent, Jean-Paul .78
Série Rose [pink series] (TV) **17**, 63
Serra, Antônio 33
Sessa, Jean-Raphael 78

Seven Deadly Sins, The
▸ *Les Sept Péchés Capitaux*
Seven Women for Satan
▸ *Les week-ends maléfiques du Comte Zaroff* [evil weekends of Count Zaroff]
Seventh Seal, The
▸ *Siodma Pieczec*
Sex Life in a Convent
▸ *Interno di un Convento* [inside a convent]
Sex Stars System (mag) 93, **34**
Sexcula (1974) 83
Sexualist, The (1973) 83
Shane, Bryan 74
Shindô, Kaneto 86
Sho Wo Suteyo Machi He Deyou / 書を捨てよ町へ出よう [*Throw Away Your Books, Rally in the Streets*] (1971) 63
Shudojo Runa no Kokuhaku / 修道女ルナの告白 [*Cloistered Nun: Runa's Confession*] (1976) 56, **57**
Siennicka, Jadwiga 50
Sierpien [August] (1946) 12
Simon, Michel 24
Simsolo, Noël 58
Sinful Nuns of St Valentine, The
▸ *Le Scomunicate di San Valentino*
Singing During the Occupation
▸ *Chantons sous l'Occupation*
Siodma Pieczec [*The Seventh Seal*] (1957) . .10
Siritzky, Alain 74
Siritzky, Alain 77
Sister Emanuelle
▸ *Sœur Emmanuelle*
Sisters of Satan
▸ *Alucarda*
Sisti, Giancarlo 47
Sjoman, Vilgot 86
Skerl, Peter 86
Slowacki, Juliusz 24, 25
Smal, Ewa 51
Smemorata, Le [the forgetful] (1982) 61
Smith, Christophe 62
Smith, Guy N. 9
Smith, Jack 8
Smiths, The (group) 53
Smiths, The (LP) .53
Snails, The
▸ *Les Escargots*
Sochnacki, Boguslaw 50
Softly from Paris
▸ *Serie Rose*
Soldi, Giancarlo 61
Sole, Alfred 86
Soleil des loups [wolves' sun] (book) 81
Soleils de l'île de Pâques, Les [*The Suns of Easter Island*] (1972) .69
Sonata in A Major, K. 209 Allegro (tune) 42n
Sonata in D Major K.119 (tune) 41n
Sonnet, Lili 78
Sorbole... che romagnola! (1976) 61

Sous la Lame [under the lame] (book) 81
Spadoni, Luciano .55
Spangles (confectionary) 8
Spelvin, Georgina .85
Spencer, Bud 48
Spielberg, Steven .87
Spinetti, Victor 46
Spooky Kama Sutra AKA *Beautiful Dead Body* (1987) 85
Spotkania [meetings] (1957) 23
Spring-Heeled Jack (bastard) 67
Stadion [stadium] (1958) 13, 23
Stanford Arms (pub) 8
Star Wars (1977) .48
Star, The (newspaper) 7
Starlog (mag) 8
Stars System
▸ *Sex Stars System*
Stefanelli, Simonetta 72
Stefano, Joseph 85
Stehl, Jessica 74
Steinke, Michael .64
Stendhal, Henri 54, 55
Stern, Roswita 51
Sticky Fingers (LP) 53
Story of a Sin
▸ *Dzieje Grzechu*
Story of O, The
▸ *Histoire d'O*
Story of the Eye, The (book) 39, 41n
Strange Case of Dr Jekyll and Mr Hyde (book) 70, 99
Strange Case of Dr. Jekyll and Miss Osbourne, The
▸ *Docteur Jekyll et les Femmes*
Strangers of the Earth
▸ *Les Inconnus de la Terre*
Strawa, Isabelle 74
Streetwalker, The
▸ *La Marge* [the margin]
Strip Nude for Your Killer
▸ *Nude per l'Assassino*
Strip-Tease (1957) **12**
Stroboscopes: Les Magasins du XIXe Siecle, Les [stroboscopes: shops of the nineteenth century] (1963) 14
Strom, Max 74
Strzebiecki, Henryk 51
Studio 5-6-7 (cinema) 6, 7, 8, 119
Studio 5-6-7 (song) 119
Study in Terror, A (1965) 67
Suarez, Bobby A. .56
Subiela, Michel 98
Sullivan, Thomas Russell 70
Suns of Easter Island, The
▸ *Les Soleils de l'île de Pâques*
Suor Emmanuelle [*Sister Emanuelle*] (1977) 56, **57**
Suor Omicida [*Killer Nun*] (1978) . . .53, 56

Super Troopers (2001) 88
Supervixens (1975) .8
Suspiria (1977) **60**, 61, 69
Suzuki, Norifumi .56
Svastica nel Ventre, La [swastika on the belly]
   AKA Nazi Love Camp 27 (1977) **47**
Szał Uniesien [Frenzy of Exultations]
   (painting) **2**, 4, 40n
Szaro, Henryk 51
Szemberg, Jolanta .50
Szeski, Jerzy 51
Szkola [School] (1958) 13, 27
Sztandar Mlodygi [banner of youth] (1957) **12**
Sztuka Ulicy [art of the streets] (1958) 12
Szuttenbach, Lechoslaw 51

T

Ta paidiá tou Diavólou / Τα παιδιά του Διαβόλου
   [Island of Death] (1975) 85
Tabah, Jean-Jacques 78
Taccini, Philippe .72
Tail Gunner (video game) 7
Tanya's Island (1980) **86**
Tarbuck, Jimmy 7
Tarkovsky, Andrei 28, 29
Tarz and Jane and Cheeta (1975) 83
Tarzan (1999) 83
Tarzan, the Ape Man (1932) **83**
Tarzan, the Ape Man (1981) 88
Tati, Jacques 92
Taurus [The Bull] (constellation) 90
Taviani, Paolo 86
Taviani, Vittorio .86
Taxi Love (1976) 60, 61
Taylor, Timothy .75
Tcherka, Gerard .30
Tent, Kevin 74
Tentacles (1977) 87
Teodorczyk, Tadeusz 50
Terayama, Shuji 28, 29, 63
Terra Incognita (1959) 13
Testament d'Orphée, Le [Testament of Orpheus]
   (1960) 46
Testament of Orpheus
   ▸ Le Testament d'Orphée
Testanière, Marie 38
Testanière, Stéphane 38
Tete [the head] (1961) 13
Teti, Camillo 72
Thatcher (bastard) 7
Théâtre de M. et Mme Kabal [Theatre of Mr.
   and Mrs. Kabal] (1967) 11, 14, 15, **18–19**
Theatre of Mr. and Mrs. Kabal
   ▸ Théâtre de M. et Mme Kabal
Thénaisie, Gisèle 21
Thérèse Philosophe (1974) 31, 41n
Thérèse Philosophe (book) 31, **33**
Thévenet, René .20

Thévenot, Françoise 25
They Call Her Cleopatra Wong (1978) . 56, **57**
Thiele, Rolf 66, 67
Thing from Another World, The (1954) . . 44n
Thomas, Gerald .77
Thomass, Michel 20
Thousand and One Nights (book) 17
Three Graces (painting) 59
Three Immoral Women
   ▸ Les Heroines du Mal [Heroines of Evil]
Throw Away Your Books, Rally in the Streets
   ▸ Sho Wo Suteyo Machi He Deyou
   /書を捨てよ町へ出よう
Thundercrack! (1975) 83
Tibertelli De Pisis, Bona 16
Tiller, Nadja **66**
Time After Time (1979) 67
Tin Drum, The
   ▸ Die Blechtrommel
Tinard, Isabelle .78
Tinebra, Alberto 55
Tinelli, Giuseppe 55
Tohill, Cathal .9, 92
Tom Thumb
   ▸ Le Petit Poucet
Tomassi, Vincenzo 47
Tomato Kecchappu Kotei / トマトケチャ
   ップ皇帝 [Emperor Tomato Ketchup]
   (1971) 63
Tombs, Pete 9, 92
Touch of Class, A (1973) 46
Touche pas la Femme Blanc [Don't Touch the
   White Woman] (1974) 79
Tourneur, Jacques 84
Tout Disparaitra [everything must go]
   (book) 78, **80**, 81
Tovoli, Luciano .55
Tracy, Spencer 70
Trash (1970) 53
Travels with a Donkey in the Cévennes
   (book) 99
Tréfouel, Jacques 21
Tréjan, Guy .38, 98
Trial, The (1962) 13
Tribunal de l'impossible, Le [court of the
   impossible] (1967) **98**
Trimble, Lawrence 24, 35
Trocchi, Alex 32, 80
Trois Filles dans le Vent [three girls in the
   wind] (1982) 49
True Story of the Beast of Gévaudan, The
   ▸ La Véritable Histoire de
   la Bête du Gévaudan
Trzech Kroli, Wieczor 11
Tu Imagines Robinson [you imagine Robinson]
   (1970) 29
Tucci, Ugo 72
Twelfth Night
   ▸ Wieczor Trzech Kroli
Twilight Zone, The (TV) 85

Two Faces of Dr. Jekyll, The (1960) . . . 70, **71**
Two Love Crimes
   ▸ Les Crimes de l'Amour [crimes of love]
Two or Three Things I Know About Her
   ▸ 2 ou 3 Choses Que je Sais d'Elle
Tylczynski, Stanislaw 50

U

Ubu Plays (plays) 19
Uher, Natalie 77
Un Amleto di Meno [one Hamlet less]
   (1973) 31
Un Été Torride [a torrid summer] (1965) . .14
Un Linceul n'a pas de Poches [no pockets in a
   shroud] (1974) 53
Un Merveilleux Parfum d'Oseille [a sweet smell
   of cash] (1969) 37
Un Monde Agité [a hectic world] (2000) . .36
Un Traitement Justifié [a justified treatment]
   (TV) **17**, 61
Una donna senza nome [woman without a
   name] (1987) 86
Uncanny, The (essay) 84
Undari, Claudio 48
Une Collection Particulière [A Private
   Collection] (1973) . **15**, 29, 31, 36, 80, **81**
Une Femme Fidèle [a faithful woman]
   (1976) 53
Une Semaine de Bonté [a week of kindness]
   (book) 13
Unendliche Geschichte, Die [The NeverEnding
   Story] (1984) 45
Ungari, Enzo 72
Up in Smoke (1978) 8
Urotsukidoji: Legend of the Overfiend
   (1989) 87

V

Vadim, Roger 53, 46
Valentina (comic strip) **66**
Valio, Michel 38
Valparaiso (1965) 29
Valys, Katia 74
Van Dyke, Dick .73
Van Dyke, W. S. .83
Vanille, Marie 74
Vanity (actress) .86
Varda, Agnès 29
Vari, Giuseppe 56
Variety (mag) 73
Vase de Noces [The Wedding Trough] AKA The
   Pig Fucking Movie (1974) 85
Vayan, Greta 54
Védrès, Nicole 63
Venantini, Venantino 48
Veneto, Bartolomeo **33**
Venus on the Half-Shell
   ▸ Escargot de Venus [snail of Venus]

Véritable Histoire de la Bête du Gévaudan, La [*The True Story of the Beast of Gévaudan*] (1973) 15, 29, 31, 36
Vernon, Howard 68, 69
Véry, Noël 21, 25, 30, 38, 62, 68
Vezzani, Giuseppe 55
Vidal, Gore 73
Video Watchdog (mag) 75
Vie de Château, Le [life in a castle] AKA *A Matter of resistance* (1962) 11, 14, **15**
Villani, Simona 54
Vinke, Isabelle 78
Viol, Le [rape] AKA *A Question of Rape* (1967) 29
Violentata Sulla Sabbia [*Raped on the Beach*] (1969) 80, **81**
Violostries (LP) 69
Visconti, Luchino 60, 61
Vivre la nuit [night life] AKA *Love in the Night* (1968) 37
Vlad the Impaler (bastard) 32
Vlastas, Pamm 74
Vogel, Amos 13, 14, 93
Vogue (US) **36**
Voit, Mieczyslaw 50
Volson, Patrick 99
Voltaire (writer) 3, 41, 40n
von Bayros, Franz 45
von Radványi, Géza 64
Vortex AKA *Blondy* (1976) 37
Vukotic, Milena .72

W

Waggner, George 83
Wajda, Andrzej . . . .
Walczewski, Marek 50
Walerian Borowczyk: Cinema of Erotic Dreams (book) **92**
Walks in Rome (book) 54

Wallace, Richard 67
Waltenberger, Andrzej Rafal 51
Walter, Renaud .29
War is Over, The
▶ *La Guerre est Finie*
Ward Baker, Roy 67, 70
Warhol, Andy 27, 46, 53, 84
Watership Down (1978) 59
Wedding Trough, The
▶ *Vase de Noces*
Wedekin, Frank 64, 65, 66, 67
Week-ends Maléfiques du Comte Zaroff, Les [evil weekends of Count Zaroff] AKA *Seven Women for Satan* (1970) 7
Weeks, Stephen .70
Welles, Orson 13, 76
Wells, H.G. 67
Wenders, Wim 28, 29
What The Swedish Butler Saw (1975) . . .8, 67
White Zombie (1932) 84
Whizzer and Chips (comic) 7
Whoopee! (comic) 7
Why do They do it?
▶ *Hvorfor Gør de Det?*
Wieczor Trzech Kroli [*Twelfth Night*] (1956) **10**, 11
Wildes Leben, Ein [a wild life]
▶ *La Jeune Fille Assassinée* [a young girl murdered]
Wilhelmi, Roman 50
William, Shakespeare, ...11
Willie, John 63
Wills Tobacco (corporation) 14
Wilson, Georges .24
Wings of Desire
▶ *Der Himmel über Berlin* [Heaven over Berlin]
Winters, Shelley .87
Wisniewski, Bogdan 50

Wodkowski, Jacques 49
Wolf Man, The (1941) **83**, 84
Wolf Man, The (essay) 84
Wood, Ed 86
World's Most Beautiful Swindlers, The
▶ *Les Plus Belles Escroqueries du Monde*
Wray, Fay 83
Wurtz, Gérard 38
Wyler, William 73
Wynorski, Jim 75

X–Y–Z

Xenakis, Iannis .69
Yeats, W.B. .80, 90
Yellow Submarine (1968) 13, 87
Za vlast' Sovetov / За власть Советов [for the power of the soviets] AKA *Do Ostatniej Kropli Krwi* [to the last drop of blood] (1956) **10**, 11
Zakazane Piosenki [forbidden songs] (1946) **10**, 11
Zakrzenski, Janusz 50
Zalcberg, Gérard 68, 69
Zampacavallo, Maria Laura 55
Zapasiewicz, Zbigniew 50
Zed and Two Noughts, A (1985) 90
Zelnik, Jerzy 50
Zéno, Thierry 85
Zeromski, Stefan 50, 51
Zimowy Zmierzch [winter twilight] (1957) **23**
Zincone, Bruno 49, 77
Zincone, Elvira 55
Zirisch, Marie-Hélène 78
Złote Ekrany [golden screen] (1976) **23**
Zolat, Michel 30, 78
Zoo Zéro (1979) 36, 37
Zúñiga, Ariel 37
Zywe Fotografie [living pictures] (1954) . . .12

THE LEDATAPE ORGANISATION
"OUR SHIT BEATS THEIR GOLD"

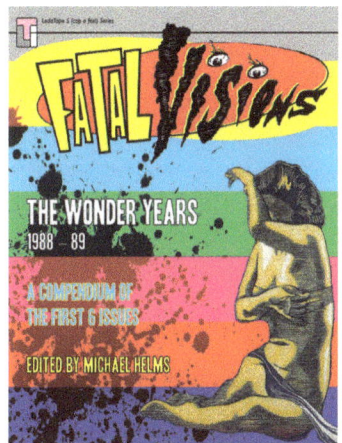 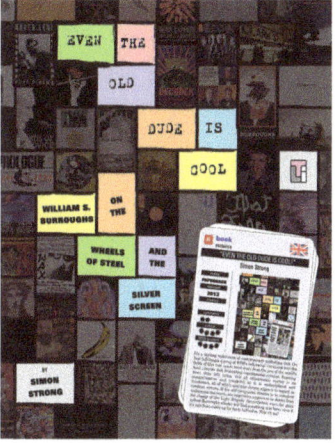 

Michael Helms
FATAL VISIONS
THE WONDER YEARS

2012, 7½ x 9¼ in., 248pp

At freaking last! A collection of FATAL VISIONS, Melbourne's own infamous trash film zine, has congealed into perfect bound format. Proving that dead tree technology has not entirely slipped into a coma this compilation covers the earliest and rarest entries in FVs decade-long publication history.

Devoted to sleaze, violence and sexploitation in the Cinema and wherever it appears on video, TV & in print, FATAL VISIONS went to places where few other Australian publications even knew existed: bottom of the package video titles, late late night TV movies, films that played announced as drive-in supports and in hard tops where they were lucky to play for one week only.

VOLUME 2
"The Golden Age"

COMING SOON!

Simon Strong
"EVEN THE OLD DUDE IS COOL!"
WILLIAM BURROUGHS ON THE WHEELS OF STEEL AND THE SILVER SCREEN

2014, 7½ x 9¼ in., 122pp

It's a searing indictment of contemporary publishing that the first full-length survey of WSB's influential intrusions into the fields of film and music must come from the pen of the world's most obscure and frustrating experimental novelist.

Boasting more than 323 items, this uh idiosyncratic survey is as comprehensive and insightful as it is undisciplined and incoherent, all of which qualities Strong appears to regard as cardinal virtues. Even the most ardent Burroughs scholar will find something new here, even if it's just been made up for funty laff value. Nice try pal.

Adrien Clerc
GUERILLA CONDITIONS
LA FOLLE ÉPOPÉE CINÉMATOGRAPHIQUE D'ANTONY BALCH AVEC WILLIAM BURROUGHS, RICHARD GORDON, ET TOUS LES AUTRES

2014, 5½ x 8½ in., 228pp

Voici le tour d'horizon de l'une des aventures les plus radicales et les plus méconnues que produisit le cinéma, celle d'Antony Balch. Réalisateur, distributeur, programmateur, monteur, publicitaire et critique, l'Abominable Showman travailla entre autres avec l'écrivain William Burroughs et le producteur Richard Gordon. Avant-propos par Norman J. Warren!

French text

ENGLISH VERSION
COMING SOON!

www.ledatape.net

www.ingramcontent.com/pod-product-compliance
Lightning Source LLC
Chambersburg PA
CBHW041137170426
43198CB00023B/2979